AFRO-AMERICAN MASS POLITICAL INTEGRATION

A Causal and Deductive Model

Mfanya Donald Tryman

UNIVERSITY
PRESS OF
AMERICA

Library of Congress Cataloging in Publication Data

Tryman, Mfanya, Donald.
    Afro-American mass political integration.

    Bibliography: p.
    1. Afro-Americans--Politics and suffrage.
I. Title.
E185.615.T78 1982   323.1'196073   82-45013
ISBN 0-8191-2645-4
ISBN 0-8191-2646-2 (pbk.)

E
185.615
T78
1982

DEDICATED

In memory of my mother, whose warmth,
love, kindness and care,
radiated like the sun.

Whose dedication, perseverance, understanding and "togetherness",
made her a star among the stars,
of the Mother Universe.

And whose care, devotion, and consciousness, brought about a calm,
on the stormiest of days.

MDT

CONTENTS

*****

PREFACE

The research for this study grew out of a deep concern for the Black masses in urban America who inhabit most of the decaying central cities of the United States. Blacks in America's ghettoes lack political power as well as an economic base from which political power might emerge. At the same time, annexation, consolidation, reapportionment and Reaganomics threaten political gains that Blacks have made as a result of the political struggles of the sixties and seventies.

This study was developed in order to construct an alternative model to the one of domestic colonialism; one which suggests dynamic change among Afro-Americans. It is contended here that the model of domestic colonialism, while applicable to Afro-Americans in many respects, is not sufficient in explaining certain aspects of Black politics. The model in this study looks at self-determination, political leadership and group cohesiveness as prerequisites for obtaining political power. It is in this spirit that the model of Afro-American political integration was developed. This model suggests how Blacks may have more clout in the political arena once they have integrated primordial loyalties. Once this is accomplished, competition in the American social, economic and political system is likely to bring about more benefits as the result of racial unity.

Many people have been of assistance in putting this book together, and I would like to express my sincere thanks to them. Paul Puryear of the University of Massachusetts was instrumental with regard to financial assistance which provided research time. Graham Kinloch of Florida State University was especially helpful in his comments on model-building and theory construction. Douglas St. Angelo, also of Florida State University, provided helpful comments and encouragement. I owe my deep appreciation to Delores Campbell, Leslie McLemore, and John Jenkins, all of Jackson State University, for their assistance in proofing previous drafts and providing useful advice. Last but not least, I owe a debt of thanks to Ann Nelson for her typing and tedious work on the final draft. Any errors at this point are mine.

M.D.T.
1982

vii

INTRODUCTION

In the past, explanatory models put forth by poli-
ticial scientists and sociologists which have attempted
to explain certain political and social phenomena
applicable to or having implications for, the status
and condition of Black people in America in relation
to White people have included the pluralist, elitist,
conflict, assimilationist, <u>ad infinitum</u>. At the same
time, political scientists have lagged far behind
sociologists in their attempts to deal with American
social problems and race relations as an academic sub-
discipline.

On the other hand, almost every study on Black
politics in the past, until recently, has invariably
focused upon Black voting behavior, beginning with
Harold Gosnell's pioneer study of the influence of
Black migration upon the political machines in Chicago
during the thirties (<u>Negro Politics</u>); Some of the more
recent studies are Clayton's <u>The Negro Politician</u>,
Ladd's <u>Negro Political Leadership in the South</u>,
Prothro and Matthew's <u>The Negro and the New Southern
Politics</u>, as well as Harry Holloway's <u>The Politics of
the Southern Negro</u>.[1]

Holloway's study is broader in scope than the
others in that he uses a developmental framework by
outlining stages of political activities. Holloway
discusses three stages in this setting for Blacks
which include non-participants, semi-participants,
and full participants. Holloway suffers the recurrent
tendency to analyze Blacks in the "conventional" framework of democratic participation, i.e., voting behavior.[2]

This type of approach is an off-shoot of Almond
and Verba's <u>The Civic Culture</u>, which proclaims that
the United States is the most democratic and has the
most efficacious civic culture of five countries
studied which include Great Britain, Italy, Mexico,
and Germany.[3] Thus, past studies in general and political scientists in particular have always put the
emphasis upon voting with regard to Blacks as well as
the prerequisites for a stable democracy.[4]

Hanes Walton's <u>Black Politics</u>, from a methodological perspective, goes further than other studies of
Black politics which focused only upon the vote; he

points out that an analysis of Black politics must be macro rather than micro and must include not only the influence and effect of the Black vote in the political process but must also study the impact of the following: Black political parties, Black machines, Black pressure groups, Blacks in third parties, and Black leadership and its relationship to the Black community upon Black political life.[5] Walton refers to this concept as macroanalysis or full systems analysis. Walton argues that by using a developmental or evolutionary approach involving macroanalysis or full systems analysis one avoids the weakness of the electoral analysis by using a much broader framework. Walton goes on to speak of four stages of Black development which include non-participation, limited participation, moderate participation and full participation, all of which would be included in full systems analysis. Viewed from this perspective, Walton's approach is similar to that of Holloway's with respect to Black political participation and the stages involved. Neither the analysis of Holloway, however, nor that of Walton goes far enough since the emphasis is upon political participation and engaging in "conventional" forms of politicking. Furthermore, Walton calls for a macroanalysis of Black politics which is laudatory, but his elemental assumption is incorrect. That is, his call for a macroanalysis of Black political phenomena is still seen here as a micro approach since he fails to see Blacks engaged in political processes which may constitute an approach which is more explanatory in a comparative framework. As a result, his macro approach is still micro in that his analysis is confined to "normative" explanations of the American political process which conform to democratic norms such as voting, lobbying, compromise, bargaining, campaigning, and the like. In short, Walton's analysis of Black political participation utilizes the same approach and assumptions of most western political scientists.

The approach employed in this study is that Black politics cannot be fully explained through conventional and normative avenues such as voting, lobbying, bargaining, compromise, etc., within the American political system. In essence, Black politics constitutes an epiphenomena to conventional themes put forth by social and political scientists in explaining to us what Black politics are all about. In other words, political processes and interactions that cannot be explained in the context of democratic participation as the West knows it.

It is suggested here, however, that Afro-American or Black politics is an epiphenomena only in that studies on Blacks in the past have failed to see Black politics in a nondemocratic framework linked to political processes within the larger American political system. Obviously, ideological biases have been at work here just as it has been assumed that developing nations would automatically turn to democratic forms of government, (which also has implications for American foreign policy and foreign aid). It is proposed in this study that a model of Black political development is applicable to Afro-Americans and that it can be viewed in a framework of comparative politics in two respects. First, it attempts to compare variables and concepts emanating from two different types of "nations", which will be defined and conceptualized. Second, it is viewed as comparative in that it views Blacks in the context of a developing "nation" in the same context that Third World nations are perceived, and political problems that are incurred in the process.

A basic premise upon which this study is based is that Afro-Americans can be viewed as a nation within a nation. Rather than just focus upon only the political activities of Blacks within the larger American political system, this study also looks at political processes among Blacks as a separate political system or entity. This will be perceived as an avenue of investigation in contrast to the aforementioned studies on Black politics which appeared to view Black suffrage as a panacea once it was obtained, for all of the political and social ills in the Black community. One competing paradigm, however, for viewing Blacks is what has come to be known as the colonial model. For instance, Kenneth Clark's Dark Ghetto, and Robert Blauner's "The Ghetto as Internal Colony", support the thesis that Afro-Americans are a colonized people subjugated through what has come to be known as internal or domestic colonialism.[6]

Their premise is based not only upon the recognition of Blacks as a colonized people, but also upon the fact that Blacks have never assimilated, integrated, and become acculturated as ethnic groups in the past have done in the context of what sociologist have referred to as the "melting pot" theory. This theory argues that because of the egalitarian nature of American democracy every ethnic group eventually loses its distinct ethnic identity, language, customs, etc., in the process of "Americanization."[7] Indeed, if Blacks have not been able to integrate and assimilate, it must be argued here that more than just the ethnic factor is at work. Since Blacks have been recognized on the basis of their <u>race</u>, which can only be lost through amalgamation, miscegenation, or annihilation, there are also implications that can be drawn for a model of Afro-American political change as a competing paradigm to both the assimilationist and colonial explanations of the social and political conditions of Afro-Americans. If Blacks have not, in fact, become a part of the American political system and political process, could it not be argued that they are part of an Afro-American political system or "nation" and political process: A semi-independent process of political interactions engaged in particular types of political change? Seen in this context, Afro-Americans can be compared with other developing nations and polit- ical development theories often applied to them. This study is unique in that it is an attempt to develop a model of politics applicable to Afro-Americans in America, a process of political change among an ethnic group in what is already a sovereign nation.

It has been commonly accepted by political scien- tists that stages of political development have gone through the following: traditional, colonial, nation- alist, revolutionary independence, and the drive toward "modernity" or political development. But if one contends that the colonial model as a stage in political development is valid and applicable to Afro-Americans, one could also argue that a model of political change is also applicable to Blacks sub- suming the nationalist and revolutionary independence stages. However, several reservations would have to be kept in mind. First, such a model of political change should not suggest that Afro-Americans have become "liberated" from a colonial status through violence or a physical upheaval. Second, and related to the first reservation, it suggests that one could speak of cultural and mental "liberation" or "decolo- nization" as more pertinent in a model of Afro-Ameri- can political change than emphasize colonialism and resulting decolonialization in the form of violent revolution. This is not, however, an attempt to draw the linkage between the stage of colonialism and nationalism resulting in political independence; rather, it suggests that a model of political change can be seen as an _alternative_ to the colonial model in viewing Afro-American politics. It is in this regard that "cultural decolonization" may be suggested as part of a competing paradigm of the political change stage. If one should argue that Afro-Americans are comparable to a developing "nation", it appears relevant to review the literature on political development in comparative politics. Given the shortcomings of studies dealing with Black politics in the foregoing discussion, and the suggestions of how Blacks can be viewed in a model in a comparative context, such a literature review provides a fruitful avenue for establishing the parameters of the research.

However, it is by no means an attempt to exhaustively cover and critique the voluminous literature which has flowed forth since the inception of the term political development. Rather, what will be dealt with here is the origin of this term, its "unilinear development" in the academic realm of political development theory (as well as attempts which were made by scholars to look at political development on a unilateral path), how it is dealt with as an independent and dependent variable, the "development syndrome", and the need for stages of development and transition. By giving one such an overview of the main aspects of the literature hopefully will provide a fruitful approach and will be reflected with some contrary notions in some of the propositions set forth in the model of Afro-American political development and the criticisms offered of the literature. This will constitute Chapter One.

Chapter Two will be composed of the domestic colonial model. Given the controversy it has aroused in recent years, it warrants serious attention as a competing explanation of the political and social conditions of Afro-Americans. This will not be an attempt to either support or oppose the model, but to suggest what might be useful concepts, categories, and indices if one were to investigate such an approach to Black politics in more detail. Chapter Three will constitute the methodology for the model. In Chapter Four, the conceptual approach to the model is outlined and several steps in model-building are constructed. Chapter Five establishes various causal relationships between the variables in the model and completes the model-building process and model of Afro-American political integration. Chapter Six constitutes the conclusion of the work and pulls together the entire work, and suggest the prospects for Afro-American political integration in the future.

Notes

1. Harold Gosnell, Negro Politicians: The Rise of Negro Politics in Chicago, (Chicago: University of Chicago Press, 1967); Edward T. Clayton, The Negro Politician, (Chicago: Johnson Publishing Co., Inc., 1964); Everett C. Ladd, Negro Political Leadership in the South, (Ithaca: Cornell University Press, 1966); Donald Matthews and James Prothro, Negroes and the New Southern Politics, (New York: Harcourt, Brace and World, 1966); and Harry Holloway, The Politics of the Southern Negro, (New York: Random House, 1969). Walton points out the significance of past studies on Black politics from the electoral angle. "Heretofore, those students of the American political process (black and white) have begun their scholarly analyses with the elemental assumption that if blacks could not vote, they had little chance to have any meaningful effect on the political process." Hanes Walton, Black Politics, (Philadelphia and New York: J.B. Lippincott, Co., 1972), p. 2.

2. Harry Holloway, The Politics of the Southern Negro, pp. 3-7.

3. Gabriel Almond and Sidney Verba, The Civic Culture: Political Attitudes and Democracy in Five Nations, (Princeton: Princeton University Press, 1963).

4. This is one of the main themes in Seymour M. Lipset's Political Man: The Social Basis of Politics, (Garden City: Doubleday, 1960).

5. Walton, op. cit., p. 8. Other studies which have emphasized the nature of Black life include W.E.B. DuBois, The Philadelphia Negro, (New York: B. Blom, 1967); St. Clair Drake and Horace Clayton, Black Metropolis, (New York: Harcourt, Brace and World, Inc., 1970); and Gunnar Myrdal's classic, An American Dilemma, (New York: Harper and Row, 1969).

6. See Kenneth Clark, Dark Ghetto, (New York: Harper and Row, 1967); Robert Blauner, "The Ghetto as Internal Colony" Social Problems, 16, (Spring, 1968), pp. 393-408. This by no means is exhaustive of the literature on internal or

domestic colonialism. Similar and provocative themes are put forth by Stokley Carmichael and Charles V. Hamilton in their book Black Power, (New York: Random House, 1969); and Harold Cruse's two works, The Crisis of The Negro Intellectual, (New York: William Morrow and Co., 1967); and Rebellion or Revolution, (New York: William Morrow and Co., 1968). The concept of domestic or internal colonialism will be used interchangeably from here on.

7. See the previous footnote to Myrdal on this point. For a discussion of the melting pot theory with regard to the Black political experience and as a means of analyzing it, see James Q. Wilson's Negro Politics, (Glencoe: Free Press, 1960), especially pp. 25-34.

CHAPTER I

POLITICAL DEVELOPMENT AND MODERNIZATION

The origin of the concept, political development, began shortly after World War II. This concept concurrently opened up a new sub-field of comparative politics and political science. But the origin of the concept was not due as much to intuition or clairvoyance on the part of political scientists as it was to facing the academic and political reality of the emerging and newly independent nations in Africa, Asia, and Latin America and the consequences and impact that they may have on political science. At the same time, if there ever was a pretense of "value neutrality" or "objectivity" in political science it was destroyed with a "swipe of the pen" and by the embryonic stage of the concept itself. As western observers began to study political development their previous committment to ethnocentrism centered around western political studies was broadened in the study of new nations -- new nations with distinct and different geographical, cultural, political and social entities. Karl Von Vorys puts this into perspective:

> Political science for long has suffered from a certain ethnocentricity. As a systematic study it is rooted solidly in Western civilization. European and American cultures inspired most of its theory; European and American states provided most of its data.[1]

Grundy takes note of the more subtle ethnocentrism that permeates much of the literature on political development.

> In recent years tremendous concern has been expressed about the problems of what had first been identified as "backward," than euphemistically "underdeveloped" and now more positively "developing" or "emerging" areas.[2]

The question that should be raised, because of the very adjectives used to describe the developing nations, is "emerging" or "developing" toward what? The very connotations of the terms, in the eyes of most political development theorists, equated the concepts with democracy and development as the West knows it.[3] Added to this problem was the ambiguity associated with the term in intellectual conceptualizations. One scholar in the field of political development, Lucian Pye, noted at least ten different yet overlapping, meanings attached to the term.[4] But if the term political development has been ambiguous and value laden in its implications, the use of the term modernization can be classified in the same basic category. The term modernization implies that a society is democratic, healthy, educated, industrial and affluent with available, inanimate power and mechanical tools or by the extent of competitive allocation of roles and rewards.[5]

While the term political development has many overlapping meanings attached to it, Huntington suggests that there is a consensus among scholars upon nine characteristics associated with the term modernization which include the following: modernization is a revolutionary process, a lengthy process, a phased process, a homogenizing process, an irreversible process, and a progressive (emphasis mine) process.[6]

However, one can take issue with the last two characteristics of modernzation as an "irreversible" and "progressive" process. To speak of modernization as an "irreversible" process would suggest, as Huntington has elsewhere, that it is a unilateral process, when in actuality there may be political decay.[7] Nevertheless, it should not be implied that traditional or developing nations are the only ones that are "decaying" (even in the context that Huntington uses the word), for modern nation-states may also be "decaying." Furthermore, what Huntington suggests here appears to be merely a new twist to an old line (or perhaps, should we say lemon...or old "line"?). Western stereotypes, prejudices, and just plain 'ole ignorance has long typed people of the "Third World" as backward, uncivilized, traditional, etc. In fact, the very term Third World denotes, in the view of this author, a certain "coming of age" of a people as opposed to the First World, which apparently has already "arrived" and "made it" (assuming we all know intuitively, if not euphemistically, what these terms mean for people in the West). The question is--has Huntington really contributed anything new to our knowledge with the concept of political decay when perceived in this light?

2

It appears that concepts such as political decay merely involves neologisms to reassert an old theme.

On the other hand, to suggest that modernization as defined by the West is a "progressive" process appears to tell us that there is some inherent value in "progress" as opposed to what may be (or have been) the present state of affairs in a nation. This appears to be especially true in such transitional societies in which mobilization causes disorder, confusion and chaos in the drive toward "modernity." Or perhaps this can rightfully be interpreted unwittingly as a condemnation of European colonialism by some of the same scholars who tended to rationalize away colonialism's very existence.[8] In essence, even the suggestion that the Third World is now "developing" after the indigenous revolutions removed the yoke of colonialism may be a rather subtle admission that they were not "developing" but perhaps "decaying" under the reign of colonialism. It further appears to be extremely ironic that western theorists suggest that the Third World is now "developing" or "progressing" toward some model of the West given past western perceptions of the "Dark Continent" (Africa). This is especially true since Africans were always thought of as being "different." This point appears to be all too obvious for those of us with an epistemological foundation of Africa and African culture to warrant documentation.

Nevertheless, even with all the confusion between the concepts of political development and modernization as well as the ambiguity over the various perceptions and notions of what the terms within each conceptual framework denote, there have been more recent attempts to distinguish between the two as well as clarify the meaning of what each term should mean. Huntington has asserted that political development is distinct from modernization and often is impeded by the latter.[9] Huntington has also stated that the term "political development" be dropped because of its teleological implications, for the less dogmatic term of "political change."[10] On the other hand, Binder et. al. make a distinction between the terms political change and political development, favoring the retainment of the concept of political development while enriching its meaning. They propose that development is a process without an end point consisting of a political system's ability to find adequate resolutions to its crises

3

that are faced in the process of political development.[11]

So far, the discussion of the term political development has been limited to its origin, its ideological, its ethnocentric, and its teleological ambiguities, vis-à-vis the concept of modernization and the consensus and conflict that has developed around their meaning, as well as attempts to clarify and distinguish more recently between the concept of political development and modernization. By no means has this been an attempt to discuss the concept in a vacuum, but rather to criticize some of the more overt implications of the term.

It does appear somewhat ironic that Huntington suggests using the more neutral term political change in favor of development, given the more subtle and covert ramifications of his own term political decay when perceived and critiqued in the fashion above. In short, the term political change in preference to political development being a more neutral term even though he (Huntington) proposed that development might be decay. In this context, Huntington causes both ambivalence on the one hand and clarification on the other, i.e., decay in the first instance and change in the latter. Let us now turn to the term political development in the context that it is used both as an independent and dependent variable.

Political Development as a Dependent Variable

Up until the middle sixties, most of the literature treated political development as a dependent variable. This approach emphasizes political modernization and/or political democracy as goals and conditions of political development, stressing massive socio-economic and psychological forces as those conditions necessary to achieve those goals.[12] This dependent variable approach, however, was geared to imprecision as far as defining political development, based upon the assumption that everybody knew in some intuitive way what political development was. From this perspective of looking at political development as a dependent variable, five distinctive approaches are discernible. Let us proceed with the dialectics of each approach stressing political development as a dependent variable.

4

The legal-formal approach. This approach discusses political development mainly as a function of
the legal-formal apparatus of government, prescribing
such features as equal protection of the law, regular
elections by secret ballot, single-member or propor-
tional representation; in sum, a stress upon democratic ideals and liberties which is all too obvious
in its suggestive power. The legal-formal approach
was the only one in the study of political development
until 1950, and even up until then it was a stress
upon western states rather than developing ones.[13]

Pye states that the legal-formal approach and the
resultant colonization of people in the Third World
was the result of the manifestation of the universality
of European law as being applicable to traditional
societies throughout the world.[14] What is both significant and ironic with regard to this assertion is
the "manifest" assumption Pye makes with regard to
the colonization of African people which was similar
to the Manifest Destiny doctrine of the United States
in the nineteenth century which rationalized the West-
ward Movement and subsequent annihilation and "reservation" of the American Indian. One should ask the
question as to just what assumption on the part of
Pye should make one think that European law should be
universal? Surely, it was not that other countries
and traditional societies did not have laws. The
irony of this legal approach to political development
is that law, as Hah and Schneider have pointed out,
"has most of the characteristics of the colonial ethos
of the nineteenth century, which concerned itself
with such problems as constitutional government, rule
of law, and parliamentary democracy."[15] Thus, the
logical question which follows is how could one advocate law or the legal approach as a mechanism in the
process of political development or change when it was
so instrumental in hindering indigenous political
change in the first place? Since exogeneous political
and administrative institutions had the vested interest
of the colonizer at stake, European law in colonial
countries was geared to protect that vested interest.

The economic approach. This approach to the study
of political development arose as a reaction to the
excessive legal-formal interpretation of development.[16]
It views development as a function of the level of
economic development necessary and sufficient to serve

the material needs of members of the political system. Perhaps the economic approach best exemplified the American equation of political development with political democracy since western political development was deeply rooted in the economic philosophy of capitalism. A good example of a study that takes this approach is that by Ilchman and Bhargava.[17]

One of the methodological problems in this approach is the criticism often made that there is a too-close relationship between economic and political development and democracy. Such a conclusion is found in the work of Almond and Coleman as a result of their working hypothesis; that there is a positive correlation between economic development and political competitiveness--an essential attribute of a democracy.[18] However, economists themselves have come to recognize that in developing nations political factors are often more important than strictly economic ones.[19] Additionally, such an approach fails to recognize the discontinuities inherent in major economic policies and political change as well as the "lack of appreciation for the science of leadership and organization."[20]

The shortsightedness of the economic approach and scholars who approach political development in this manner is also inadequate because of their inability to perceive past economic exploitation in the quest for political development. Somehow, both political development theorists (economic or otherwise) as well as social science theorists in general appear to overlook the significance of such exploitation in the name of democracy in their discussions of the role of economics in fostering political development. Such negligence should not be dismissed as mere academic oversight, but rather the prejudicial nature of western scholars to perceive western history in its proper perspective.

The administrative approach. This third approach to political development discusses it as a function of the administrative capacity to maintain law and order efficiently and effectively and to perform governmental output functions rationally and neutrally. This approach is one that was best articulated by Max Weber in which he saw bureaucratization as an institutional form inherent in all democracies and characterized by neutrality, rationality, and achievement.[21] Further-more, and more important in this approach, is the ability of government to carry out public services while at the same time maintain law, order and stability in implementing the above characterizations. Again, one is confronted with an ironic situation in the literature on political development. It appears that the administrative approach is one that emphasizes bureaucratic stability when political change may be an unstable and unpredictable phenomenon. It emphasizes maintaining law and order when in actuality political change may constitute the need for disorder.[22] Of course, if one should argue that political order is the only way for development to take place, then disorder is a disruptive process. The political upheavals taking place today, however, should not lead one to any absolute assertions on the role of order and disorder, especially since political development and political change is a continuing process in the Third World.

A second criticism, interlocking with this one, is that being obsessed with outputs and goals on the part of the administrative structures fails to take into consideration the question of legitimacy. Political parties, factions, and interest groups in developing nations may see the incumbent leadership as illegitimate or illegal and not in the best interest of the nation. Thus, the administrative approach does not take into account the validity of interest group articulation and aggregation which may not be institutionalized (a theme we will come back to later in viewing political development as an independent variable, in more detail), but representing popular demands and external forces to the institutional norms and procedures. In brief, it assumes that the leadership in power should provide the means to stay in power at all costs.

Still another problem of both the administrative approach and those scholars who advocate it is the ambiguity of such administrative concepts as neutrality, rationality and achievement when applied to developing nations as well as to the West and more particularly the U.S. In the interest of academia, one must ask the pertinent questions of what type of political and administrative structure, at what structural level, and at what time period in the development of the U.S.? There appears to be gross generalizations with regard to such reference points when scholars suggest that administrative structures in the U.S. are achievement-oriented. Especially when nepotism, ascription, patronage, graft, corruption and the like were the rules of the day under political machines (although they were, for the most part, moribound institutions by the 1940's) and party organizations during the era of "machine politics" in the early twentieth century.[23] In this respect, the shortcomings of the administrative approach are not just applicable to developing nations, but to developed ones as well. This is especially true when there is a failure to locate the particular structure (political or administrative), the level of that structure (local, state, or federal), and the time period under discussion (for example, from the late nineteenth century through the middle of the twentieth local American political structures were permeated with corruption).[24] Local and state structures in the South were notoriously corrupt morally and politically as late as the 1960's in their treatment of Blacks with regard to the vote.

The Weberian model (that is, the emphasis upon rationality, neutrality, efficiency, etc.,) and the administrative approach to political development have come under attack by scholars for this emphasis upon certain Weberian criteria as best suited for bureaucratic functions. This is what has been referred to elsewhere as the "bureaucratic trap", i.e., assuming that the Weberian model of bureaucracy and administration are best suited for political change and modernization.[25]

The social systems approach. This approach views political development mainly as a function of a social system that facilitates participation in political processes at all levels, and that bridges geographic, religious, caste, tribal and other cleavages. This aspect constitutes a fourth approach to political development.[26] The social systems approach assumes that all major groups have some access in the arena of political decision-making. Cross-cutting memberships and multiple loyalties are the result of voluntary associations. Vertical links in this setting allow for the articulation of demands from lower-level groups to be aired in the decision-making process.

Within the social systems approach one may discern

8

what has also come to be known as the leadership approach,[27] in which the emphasis is not upon types of political development but rather strategies of political development in which the elite must contend with two dilemmas -- the manipulation and direction of social change and the maintenance of legitimacy. Such strategies on the part of the elites to obtain these ends may include charismatic leadership, nationalist ideology and the risk of routinization or national disenchantment which may result.[28] It has been argued that the "routinization of charisma", to borrow a Weberian concept, on the part of leadership while at the same time rationalizing the civil service in order to implement policy, and the subsequent direct control over the leaders subordinates and succession to his office, is what led to the downfall of Kwame Nkrumah and the military coup that replaced him in Ghana in 1966.[29] In this light, it is contended that while Nkrumah routinized his charismatic leadership, he went to the "well" once too often which led to his political demise. While continuing mass charismatic appeal, Nkrumah was not keeping one ear open for his administrators in regard to politics and programs that would have to be implemented in order for political change to be stabilized and enhance Nkrumah's leadership.[30] The consolidation of leadership strictly on the basis of charismatic appeal, can thus become a dangerous strategy on the part of the leader without effective policy outputs juxtaposed with it.

Although many arguments can be made for or against the social systems approach, in the interest of brevity only two criticisms will be offered here. One, how can it be assumed that developing nations are in the process of achieving what would surely have to be a utopian society, as the vertical link implies, in which every citizen has access to the decision-making process? When, in reality, it does not exist in western nations that go under the somewhat dogmatic rhetoric of democracy as their system of government. Furthermore, it goes without saying that many developing nations have "slapped democracy in the face" for socialism, communism and military rule as forms of alternative government. A second criticism of this approach, somewhat polemical in character, relates to the first. On what premise do western theorists base such assumptions that developing nations should have citizen access to decision-making? As a value premise what is it that makes one think that citizens, especially the rank-and-file, can or should have access to decision-making processes? After all, if one accepts the elitist theory of democracy, the masses are assumed to be uneducated, illiterate and insecure and that such participation in "democratic" processes can only lead to chaos and confusion and cause instability in the political system.[31] If this argument would ever appear to stand on any solid grounds in the continuing arguments between the pluralist and elitist proponents of democracy and community power, it would appear to have even more validity in developing nations and transitional societies in which political change often causes political instability and psychological insecurity.

The political culture approach. The political culture approach constitutes the fifth and final approach to political development as a dependent variable. In this regard, political development is viewed mainly as a function of a given political culture in society. This includes fundamental attitudinal and personality characteristics among members of the political system as equipped to be able to both accept the privileges (emphasis mine) and bear the responsibilities of a modern, democratic political process.[32] Packenham states that political culture can be viewed largely as a psychological concept working and occurring on two levels: 1) attitudinal or sets of expectations about political roles held by members of the polity, and 2) the level of personality.[33]

The question of identity as put forth by Lucian Pye explains its significance in regard to political culture and political development. Such identity is one found, first of all, either with the masses or elites in their political culture and second as one oriented to modern or traditional ways. Pye argues that the relationship between these divisions in political culture and the dichotomy between them seem to be crucial factors governing the total course of national development.[34] Pye's analysis of political development as an element of national or regional identity is useful because it takes into consideration not only tribal or caste systems per se but the role that identity plays in political development as a process. It helps to answer the question of whether or not an identity crisis can be overcome in attempting to "modernize" or whether it becomes a hindrance because of its roots in the traditional societal culture. Furthermore, it helps some of the more conservative western scholars

10

to understand why some traditional societies do not
or can not undergo political change as defined by the
West.

In sum, the normative theory of political development, i.e., one that defines the political system as
it approaches the "good" political order, is found mostly in the dependent variable approach. Although this
is not to say that all of the works found within these
approaches are categorically normative in this sense.
Generally speaking, it could be said that the contribu-
tion of such approaches has led to not only a better
understanding, as a whole, of what political development
involves, but also a better understanding of the shortcomings and premises upon which the approaches are set
forth in the first place. Perhaps the two most important variables and approaches in understanding political development are the social (systems) and psychological (political culture). They are important both
as analytical variables and as criteria for understanding political change processes. It is a combination
of these two variables that have influenced the alternative approach to political development and change.
Let us now turn to a discussion of political development as an independent variable.

Political Development As An Independent Variable

A second major approach to the study of political
development emphasizes the ability of leaders and elites
to cope with issues, demands and the needs of the society or political system cast upon them by the forces
of or the imprinted desire for modernization.[35] In
this respect the stress is upon the "will and capacity"
of leaders to cope with attempts at developmental
change. Stability is of the most importance and the
main ingredient upon which the approach is based.
Manfred Halpern states the significance of this approach:

> The revolution of modernization, however, is
> the first revolution in the history of man-
> kind to set a new price upon stability in any
> system of society; namely, an intrinsic capa-
> city to generate and absorb continuing trans-
> formation.[36]

Modernization and/or political development in this
approach are equated with stability maintained in the

11

system as a result of the political leaders "will and capacity" to cope with the "forces of change." Within this "capacity to cope" approach in looking at political development as an independent variable has developed what has come to be known as the developmental syndrome, in which there appears to be a consensus upon three elements implicit in all definitions of political development. These three elements are capacity, equality, and structural differentiation, which stresses viability as a quantitative relationship between them.[37] What is significant here is that the term viability, as stressed by Pye, suggests long-term persistence also in that the "capacity" of a polity must keep ahead of the egalitarian demands of the masses. On the other hand, terms such as equality, capacity and differentiation may be significant as a test for political development in the West as well as in developing nations. Using such a criteria one may question the "development" of the U.S. with regard to the treatment of Blacks, the U.S.S.R. with regard to the treatment of Jews, and undoubtedly "classic" colonial nations such as the Union of South Africa with regard to the treatment of Black Africans. In this context, when the capacity to control takes priority over demands for equality some western nations may be judged as underdeveloped.

This is also the dilemma between the rightest demand for control and the leftist demand for equality. It has been argued that the "developmental trap" of viability in political development is that to move too far to the right will bring about an increase in inequality and raise the capacity level for control, creating totalitarianism and dictatorial tendencies. At the same time, to move too far to the left will result in an increase in equality, bringing about chaos and disorder.[38] The real developmental trap, however, may not be that suggested by Riggs' assumption. That is, just as it is misleading to believe that patterns of political development must be guided by some democratic ideal, it is just as misleading, one could argue, to believe that the conceptual scheme of viability must be a dichotomy of totalitarianism on the one hand and chaos on the other. It may be more fruitful to view patterns of political development in the context of their own geographical, political and cultural settings rather than the tendency to make hypothetical assertions based upon the experiences and value preferences of the West. This should take into account not only the ideological orientations of the developing nations, but also what type of ideological patterns are most suitable for those nations, i.e., communism, socialism, etc. Nor should one assume, in such an examination, that such ideologies and political structures in developing nations are going to persist on a permanent basis, but look at their functional value in terms of both short-run and long-term effects. For example, can one assume, as stated earlier, that with the high rate of illiteracy and lack of education in developing nations that the masses are in a position to determine their own fate when there is a high degree of insecurity and instability among them in the process of social mobilization?

Similarly, should one assume that competitive or multi-party systems rather than a one-party system are viable in the process of political change when competition leads to further factionalism, and the quest for political development requires a unified outlook and concerted drive? The real development trap may not be either totalitarianism or chaos, but the inability on the part of developmental theorists to perceive the utility of chaos in bringing about political order, or totalitarian dictatorships giving way to more democratic forms in the long run once social mobilization has occurred.[39]

Interestingly enough, Huntington's reference to political decay and political disorder as praetorian politics are worth noting here as distinguished from political order. Kesselman states with reference to Huntington's emphasis on praetorian politics:

> Political order exists when everything is ship-shape, when all's right with the political world. Its opposite, political decay refers to praetorian politics, when the political arena is swamped by exogeneous forces (organized interests, tribes, military, students, etc). The concept thus obscures the legitimacy of the means used by government to maintain power. It ignores the danger posed by government that is strong (too) ...and the disorder that derives from officially sanctioned repression...The concept of political order is not neutral: it places the burden of disorder on subordinates who challenge elites. Decay refers only to

13

disruptions of the status quo by subordinates. Disorder that results because of rulers and ruling institutions who exert coercion falls outside the definition. Yet authoritiies may disrupt the status quo more than subordinates, and may create (or help perpetuate) a status quo that defies elemental requisites of the political community.[40]

Needless to say, the shortcomings of such an emphasis upon political order are that it fails to perceive as legitimate, demands cast upon leadership for policy inputs and decision-making in policy outputs. The earlier reference to Nkrumah bears this out. Corrupt leadership is not to be challenged by external forces, even if such leadership is not bringing about meaningful political change and is more concerned about consolidating its own power base. Focusing upon political order as a prerequisite for political change, as Huntington does, suggest that such an emphasis may in and of itself be "disorder." But what appears to be paradoxical in works stressing the independent variable approach is the emphasis upon order, stability, and the capacity of political leaders to absorb change. It appears that the capacity to cope should always run ahead of the forces of change, giving a conservative and status quo orientation (which itself appears contradictory) to the promotion of political change. But proponents of this approach do not see political development as a continuum toward some end-point which is obtained unilaterally, but rather as a means and ways of coping with the "revolution" on a continuing basis "from above."[41]

Within the capacity to cope approach in viewing political development as an independent variable there also has been identified six crises which political leadership in a developing nation must confront and overcome in order to cope with forces of change. Pye describes such crises as constituting the following: identity, legitimacy, penetration, participation, integration, and distribution.[42] Pye states that such crises are more difficult to contend with if they are of a ubiquitous nature or occurring at the same time. He points out that in England, however, these crises occurred in the order listed. A more recent and elaborate study on this capacity to cope approach to crises is the study by Binder, et. al.[43]

On the other hand, we are confronted again with

14

the dual nature of conceptualizations which are most often applied to developing nations as identified by scholars. Developed nations are faced with certain crises which may ultimately affect their stability and ability to govern. Could one not argue, for example, that there is also a legitimacy crisis in the United States among Afro-Americans, Puerto Ricans, Mexican-Americans and the American Indian? Is there not a penetration crisis with regard to reaching the poor, Black and White? Is there not an integration crisis which reached monumental proportions in the early sixties under Dr. Martin Luther King's leadership, a crisis that has been exacerbated by Black nationalists' demands for separatism and by the continuing controversy over school busing? And for that matter, is there not a racial crisis which supercedes the identity crisis developing nations are facing? The implications of these crises are all too apparent for developed nations. To say that the American political leadership can cope with them belies the very nature of their existence, which many Black Americans perceive as illegitimate.

Thus, to speak of these crises only with reference to developing nations, as suggested in the literature on political development, apparently misses a crucial concern here which has implications for this study. The crux of the matter is that many of the concepts and generalizations often applied to developing nations by scholars and intellectuals miss the point of their applicability and utility to a "developed" nation such as the United States, although such crises, for instance, have been applied to other western nations. Nevertheless, there has been an attempt in more recent years to equate particular regions of the American South to a "developing area" in the context of a comparative analysis. This will be examined in another chapter of this work.

What is important to keep in mind with regard to development theorists and theories are the many "trappings" that they themselves may be caught in when they interpret in theoretical terms political phenomena in the Third World as well as the utility of such concepts to western societies and specifically the United States. If there are certain crises, for instance, that have not been overcome in the United States, there is more than just an elite-mass gap of political integration (even if it is just ethnic minorities) which fosters nationalist sentiments and political activities which may parallel developing nations, even if the analogy is not complete. The bureaucratic trap, the trap of political decay, depending upon one's perception of Huntington's concept and what it implicitly may suggest, and the developmental trap. Let us now turn to one final area of political development literature and the possible "traps" that can or have been fallen into in the past. This is not to say, though, that this is a trap theory.

Stages of Political Development and Transition

Obviously, developing nations do not just go from being traditional societies to modern polities, if at all. There are, to be sure, certain "gaps" that must be fulfilled in the period of transition and during the initial stages of social mobilization (this is not to suggest gap and requisite theorists as necessary for successful political change as defined by the West in an earlier footnote). The period of social mobilization brings about individual and group insecurity as well as political disorder. Denis A. Goulet, realizing that progress is a two-edged sword, states:

> It exacts its price at all stages of the development process; the early steps, the intermediate periods, and the more advanced moments. "Transitional" individuals and societies thus find themselves caught...between two worlds: one dead, the other powerless to be born. At the very moment when they register "progress" they undergo unforseen disruptions and unanticipated problems.[44]

In order to attempt to deal with this problem, scholars have in the past suggested stages of development on a unilinear continuum. John H. Kautsky proposes five such stages which include: traditional aristocratic authoritarian, a transitional stage of domination by nationalist intellectuals, totalitarianism of the aristocracy, totalitarianism of the intellectuals, and democracy.[45] Kautsky argues that although there are political systems in which none of the abovementioned five types will be found in pure form, it is by putting them in pure form which allows for generalizations and comparisons to be made in political development.

Edward Shils has developed, contrary to Kautsky,

a fivefold classification rather than five stages of political development, based upon the social class characteristics of the elite. Shils suggests the following for analyzing political transition: political democracy, tutelary democracy, modernizing oligarchy, totalitarian oligarchy, and traditional oligarchy.[46] Of course, such a classification in and of itself still does not explain how traditional societies move to modern polities but rather emphasizes the characteristic nature of the elites and the type of political systems that they rule over.

A.F.K. Organski's work, on the other hand, is primarily based upon an economic premise of political development in which he concludes that there are basically four stages involved: political unification, industrialization, national welfare, and abundance. However, Organski's work is archetypical of the model of political development used before 1965 (1962), emphasizing economic development with political development as a dependent variable, stressing material wealth and abundance as the primary characteristics of a nation that has achieved "modernization" in the context of the previous discussion of the concept and its implications. It should be noted, however, that this is not an attempt to discuss exhaustively studies on political transition, but merely to point out initial types of studies that were taken in that direction. By doing so, we can get at the ambiguity of the concept and the emphasis in the literature as well as the direction that will be taken later in this research.[47]

It was because most studies on transition and political development implied that it was a unilinear process and explicitly revealed a "magnetic pull" toward democracy that Huntington initially suggested the term political decay might be more indicative of the phenomena of political development Third World nations were engaged in. Somewhat paradoxically, even though Huntington criticized stage theorists for explicitly stating political development as a unilinear process, he did not state in what manner a policy might proceed (that is, stages) to achieve political decay.

David Apter's work is interesting here because in a sense, it takes Huntington's lead by showing the dual nature of development. Apter looks at development as a process involving political decay or stagnation on

one end of the continuum and political development and
modernization on the other end. Apter focuses upon
traditional societies as the embryonic stage for change
and, although not listing particular stages of change
as Kautsky and Organski, is perhaps more academically
stimulating in his analysis for political change.
Using three authority types (hierarchical, pyramidal,
and segmental), Apter explains the reasons some societies are able to "advance" through certain stages of political development while others remain in the primary
stages of development, i.e., traditional.48 Depending
on whether the traditional base is an instrumental or
consummatory one, the traditional system can either
innovate easily by spreading the blanket of tradition
upon change itself without altering basic social
institutions, or be hostile to change and innovation
which threaten customary relationships, warmth and
intimacy, and institutions. Apter perceives two types
of developmental sequences which prevail as a result.
One, a secular-libertarian model approaching democracy
through reconciliatory traditional systems; and two, a
sacred-collectivity model approaching totalitarianism
through mobilization types of traditional systems.

     In this respect, Apter's work goes farther than
Huntington's in not merely stating that political
development really may be political decay and/or
stagnation, but suggesting what types of traditional
systems and under what conditions there may be political stagnation and/or political development. Apter
states the problem most succinctly regarding the foregoing discussion:

               Consider two traditional systems, one
               consummatory and the other instrumental
               in value type. Both are short-hoe cul-
               tures and an effort is made to introduce
               new agricultural techniques in each,
               particularly the use of tractors. In
               the consummatory system, changing
               from the short-hand-hoe system will
               so corrupt the ritual of the hoe-
               making, the division of men's and
               women's work, the religious practices
               associated with both, and the rela-
               tionship between agricultural rituals
               and the authority of chiefs that it
               would be impossible to consider intro-

duction of the tractor only in terms
of increasing agricultural produc-
tivity. In the instrumental system,
by contrast, the tractor would simply
be viewed in terms of its ability to
expand agricultural output and would
not affect the ultimate ends of the
system. In the first instance, such
an innovation represents a threat to
the system. In the second instance,
it is far likelier to strengthen the
system in increasing farm income.[49]

Several subtle impressions are worth taking note
of in Apter's work with regard to political development theory. One, which is rather revealing is the
complexity of traditional systems which is conceptualized in a framework as a confrontation between traditionalism and "modernization" or western technology.
This framework runs contrary to western notions of
traditional systems in the past which viewed them
as simplistic and ritualistic in nature. Two, and
related to this first impression, is the disruptive
nature of modernity with its impact upon traditional
societies. Because western culture is often perceived
as a foreign element intervening and interfacing with
traditional culture, it may be the very source of
political decay and stagnation since it often causes
social and political turmoil. It is this element
that is often overlooked by scholars, i.e., seeing the
West as the antithesis of political development rather
than the only source of it. As such, contact with
"modernity" can either initiate political change or
throw the traditional political and social system into
turmoil and stagnation. A third impression is somewhat
implicit in the foregoing statement. That is, the West
may not just be the source that initiates political
decay in traditional systems, but may be the prototype
of political decay. Just as Huntington suggested that
political development is not a unilinear phenomena in
the first place, it also appears clear to this observer
of politics that the West should not be perceived as
the standard for political development in such an
arbitrary manner as it has been in the past. Who is
not to say, for example, that the high crime rates,
air pollution, immorality, prostitution, etc., that
has come with western industrialization do not
represent political stagnation and decay at the other

end of the continuum? In short, what developing nations are struggling to achieve in the name of modernization (if that means that it must be some facsimile of the West) may have as an end result political decay. This would appear especially true if development and the importation of western technology and industrialization have a correlation with high crime rates, immortality, pollution, etc. [50]

This chapter has attempted to highlight the concept of political development in order to bring out the more conspicuous aspects and variables with which it is associated and the western biases associated with the concept. Given the ambiguity of the term, it appeared necessary here in order to put the concept of political development into perspective with respect to Afro-American political change. Many of the criticisms and comparisons of the concept of political development with the West are pertinent here because it has implications for the model of Afro-American political change in Chapter Four. Our discussion now moves to Chapter Two in which we discuss the domestic colonization of the Afro-American in the United States.

Notes

1. Kark Von Vorys, "Use and Misuse of Development Theory", in Contemporary Political Analysis, ed. by James C. Charlesworth, (New York: Free Press, 1967), p. 350.

2. Kenneth Grundy, "Nkrumah's Theory of Underdevelopment", World Politics , 15, (April, 1963), p. 438.

3. Willner suggest that such studies and scholars which equate political development with democracy, or the reasons that new nations have failed to develop democracy, can be characterized and categorized as "gap" and "requisite" theorists. "Gap" theorists attempt to find explanations for the failure of democracy taking root and barriers to democratic norms and development. "Requisite" theorists, the corollary of "gap" theorists, merely tend to elaborate more on the same themes by "specifying the 'prerequisites' or attributes of democratic societies." Ann Ruth Willner, "The Underdeveloped Study of Political Development", World Politics, 16, (April, 1964), p. 472. Similar themes on western ethnocentrism in studying political development are found in Mark Kesselman's "The Literature of Political Development as Ideology: Order or Movement?", World Politics,

25, (October, 1973), p. 153; Ali A. Mazrui, "From Social Darwinism to Current Theories of Modernization", World Politics, 20, (October, 1968), pp. 76-80.

4. Lucian Pye, Aspects of Political Development, (Boston: Little, Brown and Co., 1966), Chapter Two. Von Vorys also highlights this ambiguity, "The concept of political development itself could stand a more uniform definition...Views differ...on the questions whether political development denotes progress toward a specific objective and if so what this specific objective may be." Op. cit., p. 355.

5. Von Vorys, op. cit., p. 359. Whitaker presents a good critique and objections to the term modernity in a discussion of northern Nigeria. See C.S. Whitaker, Jr. "A Dysrhythmic Process of Political Change", World Politics, 19, (January, 1967), pp. 190 - 217.

6. Samuel P. Huntington, "The Change to Change", Comparative Politics, 3, (April, 1971), pp. 288-90.

7. Samuel P. Huntington, "Political Development and Political Decay", World Politics, 17, (April, 1965), pp. 386-430.

8. Some of these gross ethnocentric rationalizations will be discussed in the next chapter on colonialism.

9. Samuel P. Huntington, Political Order in Changing Societies, (New Haven: Yale University Press, 1968).

10. Samuel P. Huntington, "The Change to Change", op. cit.

11. Leonard Binder, James S. Coleman, Joseph LaPalombara, Lucian Pye, Sidney Verba and Myron Weiner, Crisis and Sequences of Political Development, (Princeton: Princeton University Press, 1971).

12. Robert A. Packenham, "Political Development Research", in Approaches to the Study of Political Science, ed. by Michael Haas and Henry Kariel, (Scranton: Chandler Publishing Co., 1970), pp. 169-93.

13. Robert A. Packenham, "Approaches to the Study of Political Development", World Politics, 16, (October, 1964), pp. 108-20. All five approaches are discussed elaborately in this article along with the extensive bibliography that is provided.

14. Lucian Pye, Aspects of Political Development, pp. 122-25.

Pye's more elaborate discussion on the legal-formal appraoch begins from p. 113.

15. Chong-Do Hah and Jeanne Schneider, "A Critique of Current Studies of Political Development and Modernization", Social Research, 35, (Spring 1968), p. 133.

16. Ibid.

17. Warren F. Ilchman and Ravindra C. Bhargava, "Balanced Thought and Economic Growth", Economic Development and Cultural Change, 14, (July, 1966), pp. 385-99.

18. Gabriel Almond and James Coleman, The Politics of the Developing Areas, (Princeton: Princeton University Press, 1963).

19. Hah and Schneider, op. cit.

20. Ibid., p. 136.

21. Robert A. Packenham, "Approaches to the Study of Political Development." Also see Max Weber, The Protestant Ethic and the Spirit of Capitalism, (New York: Scribner, 1948), and Lucian Pye, op. cit., especially pp. 14-23.

22. For perceptive insights on this point and how bureaucracy can hinder political development, see F.W. Riggs, "Bureaucrats and Political Development: A Paradoxical View", in Bureaucracy and Political Development, ed. by Joseph LaPalombara, (Princeton: Princeton University Press, 1963), pp. 120-67.

23. For instance, see Alex Gottfried's article "Political Machines", in the International Encyclopedia of the Social Sciences, 12, (1968), pp. 248-52; G.M. Kammerer and J.M. DeGrove, "Urban Leadership During Change", as well as the other articles that can be found in the Annals of the American Academy of Political and Social Science, 357, (May-June, 1964). Also, see Robert Michel, Political Parties, (New York: Dover, 1959), for a good analysis of political bosses in the context of European socialist parties.

24. Some of the best studies with regard to structures and functions was initially produced by Talcott Parsons. For example, see The Social Theories of Talcott Parsons, ed. by Max Black, Talcott Parsons and Robert Bales, (Englewood Cliffs: Prentice-Hall, 1961), and Edward Shils, Working

Papers in the Theory of Action, (Glencoe: Free Press, 1953).

25. On this point, see Merle Fainsod, "Bureaucracy and Modernization: The Russian and Soviet Case", in Bureaucracy and Political Development (op. cit.), pp. 233-267. This is also noted by LaPalombara in the same book, pp. 10-11; John Buecher, Public Administration, (Belmont: Dickinson Publishing Co., 1968); and Berton Kaplan, "Notes on a Non-Weberian Model of Bureaucracy", Administrative Science Quarterly, 13, (December, 1968), pp. 471-83

26. Robert A. Packenham, op. cit. On this approach see also Rupert Emerson, From Empire to Nation: The Rise to Self Assertion of Asian and African Peoples, (Cambridge: Harvard University Press, 1960).

27. Hah and Schneider, op. cit., p. 145.

28. Ibid., Also, see Hah's reference to Seymour Lipset, The First New Nation, (New York: Basic Books, 1963).

29. Henry Bretton, The Rise and Fall of Kwame Nkrumah, (New York: Praeger, 1966). This is not the only interpretation of Nkrumah's fall from power. Other views include extravagancy, not enough concern with domestic affairs in his involvement with Pan-Africanism, and taking Pan-Africanism too far. See Rukudzo Murapa, "Nkrumah and Beyond: Osagyefo: Pan-Africanist Leader", Black World, 21, (July, 1972), pp. 12-20.

30. Ibid.

31. On this point, for example, see Thomas Dye, The Irony of Democracy, (Belmont: Wadsworth Publishing Co., 1970); and William Kornhauser's The Politics of Mass Society, (New York: Free Press, 1959). This is not to say, though, that the social systems approach is of little or no utility. It is only to point out some of the shortcomings of the approach when development theorists proceed under certain assumptions. To the contrary, the social systems appraoch represents, in the mind of this author, a great improvement over the legal-formal and administrative approaches.

32. Robert A. Packenham, op. cit.; Almond and Verba, The Civic Culture; and Daniel Lerner's The Passing of Traditional Society, (Glencoe: Free Press, 1958).

33. Robert A. Packenham, "Approaches to the Study of Political Development", p. 117.

23

34. Lucian Pye and Sidney Verba, Political Culture and Political Development (Princeton: Princeton University Press, 1965).

35. Robert A. Packenham, op. cit.

36. Manfred Halpern, "The Revolution of Modernization", in Comparative Politics, ed. by C. Macridis and Bernard E. Brown, (Homewood: The Dorsey Press, 1968).

37. Lucian Pye, Aspects.

38. Fred Riggs, "The Theory of Political Development."

39. However, this is not to say that studies have not been done on the short and long-run effects of dictatorships or the role of ideology, only to say that not enough have been incorporated under the rubric of political development. For a good study of the effects of terror and totalitarianism, for example, see A. Dallin and G. Breslauer, Political Terror in Communist Systems, (Stanford: Stanford University Press, 1970); and Alexander Eckstein, "Economic Development and Political Change in Communist Systems", World Politics, 22, (July, 1970). For a look at the role that ideology plays in political development, one may look at Ideology and Discontent, ed. by David Apter, (New York: Free Press, 1964).

40. Mark Kesselman, "Order or Movement", pp. 142-43. Kesselman presents an excellent critique of Huntington in this article. His argument is a reference to Samuel Huntington, Political Order in Changing Societies, (New Haven: Yale University Press, 1968).

41. Manfred Halpern, op. cit. Other studies that one may look at that take this approach include Joseph Nye, "Corruption and Political Development", American Political Science Review, 61, (June, 1967), pp. 414-427; and S.N. Eisenstadt, "Modernization and Conditions of Sustained Growth", World Politics, 16, (July, 1964), pp. 576-594.

42. Lucian Pye, Aspects of Political Development, see especially pp. 62-67.

43. Binder, et. al., Crisis and Sequences in Political Development.

44. Denis A. Goulet, "Development for What?" Comparative Political Studies, 1, (July, 1968), p. 302.

45. John H. Kautsky, Political Change in Underdeveloped Countries:

24

Nationalism and Communism, (New York: John Wiley and Sons, Inc., 1962).

46. Edward Shils, _Political Development in the New States_, (The Hague: Mouton and Co., 1962).

47. A.F.K. Organski, _The Stages of Political Development_, (New York: Alfred A. Knopf, Inc., 1965). One may also look at, with regard to this point, W.W. Rostow, _op. cit._, and Robert E. Ward and Dankwart A. Rustow, _Political Modernization in Japan and Turkey_, (Princeton: Princeton University Press 1961), and the previous reference to Binder, et. al., _Crisis and Sequences of Political Development_, which is a more contemporary study.

48. David Apter, _The Politics of Modernization_, (Chicago: University of Chicago Press, 1965).

49. David Apter, (ed.), _Some Conceptual Approaches to the Study of Modernization_, (Englewood Cliffs: Prentice Hall, Inc., 1968), p. 115. A similar work, but with a somewhat different emphasis, is that of S.N. Eisenstadt, "Breakdowns of Modernization", _Economic Development and Cultural Change_, 12, (1964), pp. 345-367. Seen in twenty-twenty hindsight, perhaps Huntington should have followed Eisenstadt's lead, in which Eisenstadt assumes that in the early stages of development, polities and political leadership are faced with political and economic problems, which, if not solved, may lead to political stagnation yet causing conditions distinctively different from the traditional society out of which change was attempted.

50. This is by no means a novel assertion. That is, to associate the West with political decay. In fact, western thinkers and philosophers had a _weltschmerz_ view of the West during the thirties and forties. It is somewhat novel when injected into the literature on political development, since, developing nations were often perceived on a teleological course toward some "good" associated with the West (although even as a _leitmotif_ it has been pointed out as an erroneous assumption) when it was never questioned as to whether the West represented a developed utopia in the first place. In essence, even the association of political development as a unilinear process never questioned political decay and stagnation on the other end of that continuum. It does seem somewhat ironic, though, that the shift from the West as a decaying social order to developing nations and the subsequent question of decay, brought about a total refocusing as to what types of polities may be in decay. For a look at some of the literature that

associated the West with a dying social order, although it
was not with regard to political development theory, see
Huntington's "The Change to Change", op. cit., especially
pp. 290-93. Huntington speaks of two schools of pessimism,
one centered around a cyclical theory of humanity in general,
and a second focusing exclusively upon western society, p.
290.

CHAPTER II

DOMESTIC COLONIALISM AS A SOCIAL PROCESS

A popular theme that has arisen in the last decade
has been the development and elaboration upon what has
come to be known as the colonial model. This model
has been articulated upon in scholarly literature and
heatedly debated in academic circles. This model has
risen as a competing one to that of the assimilationist[1] and culture of poverty[2] models in attempting to
explain why Afro-Americans have not become integrated
in the same manner as other ethnic groups in America,
even though this is not to say that such ethnic groups
have not maintained part of their cultural heritage
in the process.[3] The model of domestic colonialism
suggests that certain characteristics of colonial
systems are analogous to Afro-Americans in America
in terms of similar experiences shared. In the discussion, however, that will follow, certain reservations should be kept in mind. To begin with, the
analogy perceives a'la Blauner, internal colonization
as the "common process of social oppression", or what
Blauner refers to as the "colonization complex",[4] in
which certain elements associated with colonial domination have been the same regardless of the type of
political and economic system of colonialism, or the
"Mother Country" which colonized. The emphasis here
will be upon the "subordinate" rather than the "super-
ordinate", in short, the colonized rather than the
elites who dominated them. Past studies on "classic"
colonialism have tended to take this latter approach,
rather than emphasize the resulting social and psychological behavior which results in the "colonial mentality." Curtin notes that nine-tenths of recent
scholarship looking at the colonial period focuses
upon European conquests, politics and colonial government and the like while almost nothing is said about
how Africans responded to colonial rule or how colonial
politics affected the African personality.[5]

In this respect, three objectives should be kept
in mind. First, we want to "validate" the model of
internal colonialism as argued by its proponents, by
setting up the parameters of the framework of analysis
while distinguishing it further from "classic" colonialism. Second, once the parameters of analysis in the
context of internal colonialism are defined, a dis-

27

cussion of colonialism as a social process will be pursued. This will look at the impact of colonialism on an indigenous people and the behavior and attitudes resulting from this social process. For the purposes of comparative utility by revealing similarities, the analysis will distinguish colonialism as a social process in the "internal" and "classic" colonial settings under four sub-headings: forced entry, impact upon social and cultural organization, domination and manipulation of political and economic institutions, and racism. A third objective here is to set the stage for the "decolonial" or political change model in the next chapter. It is proposed that the many writings that have become fashionable on internal colonialism and racial oppression are not sufficient to explain aspects of political change that are taking place in the Black community.

This is not to say the colonial model is no longer of utility in explaining the political conditions of Afro-Americans, but that it is of limited value if it shields one from another perspective that has academic value as well as a prescriptive orientation. In this sense, the model to be developed in the following chapters can be viewed as a competing explanation or alternative to the emphasis of the colonial model of exploitation and oppression. Also, in this regard, the model of political change assumes that the emphasis upon structures in the American political system that foster or perpetuate oppression can, somewhat para-doxically, cause political change. This argument will be developed further in the model of Afro-American change and political integration.

It should be kept in mind here, nevertheless, that the utilization of the term internal colonial model does not represent or constitute an empirical analysis per se, and hence as a model is limited to theoretical assumptions that have not been tested. As such, it represents an approach to studying the social and polit-ical conditions of Afro-Americans which, until more recently, past explanations such as the "assimila-tionists" and "culture of poverty" models have failed to do in this perspective. From this vantage point, the literature drawn upon here should be viewed as selected not just upon the basis of supporting or making an appropriate "fit" with the colonial analogy, but rather as past and present research upon social,

28

political and economic aspects of Afro-Americans that
will provide fruitful parameters for investigating
Blacks under colonial conditions. Thus, this observer
of politics is not just attempting to support the
colonial model, but to suggest it as a competing one
and some of the limitations of it with regard to
political change.

Furthermore, in suggesting it as a competing model,
it attempts to show that the domestic colonial model
is analogous to classic colonialism in the dependent
relationship that still exists, especially but not
exclusively, in the Black ghetto. Empirical indices at
the end of the chapter will be utilized to validate
this discussion and serve as empirical referents for
further investigation and research on domestic colonialism.

Domestic and Classic Colonialism

What is colonialism? How is domestic colonialism
distinguished from classic colonialism? What is it
that leads man to dominate man as has happened in the
Third World? What does it involve? And how does it
affect the colonized? What is the motive for entering
into, and subjugating an "alien" culture? These are
but a few of the questions that we want to raise and
provide tentative answers to in this chapter. From
a historical viewpoint, Curtin notes two traditions
of western historiography that tended to neglect an
emphasis upon Africa:

> One was a deep ethnocentric bias:
> history was the study of "our" past,
> which emphasized English history in
> England, French history in France, and
> American history in the United States.
> Africa was simply beside the point.
> And history was elitist--concerned with
> those who governed countries, won
> battles, invented, discovered, and
> innovated.[6]

Curtin goes on to utilize the concept of colonialism as "a government by people of one culture over
people of a different culture--usually of European
over non-Europeans", in which a distinction must be
made between race and culture, i.e., physical traits

and a way of life that is learned, asserting that the latter was more important than the former in colonialism, and that a distinction must be made between internal and external (domestic and classic) parameters, points to the fact that although South Africa achieved its independence from Britain in 1931, it in no way changed the status or experience of the majority of South Africans.

Proponents of domestic colonialism argue, interestingly enough, that a similar parallel with Blacks during the American Revolution existed. Although the 13 colonies achieved independence from Britain, it in no way changed the status of Blacks, who were slaves. Blauner would also suggest, in similar fashion to Curtin, that in the traditional sense colonialism not only involves political domination but also economic, in which the colony exists subordinated to, and dependent upon, the "Mother" country.[8] Blauner also takes note of the internal-external distinction of colonialism with regard to Blacks. He suggests that domestic colonialism differs from the classic sense in the internal setting in that the group culture and social structure of the colonized in America is less developed and less autonomous; and that Blacks constitute a numerical minority, they are ghettoized more totally and more dispersed than people under classic colonialism.[9]

Balandier speaks of two characteristic features of colonialism as having a causal relationship. In short, economic imperialism and exploitation under colonial domination is based upon the seizure of political power.[10] The concept of colonialism has also been defined as well as conceptualized, and H. Laurentie defines the "colony" as one in which a European minority not only imposes itself upon a majority of a different culture with a force disproportionate to its numbers, but a force that is also extremely contagious by its nature and causes social distortions in the relationship.[11]

On the other hand, the most provocative Harold Cruse, one of the most articulate proponents of the domestic colonialism school of thought, makes the following differentiation between classic and domestic colonialism:

The only factor which differentiates

the Negro's status from that of a
pure colonial status is that his
position is maintained in the "home"
country in close proximity to the
dominant racial group. It is not
at all remarkable than that the
semi-colonial status of the Negro
has given rise to nationalist
movements.[12]

In another passage linking Afro-Americans with
the colonial analogy, Cruse states:

The American Negro shares with colonial
peoples many of the socioeconomic factors which form the material basis for
present-day revolutionary nationalism...
the Negro suffers in varying degrees from
hunger, illiteracy, disease, ties to the
land, urban and semi-urban slums, cultural
starvation and the psychological reac-
tions to being ruled over by others not
of his kind. He experiences the tyranny
imposed upon the lives of those who
inhibit underdeveloped countries.[13]

What Balandier refers to as a "social distortion"
and Cruse as the "psychological reaction", Mannoni
refers to as one of "misunderstanding" between "civilized" and "primitive" men in which a unique situation
is created, that of colonialism, in which illusions
are generated on both sides which is the result of
psychological mechanisms.[14] Even though Mannoni's
psychological arguments have achieved a degree of
legitimacy in their own right since past studies have
tended to focus upon colonial structures and politics,
his work has come under fire. Balandier, for example,
notes that colonialism cannot simply be viewed as a
relationship between the exploited and exploiter, or
the dominant and dominated. Balandier states that one
must also look at the ethnic divisions among the people
colonized and the extremely heterogeneous character of
the cultures that are found in the colony. Fanon, who
speaks of "psychic injury", also argues with Mannoni's
contention that such a "misunderstanding" is not based
upon racism but rather economic factors that keep
Blacks "in their place" in South Africa. Fanon contends
that South Africa has a racist societal structure.[15]

Like Mannoni, Cruse, and Fanon, Memmi also emphasizes the psychological and cultural destruction that
takes place among the colonized, but in his various
writings does not limit his research to only the
behavior generated, but also to economic and institutional arrangements which he contends are missing in
Fanon's works.[16] Memmi also attacks Fanon with regard
to the psychological concept of "deficiency", i.e., the
inferiority complex that lingers on among a people even
in the decolonial or revolutionary independence stage.
Memmi argues that Fanon harbors a certain degree of
revolutionary romanticism in that he tends to overlook
this reality because it is embarassing and repulsive,
assuming like so many social romantics that the victim
of oppression remains proud and intact even in the face
of such oppression.[17] But Memmi is somewhat ironic
in that he argues that economic and institutional
arrangements play no small part in domination and
colonialism, yet makes the same fallacious assumption
as the "culture of poverty" theorists by suggesting
that such arrangements correspond to certain "deficien-
cies" within the colonized, implying that it is the
colonized who are "deviant" rather than what may be
the pathological social and political structures that
have created this condition.[18]

The colonial model, however, like the assimilationist and culture of poverty models, has also come
under attack as an alternative in explaining the
social, economic, and political conditions of Blacks
in America. These criticisms deserve some attention
before moving on to the four sub-topics of domestic
colonialism as a social process. One of the more vocal
critics of this model is Nathan Glazer who argues that
if one takes the pessimistic view of Blacks as "different" from White ethnics and that Blacks are really
"bad-off", one could also make the provocative argument that other ethnics are also in "bad shape" rather
than "ship-shape".[19] Furthermore, Glazer makes the
distinction between: 1) Blacks in the South and the
racism encountered, and 2) Blacks who migrated to the
North, which is more conducive to the colonial analogy;[20] but, if one argues that the experience that
Blacks have encountered in the North with regard to
racism were really no different, especially in the
realm of housing and school segregation, it would tend
to suggest that de jure and de facto segregation may
be tantamount to the same thing. The main thrust of

Glazer's argument is aimed at critiquing three main premises of Blauner in distinguishing Blacks from other ethnic groups. These premises of Blauner can be summarized as follows: 1) ethnic ghettoes arose more from voluntary choice as well as the choice to live among ones fellow ethnics in segregation, whereas Blacks were brought to America as slaves under "forced migration", 2) immigrant ghettoes tended to be one or two generation phenomenon, Black ghettoes persist as a phenomena over a longer time span, and where ethnic ghettoes (other than Blacks) tend to persist, it is because they are in big business and profit, and 3) European ethnic groups generally achieved economic control of their communities in less than a generation, whereas with Blacks economic, political and administrative control of education, the police, teachers, etc., remain in the hands of Whites who live outside of the Black ghetto.[21]

Glazer argues that although all three of these positions can be supported, the differences are smaller and the similarities (between Black and other ethnics) are greater. In short, that Blauner has exaggerated, or at a minimum, overstated his case. With regard to the first point, Glazer states that Afro-Americans migrated to urban areas on a voluntary basis, were not forced, and according to an empirical case study of New York by Kantrowitz, segregation and ethnicity is often, although not conclusively, a voluntary phenomenon. On Blauner's second assertion, Glazer argues that the ghetto duration (emphasis mine) of dwellers is not uniform even among White ethnic groups, and that White ghettoes have a longer life than suggested, while Black ghettoes are more mobile than suggested. Finally, Glazer responds to Blauner's third premise that depends upon whether we speak of the 300 year history of Blacks in America (which would tend to support Blauner), or their relatively new arrival in the cities as latecomers.[22] But Blauner's arguments have credence precisely because the colonial model of domination speaks of the ghetto as "internal colony", rather than the colonization of Blacks on a national level as a whole. Contrary to Glazer's impression of Afro-Americans as "latecomers", one would have to question the political and economic status and conditions of Blacks in the rural South for 300 years, rather than after World War II. Since the "forced migration" of Blacks predated the arrival of the new immigrants in the

late ·19th and early 20th century, it is questionable
to label Blacks as "latecomers" unless one can categorize their status while in the rural South.

But if the colonial analogy has come under fire by
Glazer in the distinctions that Blauner asserts are
prevalent between White ethnics and Blacks and their
social mobility and the immigrant experience in the
context of the ghetto, it has come under criticism as
a model in more general terms, i.e., not limiting the
parameters of the analogy specifically to the Black
ghetto and urban areas, but to Afro-Americans from a
legal standpoint. Hayden points out three such objections, although the last is more from a historical
perspective than a legal one: 1) Afro-Americans are
nationalized Americans, not of a separate national
identity, 2) the U.S. Constitution supports equal
citizenship for all, and 3) racism is based in historical prejudice rather than economic profit.[23]

While many criticisms could be launched against
this "legal assault" on the colonial model, in the
interest of brevity let us assume only three opposing
arguments for each point. One, for Hayden to suggest
that Blacks are nationalized Americans is in no way
related, to the treatment they have encountered under
the system of racism or under the system of slavery.
When the U.S. was in its embryonic stage, the first
conceptualization of Blacks in social and legal terms
was as "three-fifths" of a man for purposes of tax-
ation and representation. With regard to Hayden's
second point, it is mainly a matter of closing the
gap between theory (equal citizenship for all) and
practice (the systematic treatment of Blacks to
"second-class citizenship"), which has been all too
apparent historically for elaboration here. Finally,
for Hayden to say that racism is based in historical
prejudice rather than economic exploitation denies
the lessons of colonialism to begin with, i.e., economic profit and a "superior" technology was part of
the impetus for colonialism, rather than just prejudice.
We will elaborate more upon this theme later. But this
is not to say that prejudice did not play a role in
colonialism, only that it was perhaps subordinated
and used as a rationale for cultural and racial domination.

In speaking of colonization as a "social process"

which, as noted earlier is distinguished from colonialism as a social, economic and political system, the
former is a common experience that colonized people
have shared as a result of oppression throughout the
world. Keeping this in mind as well as the distinctions made between internal-external or domestic-classic
colonialism, let us proceed keeping two overall objectives in mind here. First, as noted earlier, the main
emphasis is upon the "dependency" and behavior that's
created if one argues in the context of domestic
colonialism. This is not to say, however, that all
Blacks, therefore, suffer from some type of behavior
resulting from domination and discrimination. But it
is to note that all Afro-Americans, irrespective of
class, have been subjected to cultural domination to
some extent. A second overall objective will be to
suggest some empirical indices that would tend to
support assertions made here. Realizing that behavior
is complex and not easy to test and that the attitudes
and behavior of a people are not necessarily congruent,
it should be kept in mind that such indicators only
represent tentative and suggestive ones rather than
absolute ones.

Forced Entry

To state in somewhat proverbial terms, let us
begin with the beginning, i.e., the origins of colonialism and the concept of "forced entry", and rationales
that were subsequently developed to justify it. Sartre,
for example, in an illuminating work on colonialism,
argues that in order for colonialism to be effective
it must deny the humanity of the colonized in order to
eliminate nagging self-doubts among the colonizer
about the humanity of the oppressed, perceiving the
natives as "exotic" in order to justify the treatment
of them as "objects" rather than human beings.[24]
Kinloch, in a somewhat similar vein, argues traditional
"American" values such as materialism, individualism,
and the moral philosophy embraced in "manifest destiny",
--an ethnocentric definition of one's culture as more
civilized than another and divinely ordained by
religion to overcome the latter, allows for an inferior
view of others. Kinloch states: "Other race groups
are viewed from this value standpoint: Indians were
'savages', Negroes, 'barbaric', Orientals, 'clannish',
and 'treacherous', Mexicans, 'inferior', and various
white ethnic groups, "un-American."[25]

This, in no small way, was the types of attitudes developed also among southern slaveholders to justify their domination of Blacks during the antebellum period in America. It was argued that Blacks were heathens, savage and uncivilized.[26] Apter, in his stimulating work The Political Kingdom of Uganda, speaks of three stages in the classical context of colonialism which are associated with a moral superiority and rationalization of domination which involve: 1) a pioneering stage in which the conquerors have the feeling of bringing a "new" civilization to a conquested country, 2) a "political-administrative" stage, involving institutionalization and ethical justification for such rule, and 3) a bureaucratic stage, when the moral fervor has died along with the ethical justification, and rule is rationalized more in terms of the technical advantages accrued to the ruling group than the moral-ethical justification.[27]

Conceptually speaking, under the notion of internal colonialism from a historical viewpoint, once slavery became economically profitable rationalizations were developed to justify the subjugated position of Blacks as slaves.[28] Kinloch notes this with regard to Blacks as well as the American Indian concerning structural characteristics:

> The structural characteristics of American society are surprisingly colonial: a minority group of white Protestants migrates to another society, attempts to drive off or exterminate the indigenous Indian population for economic reasons but rationalized in religious and philosophical terms, sets up a plantation slavery system, and imports other race groups for economic purposes, submitting them to social and economic discrimination. Under these circumstances, race is a very "real" social category, utilized as a mode of social control and economic exploitation...[29]

On the other hand, Balandier, like Apter, suggest that economics and technical advantages were more important in the process involving forced entry which was followed by revolution for independence, citing history writers: "Most historians...have shown how such upheavals were made necessary by 'colonial imperialism (which) is merely one manifestation of economic imperialism'. [30]

Curtin puts forth yet another view in stating that in:

> ...recent years prominent Marxist historians and economists have dropped the idea that economic motives prompted the Europeans to conquer Africa; at least one attibutes the exploitation of Africa to the poverty of European capitalism, rather than to its desire for expansion. [31]

Curtin goes on to point out, however, that this is not to say that such motives were not materially motivated, only that such initiatives which tied it to aspects of the European economy never had a prominent body of advocates. Again the parallel can be made here between the classic motives for colonization and the domestic motives in the United States, in that southern slave owners also needed a "cheap" source of labor, in order for slavery to be profitable. [32]

In summation, perhaps the best parallel leading to colonialism in the classic sense and the domestic sphere under this subheading (forced entry) is that of Cruse:

> From the beginning, the Negro has existed as a colonial being. His enslavement coincided with the colonial expansion of European powers and was nothing more or less than a condition of domestic colonialism. Instead of the United States establishing a colonial empire in Africa, it brought the colonial system home and installed it in the Southern states. When the Civil War broke up the slave system and the Negro was emancipated, he gained only partial freedom. Emancipation elevated him only to the position of a semi-dependent man, not to that of an equal or independent being. [33]

Blauner states that a prerequisite for colonialism may have been the slave trade linked with domestic colonialism in America since it decisively changed the percent of the population in Africa, making conquest a foregone conclusion.[34] Most significant in the fore-going discussion, if one accepts the colonial analogy, is that the source or origin for colonialism was the same in the United States and in Africa. Kinloch, for example, takes note of the many social and structural similarities between the United States and South Africa and their evolution as colonial societies. The main point of the discussion here was to point out similar-ities in the origins of colonialism which laid the groundwork for proponents of the domestic colonial model in comparing it with colonialism in the more tra-ditional sense of the word. As such, if one were to argue this position, he would have to take into account that in the instance of Afro-Americans, colonialism was "exported", to use Cruse's term, to the Mother country.

Impact Upon Social and Cultural Organization

Here we are concerned with colonialism as a dis-ruptive process, which arose out of similar origins in the conquest of Africa, and has vastly affected the social and cultural organization and cohesiveness of Afro-Americans in particular and Africans in general. One of the most striking parallels between colonialism in Africa and colonialism in America as a social pro-cess is the separation of cultures and language along tribal lines, although perhaps with different conse-quences. With regard to early American colonialism under the system of slavery, Africans were systemat-ically separated along tribal and linguistic lines to prevent communications which may have led to slave revolts and violent upheavals for uhuru. Singer states the diversity of backgrounds Afro-Americans came from:

> Africans who were brought to North
> America, as well as to other parts of
> the New World, were representatives
> of a variety of societies, cultural
> backgrounds, language groups, and so
> forth. Consequently, as a totality
> they can only be viewed as a social
> category, that is as "Africans" or
> "slaves."[35]

But the impact of slavery upon cultural and social organization must be distinguished from the "diversity" of ethnic (tribal) backgrounds in this colonial "partitioning", if one is to suggest that this type of socio-cultural separation is tantamount to the territorial partitioning under the more traditional system of colonialism. Emerson and Kilson make this point in arguing that North American slavery, which conceived of slaves as mere property, cut the Afro-Americans indigenous organization into shreds by its disregard for the slaves past social, cultural, economic and political institutions.[36]

On the other hand, the argument still lingers as to whether Afro-Americans have had all of their social and cultural ties erased under early American domestic colonialism, or whether traces still exist in contemporary Afro-American culture of their African heritage. Frazier, for instance, has noted that almost all remnants of social organization disappeared under slavery.[37] But Blasingame and Dalby, to mention but two scholars, have argued that Afro-Americans still maintain African ties in their culture and social relationships, taking note of Black dance, music, folklore, names and certain linguistic patterns.[38]

If one presumes that the family is the smallest unit of social analysis, the disintegration of the Black family under domestic colonialism and slavery had its greatest impact. The Black family was systematically broken up, the male head sold as mere chattel, there was no legal status as citizens or human beings for familial members, children were automatically born into slavery, and slavemasters were not held responsible to higher authorities for the way that they treated "their" slaves.[39]

Blasingame, in rather illuminating passages, notes not only the dissolution of the Black family under slavery, but also the cruelty and severity often incurred in the process:

> The most serious impediment of the man's acquisition of status in the family was his inability to protect his wife from the sexual advances of whites and the physical abuse of the master...By all odds, the most brutal aspect of slavery

> was the separation of families. This
> was a haunting fear which made all of
> the slave's days miserable... Nothing
> demonstrated his powerlessness as much
> as the slave's inability to prevent
> the forceable sale of his wife and
> children...It is obvious, when all of
> the factors contributing to dissolution
> were added together, that the slave
> family was an extremely precarious
> institution.[40]

Furthermore, as Frazier has pointed out, not
only was the Black male denied all sociological and
economic functions associated with being a father
and husband, but his role was relegated mainly to a
biological one of physical reproduction as a "buck."[41]
It is from this vantage point that more recent studies
which have emphasized the role and impact of slavery
upon the Black family have assumed their legitimacy,
i.e., seeing the Black family structure and life-style
as "deviant," such as the "tangle of pathology" in
The Moynihan Report and the "culture of poverty" theses
that have been put forth.

For the sake of congruency, let us now draw some
parallels analogous to the more classical colonialism
in the African setting. Staples points out that the
rationale for domination and subjugation and consequent
enslavement was justified by war. He states: "In
ancient societies, and in the colonial period, slavery
was justified by the 'just' war theory--a nation
victorious in a war justified enslaving the heathens."[42]
The rationale for domination should be distinguished
from the purpose for domination that was alluded to
earlier, in which such a distinction in the latter case
lies in the economic motives underlying the subjugation
rather than reasons advanced to explain and justify it
by the colonizer.

Black African families, by-and-large, stayed intact
to a much greater extent in the context of classical
colonialism than did the Black family under domestic
colonialism. Cultural and social organizational links,
although undoubtedly impeded upon, were not cut off
from the traditional identity as in the case of Afro-
Americans. In fact, Curtin suggests that:

> African historians from the new uni-
> versities in typical Africa have not,
> in fact, been very much concerned to
> argue about the colonial period in the
> whole of Africa...They are not much
> concerned about the loss of African
> culture, because they recognize that
> African culture is not lost in their
> countries.43

But in a broader perspective, the more traditional colonialism had similar effects to domestic colonialism as far as tribal disintegration goes. What Pye has referred to as the "scramble" for African territory, was one of tribal disintegration which resulted in par-titioning and "artificial" boundaries that were set up which did not take into account the diversity of tribal, political and cultural orientations, often splitting tribal kingdoms in half and "lumping" various ethnic groups into homogeneous colonies, assuming that the "natives" were for the most part alike.44

In early colonial America, on the other hand, the "common experience" of Blacks was one under slavery which systematically separated Blacks of the same tribes, although for different reasons. Sekou Toure of Guinea suggests that Africa's present problems stem from this colonial heritage. Toure emphasizes that Africa's cultural foundations or sense of group iden-tity (communocracy) have been destroyed in which a sense of individualism or personal egotism has replaced it, but is alien to Africa's past and hostile to its unity. Toure states: "'The voice of the African people is without face, without name, without a sense of individualism'".45

If one draws the parallel between classical and domestic colonialism in the context of their social and cultural impact, it virtually lies in comparing the tribal "disorganization" of the African with the cultural and familial ties of the Afro-American. In the latter instance one could argue that domestic colonialism had a much greater effect upon group iden-tity and the Afro-American under the system of slavery than it did with European colonialism in Africa. The African family unit, as well as tribal identity, were kept intact for the most part during the colonial period, and African culture remained cohesive. If one argues,

41

however, the colonial parallel with Afro-Americans origination in slavery, it could be asserted that the effects were much more damaging. Tribal identity was diffused for political and economic reasons, and the Black family unit was systematically broken down. When viewed in this perspective, political and structural characteristics of the colonial society are more explanatory variables in understanding the social and cultural "disorganization" among Blacks than social-psychological characteristics inherent in the life-style of Blacks. This part of the chapter examined the impact of colonialism upon the social and cultural organization of the Afro-American and the African as a component of colonialism as a social process. This leads to a discussion of the political and economic institutions under the control of the colonialists, which follows.

Domination and Manipulation of Political and Economic Institutions

Two major concerns will highlight the discussion here. Political and administrative control and domination of subordinates, and ways and means to perpetuate that domination by colonialists will be discussed in the first part. Economic aspects of domination that are associated with colonialism, and the analogy linking the more classical aspects of colonialism with those in the domestic sphere will constitute the second part of the discussion.

Unlike other ethnic groups who came to the city and urban areas in the North, it has been argued that Blacks encountered decaying economic and political structures. Patronage was passe', "Bossism" a past phenomenon, and machine politics "reformed" (or so one is led to believe). To the contrary, one of the main contentions being put forth today is that political machines have not become outdated, they have only changed their form and function. Lowi, in an illuminating study entitled "Machine Politics--Old and New", maintains that:

> Politics under Reform are not abolished.
> Only their form is altered. The leg-
> acy of Reform is the bureaucratic city-
> state. Destruction of the party foun-
> dation of the mayoralty cleaned up many
> cities but also destroyed the basis

for sustained, central, popularly-
based action. This capacity, with
all its faults, was replaced by the
power of professionalized agencies.
But this has meant creation of new
bases of power. Bureaucratic agencies
are not neutral; they are only independent...The bureaucracies--that is,
the professionally organized, autonomous
career agencies--are the New Machines.[46]

Metropolitan government, a relatively new form to
cope with the increasing complexity of an urbanized
society and which has become synonomous with the
"bureaucratic machine" in some circles of thought, is
often seen by critics as but yet one more means to
"return" political power to the suburban White middle-
class. The rubric of "consolidation", "metropolitan
re-organization", and "annexation" are seen by its
critics as an intentional means and mechanism whereby
numerical majorities will be returned to the affluent,
albeit White, suburban areas, while still leaving
metropolitan rule among the Black ghetto masses dependent upon Whites.[47] Cloward and Piven maintain that
such elements as metropolitan consolidation, organizational vehicles, and increased voting strength in
the suburbs will delete, or at a minimum, negate Black
control of the cities in the future even with Black
majorities increasingly becoming a trend.[48]

Of course, Black control of urban areas may differ
from region to region, depending not only on their
Black majorities but also upon liberal White constituencies, coalitional politics and the like. What is important here is the degree of dependency that is maintained, whether it amounts to a colonial relationship,
and whether such dependency was intentionally created.
But there is validity in both of the above arguments
for maintaining the dependent relationship since, for
instance, there are few Black professionals and administrators percentage-wise who could staff such "bureaucratic machines" and man positions of leadership.
Furthermore, one must question whether such Black
administrators could put "politics in command" ahead
of their "professional" orientation in dealing with
their "own folk." Sjoberg, Brymer, and Farris, for
example, in a study of the urban lower class, argue
that the goals and orientations of bureaucracy toward

the poor and those orientations of the poor toward bureaucracy are antithetical to each other and that contact between the two only breed further "misunder-standing", to use Mannoni's term. They state that:

> Because bureaucratic officials find it difficult to understand the perspective of lower-class clients and because lower-class persons must increasingly cope with highly specialized and technically ori-ented systems, the social distance between the bureaucratically skilled members of American society and some elements of the lower-class may be increasing rather than decreasing...Bureaucratic structures... serve to maintain and reinforce patterns that are associated with the "culture of poverty"...bureaucratic systems are the key medium through which the middle-class maintains its advantaged position vis-à-vis the lower class.[49]

Murphy comes to similar conclusions with regard to the status quo orientation of bureaucracies: "Bureaucracies...frequently act as the custodians of the status quo and as such represent a major impediment to change".[50]

Proponents of the colonial analogy in terms of dependency argue that welfare bureaucracies, on the other hand, are but another means to keep Blacks dependent and also serves as a means of political socialization. Cloward and Piven assert that:

> Low income people are drawn into these systems as recipients. They are attracted by the promise of benefits, and once in the system, they remain tied to it by the benefits they receive...they are proffered at the discretion of the pro-fessional bureaucracy. They can be employed as threats and rewards to influence client attitudes and ensure conforming client behavior...The threat-ened denial of essential benefits is a powerful sanction to control client behavior.[51]

44

Nevertheless, the movement for metropolitan consolidation may, in reality only be one of degree as
far as the concept of political and economic dependency goes, since most urban areas are already decaying and dependent upon massive economic help from the
"outside." What is implied here is that political
independence with Black leadership in urban areas may
be of little comfort when economic initiative is still
generated from "without" rather than from "within."

Bryce-Laporte has argued elsewhere that the Black
ghetto is not only dependent upon White suburbia, but
that from an institutional standpoint the ghetto is
today much like the slave plantation. He argues that
although the ghetto is not owned or managed by a single individual, it is still "Mr. Charlie" or "the Man",
that the discrete stratification of White dominants
and Black subordinates in an urban residential context
is no crucial break from the smaller and more simplified plantation structure, merely an elaboration. He
further maintains that although specialized functions
are not as utilitarian as the plantation, it shares
the same universal function of exercising control and
custody over the different and unequal through police
patrols, garbage collectors, unscrupulous merchants
and the like. Bryce-Laporte, nonetheless, concedes
that the ghetto has a much greater degree of complexity
than the plantation.[52]

On the other hand, it has been argued that the
new Black and rising Black leadership serves only as
a "buffer" between the affluent, White communities
surrounding metropolitan areas and the poor, Black
communities located within the ghettoes. Tryman and
Glazer, for instance, in different studies have come
to the same conclusion, suggesting that an emerging
philosophy among the White "backlash" vote in metropolitan areas may be one of electing Blacks to "control" Blacks.[53] Glazer states that:

> ...we have seen a good number of cases
> now in which the backlash, instead of
> going to elect law-and-order men, have
> gone to black and liberal candidates,
> on the reasoning that the blacks and
> liberals have more credibility with
> the Black population and will be able
> to prevent riots.[54]

Salamon, in an empirical study of emerging Black political leadership in Mississippi in which he compares such leadership to developing nations, contends that such leadership may not differ in any great degree from the more traditional society in which such leaders had a privileged position even in the racial caste system since they still have access to traditional resources that the Black masses lack.[55] However, Salamon does concede that the electoral process has also opened the door for "grassroots" people to run and compete for positions of leadership, but notes that even the "grassroots" people do not constitute radical modernizers.[56]

A question that must be raised here in the context of domestic colonialism is whether such leadership tendencies, urban and rural, represent such a form of dependency under the colonial model? Will such a "strategy" be or can it be uniform? Although proponents of domestic colonialism may infer that this is a systematic strategy on the part of Whites, it does not necessarily mean that it will take place on a large scale or for that matter that it will be successful. One may look at the reforms and benefits that Hatcher has brought to the lower class in Gary, for example, to see that the election of him as a Black was not one just to "keep Blacks in their place", although Tryman states that many Whites may have voted for him just for this purpose.[57] The more recent elections of Black mayors in large cities such as Detroit, Atlanta and New Orleans would also tend to show that Black elected officials will not merely serve as overseers for the White electorate.

In summary, the application of the internal colonial model in the politico-administrative context to the Black ghetto and Blacks at-large may create a dependent relationship in some instances, but not all. It undoubtedly shares some similarities with the classical model of colonialism in Africa, such as the Dual Mandate policy of the British, in which native authority was still subordinate to the colonial administration.[58] Still, such dependency cannot be applied across the board, and, it may, as Metzger has noted, be more indicative for analytical terms as a subordinate-superordinate relationship, rather than a colonial one.[59]

Economic Aspects

The economic parallels between the ghetto and developing nations that have broken the shackles of colonialism has perhaps gained the greatest credence among those who have argued the existence of such parallels. Tabb offered one such argument:

> The black ghetto is best viewed from the perspective of development economics. In its relations with the dominant white society, the black ghetto stands as a unit apart, an internal colony exploited in a systematic fachion. There are limits to such a parallel, but it is helpful as an organizational construct.[60]

Tabb goes on to suggest that by viewing the ghetto as an internal colony or developing "nation" may be more pertinent for policy alternatives in dealing with the problem of poverty. Winegarden makes more distinct parallels between the Black ghetto and developing nations, stating:

> In a relative sense, black America may be designated as a less developed country. It displays, when compared with the surrounding white population many of the classic symptoms of the less developed country (LDC) syndrome including low income per capita, inadequate levels of skill and education, inferior conditions of health and well-being, scarcity of "native" entrepeneurship, "shortage" of capital, and a chronically high incidence of unemployment and underemployment. These and other negative elements interact generating the familiar "vicious circles" of such societies. Of course, there are deviations from the classic pattern, of which the most conspicious are the geographic dispersion of the black people within an advanced nation and their partial integration into the political and economic life. Nonetheless, the parallelism is so striking...[61]

Like Tabb, Winegarden suggests that such parallels
and comparisons may be more fruitful for analytical
and policy implications. David notes, however, that
three major objections have arisen to the colonial
analogy from an economic standpoint which include: 1)
the impossibility of characterizing or delineating
the ghetto or "ghetto economy" in physical or spatial-
temporal terms, since developing nations represent
political, national and geographic entities, 2) less
developed nations are characterized by a "mass culture"
of poverty whereas poverty in the Black ghetto is different in kind and in form, and 3) ideological preferences which see the Black ghetto economy as merely one
part of the larger American economy, rather than as
part of the Third World economy.[62] But David "objects
to the objections", so to speak, in arguing with
regard to the first criticism, that not only are Black
ghettoes covered by a glacier of poverty, but that
there are 163 such little economies in the U.S. that
do have structural uniqueness. To the second point
David answers that there is a culture of poverty in
the ghetto (although David does not suggest that it is
bred from within), that has had a long history of
economic backwardness, marginal growth (if any), no
scientific and technological achievement, a primitive
system of production, and no firmly established economic institutions or public procedures. Finally,
David argues in regard to the third objection that
such an ideological bias stems from the conservative
leanings of contemporary economic thinking which in
its world-wide application is culture-bound.[63]

Again, no across-the-board conclusions can be
drawn in relating the degree of economic dependency
in making the analogy with internal colonialism. Even
David argues that Black ghettoes represent a broad
spectrum as far as degrees of dependency and development:

> It could even be justifiably claimed
> that in some cases the condition of
> life in some ghettoes are even worse
> than in some developing countries...
> All these countries are formally in
> the same boat. The black ghetto
> community is somewhere in this spec-
> trum. Some black ghettoes are at the
> top of the poverty spectrum, others at

an intermediate stage, while others are at the bottom.[64]

On the other hand, although Tabb draws parallels between economic aspects of internal colonialism with that of classical colonialism, he argues that a competing "model" to that of internal colonialism is Blacks in the ghetto as a "marginal working class." Tabb notes the existence of a dual labor market in the Black ghetto, one for White and one for Black, the former relatively high paying, with stable employment, and with good working conditions, and the latter with less attractive arrangements in each respect.[65] Tabb further asserts that White immigrant groups, under the influence of American capitalism, have in the past played this role and that because of the economic conditions of Blacks in the ghetto today, they now must play this role.[66] Nevertheless, criticism of this explanation lies in the fact that Afro-Americans have always been the "last-hired-first-fired", as the proverbial expression goes, moreover, it does not take into account that Afro-Americans, for the most part, have always occupied the lower-paying, dirtier, and less-skilled menial jobs. Consequently, it is not a phenomenon that arose with their migration to urban areas after World War II, i.e., depending upon the time period that one uses as a point of reference and if one assumes that Blacks are not analogous to White ethnics and the immigrant experience. However, if one accepts Tabb's model it does offer explanatory power if one assumes that the White immigrant and Black experience have enough similarities to be comparable.

A much more devastating thesis with regard to Afro-Americans as a working class is that which has been put forth by Yette, Wilhelm and Boggs, which suggest that the masses of poor Blacks, unskilled and untrained, represent a "dysfunctional commodity" in a highly urbanized and technological society.[67] In a sense, this thesis can be viewed as the antithesis of the domestic colonial model. If the latter (domestic colonial) is argued that Afro-Americans are dependent upon the Mother country for survival, the former (dysfunctional commodity) argues that the Mother country was once dependent upon the lower-class, Black masses to perform the low paying and unskilled jobs in America, but such dependence is minimized given the technological revolution and computerized society that we live in today.

Wilhelm, in what may to some appear to be exaggerated terms, states:

> ...the trend of technological development implemented in terms of economic incentives and racism points to what seems to be an inevitable dispensability for the black race...Under the economy of past technological configuration, it was incumbent for White America to balance racial values against economic incentives. But with the introduction of automation, the necessity virtually disappears, since it is economically feasible to negate the traditional rationale for the Negro's existence...The purged Negroes amount to waste by economic standards, and undesirables by racial feelings in White America. The combination makes not only for poverty, but neglect approximating complete oblivion.[68]

Yette, also in tracing the economic dependency upon Blacks in the past to fulfill menial but yet necessary jobs, argues in somewhat similar rhetorical terms:

> Black Americans have outlived their usefulness. Their raison d' etre to this society has ceased to be a compelling issue. Once an economic asset, they are now considered an economic drag. The wood is all hewn, the water all drawn, the cotton all picked, and the rails reach from coast to coast. The ditches are all dug, the dishes are put away, and only a few shoes remain to be shined.[69]

If one is to suggest any one major objection to this thesis, which the authors uphold as relevant to the economic status of the Black masses, it may be world opinion. In international relations that are becoming increasingly polarized between East and West, the Third World and developed nations, such a policy leading to physical "extinction" may be impractical as well as imprudent. It would appear contradictory also with regard to the image of America as leader of the "Free World", and the continuing protest, for instance, in America against the oppression of Russian Jews. Let it suffice to say that this argument is put forth here only as a competing thesis to explain the conditions of the Black masses in the economic sphere to that of the colonial analogy and the "marginal working class" theses. Undoubtedly, it represents the most critical argument with regard to the economic status and conditions of the Black masses, who still predominate the ghettoes of America.

By a twist of irony, Wilhelm and Yette's thesis suggests not that Blacks are in an economic state of "dependency", but that America is gaining its economic independence from Black menial labor in a computer and technologically oriented age. It is doubtful, however, if this "dysfunctional commodity" thesis will lead to physical annihilation of Afro-Americans, and it is questionable if it is analogous to classical colonialism in this regard, although undoubtedly there have been mass killings of Third World people in colonial nations such as Vietnam and South Africa. It does serve some utility also in the fact that it calls attention to the plight of the Black masses, who still live in penury, rather than upon the Black middle class, on which many studies tend to focus. In perspective, all three of these competing theses (domestic colonialism, marginal working class, and dysfunctional commodity) serve this purpose of focusing upon the Black masses, who are still poor, confined, and "dependent" from an economic standpoint, and it is here, from the notion of dependency, that all three theses gain some validity with the idea of internal colonialism. As suggested above, the degree and form of such dependency may differ from ghetto to ghetto and one should not attempt to generalize here in making broad-based assertions about internal colonialism. Rather, it should be looked at as representing a competing explanation to other themes[70] that have been put forth which purport to speak of the proper paradigm for analyzing the conditions of the Black masses in America.

Racism

Perhaps one of the most controversial concepts related to race relations in America and the focus of a continuing polemic today is racism. In the context

of our discussion here, we want to focus upon two particular aspects of racism--its origin and the negative
identity that is created (stigma), rather than the psychological advantages accrued to those who dominate
and practice it.[71] In this vein, as noted earlier,
the emphasis here is upon the dependency created in
psychological terms among subordinates.

Origin

     There is considerable controversy as to what gave
rise to racism in America. Some have attributed it to
rationales needed to justify the position of Blacks in
slavery, in which Blacks are perceived not as humans,
but as Kinloch suggests, "objects" or "things", often
with paternalistic overtones,[72] in order to justify
degenerate practices toward them. Blauner argues that
it was the technological and cultural superiority of
Europeans and their initial contact with Africans that
laid the basis for racist ideologies to reinforce this
attitude.[73] In this regard, some have also asserted
that economics, not race per se, was responsible for
the enslavement and subordination of Blacks in America.[74] In this sense, the genius of Marxist analysis
lies in maintaining that there is an economic basis to
exploitation, especially in capitalist countries,
although it is debatable as to the accuracy or applicability of Marxist class analysis to Blacks if one contends that race and race doctrines are more important.
Consequently, themes which projected Blacks in stereotyped, docile roles such as Elkins' Sambo-type merely
tended to reinforce the view of Blacks as inferior and
as property rather than as human beings.[75]

     In a somewhat similar vein, Kuper argues that race
became an important variable in colonialism because it
has been selected as such:

          Where racial difference becomes an
          important principle in the structur-
          ing of a society, it is because it
          has been selected, and socially elabo-
          rated, as a criterion of stratification,
          following conquest and colonization
          by people of a different race or
          consequent of enslavement. Racial
          differences is not a sufficient con-
          dition for racial discrimination.[76]

Subsequently, such ideas embraced more dogmatic content in the form of Social Darwinism, Scientific Racism, and Biblical quotations to justify subordination of one people, and domination by another.[77] On the other hand, Winthrop Jordan contends that economics may not have been as responsible for developing racial ideologies as prejudicial attitudes held by Europeans, and especially the English, as early as the sixteenth century in the Elizabethan Period. Arguing that the English associated Black with evil even before contact with Black Africans, and that the English made contact with such Africans at about the same time that they came into contact with apes such as the Orangutan, Jordan asserts that such racist doctrines that developed later may have been a foregone conclusion.[78]

But the concept and origin of racism in the context of colonialism lies in its value of how colonial superordinates perceived the colonized. Kuper suggests the significance of race in this regard:

> The institutionalization of race, and the subjective awareness of it, are not, of course, new phenomena. The spread of colonialism over the world was a manifestation of this internationalization of race; and the colonizers' experience of races living in different territories throughout the world encouraged a more generalized conception of racial difference... propelled by the dynamic of material interests and ideological needs, they emerged quite readily out of domination over great empires. And critical analysis of colonialism, of racist theories, and of imperialist domination over subject peoples added to the international dimension of the race question.[79]

It is no coincidence, therefore, when viewed from this perspective, that it was people of color in Africa and Asia that were colonized and enslaved, with race playing no small part in this process. Whether the origin of racism in relation to colonialism can be attributed to economic exploitation and rationales, cultural and technological superiority, or to prejudicial attitudes on the part of conquering Europeans may be secondary. The significance of the argument lies primarily in the role race played in justifying dominate-subordinate relationships that existed in both the domestic and classical spheres of colonialism.

Negative Identity and Stigma

Under the notion of colonialism, one should ask the question: What is the socio-psychological effect of being ruled over, dominated, and exploited by others not of one's kind? That is, assuming that the emphasis of colonialism is upon the impact and effect on the colonized, rather than the colonizer. It is a question such as this that should be kept in mind in the present discussion, if one should interpret the experience of Afro-Americans as domestic colonialism. Pettigrew suggests that not only is it debatable to contend that Afro-Americans are comparable to the immigrant by analogy, but that the analogy often overlooks the special and debilitating "stigma" placed upon Blacks from slavery to contemporary times, not withstanding certain stigmas placed upon other White ethnic groups, and the inferiority associated with the social status of Black people.[80] The concept of stigma is used by Pettigrew in the social psychological sense: "stigma signifies a handicap which disqualifies an entire class of persons from full social acceptance."[81] Pettigrew goes on to note that while it may not be associated only with physical appearance or a permanent handicap, it does evolve around the idea of inferiority.

However, such stigma does appear to have racial overtones in America, though the following may seem absurd to some, it is perhaps more relevant than academic. First consider, if you will, the noted Black historian C. Eric Lincoln's passage:

> Mary had a little lamb
> Its fleece was white as snow
> And everywhere that Mary went
> That little white lamb could go.
>
> Mary had another lamb
> Its fleece was black, you see
> They thought he was a "you-know-what"

And hung him from a tree.[82]

A similar Afro-American "folk-saying" that depicted White as "good" and Black as "bad" went:

> If you're White, you're alright
> If you're Brown, stick around
> But if you're Black, stay back![83]

And finally, Fanon's debilitating experience in a crowd of Whites in Malagasy when a child simply remarked:

> Look, a Negro![84]

While the foregoing passages may appear to have more aesthetic than academic relevance, it does have more than just a rhetorical ring of truth to it. Lincoln suggests that although there is no trace of color-consciousness among the various African tribes in the precolonial era, 250 years of slavery, 100 years of marginal participation in a ubiquitous, pervasive White culture in America, and being severed from one's parent culture with such finality, it is not unpredictable to think that Blacks would adapt a modification of the cultural values of the host society.[85] There is, of course, documented evidence of many incidents and practices in which Blacks have attempted to emulate and imitate physical and cultural characteristics identified with Anglo-Saxon culture. Emerson and Kilson, for instance, note that such emulation of a dominant culture by an oppressed group is not limited to Afro-Americans. They draw parallels between Black women at the turn of the century in America changing from African cosmetic standards for treating the hair to that of White women's standards, and that of Black women in Carribean communities, urban Brazil and urban West Africa.[86] The authors draw the same parallels with these countries with regard to being ashamed of one's skin color.[87] This is not to say, however, that such emulation and imitation continue on a large scale today, especially with the increased Black consciousness of the sixties. To the contrary, the model to be developed in the next chapter will contend that the dominant culture of America is in conflict with the emerging one in "Afro-America." Such assertions here provide investigative avenues if one were to pursue the domestic colonial model and the socio-psychological effects upon a colonized people. The domestic colonial model also provides the foundation which suggest the need for a competing model.

Not only has there been a certain stigma associated with color, but there has been documented attempts of Blacks separating themselves from other Blacks with regard to "status." For example, Dollard's pioneering socio-psychological study on race relations in the South revealed not only a caste system that separated Whites and Blacks, but also a class system of stratification among Blacks themselves in which certain benefits were to be accrued to Blacks with a "higher" status by keeping distance between themselves and the "lower" class of Blacks.[88] Similarly, Warner developed a bi-model approach to race relations in the Old South which depicted it as a political and social system divided into two mutually exclusive categories labeled color-caste. Each category of caste was divided internally by social class. Certain endemic southern norms governed class and caste relations respectively, and in the Warner two-category model there was seldom any ambiguity as to what norms were appropriate in any social relationship, i.e., Black and White as well as relations between Blacks themselves.[89]

The noted Black sociologist, E. Franklin Frazier, unlike Dollard and Warner, extends the "intra-class" cleavage of Blacks to the urban North. Frazier points out that even though the "old" Black middle class is distinguished from the "new" Black middle class with the latter placing less emphasis upon family stability and thrift, the new Black middle class places a similar emphasis on a "light" complexion, whereas the old Black middle class valued mulatto ancestry.[90] Frazier states that even though this new Black middle class diligently and self-consciously attempts to prove to Whites that they are intelligent, thrifty and consequently "different" from the Black masses, they still suffer from feelings of inferiority and frustration since they are still subjected to the same racial discrimination as the Black masses, even in the face of their own economic progress.[91] Here the Marxist analysis, as noted earlier, would appear to have its greatest shortcoming since, as Frazier points out, Blacks have been subjected to racism and discrimination irrespective of their class status.

Emerson and Kilson maintain that such stigma may not be limited only to domestic relations between Blacks and Whites. From a foreign relations point of view, they maintain that it is still a debatable question with regard to the desirability of sending Black ambassadors to relatively newly independent African and Asian states, suggesting that such nations may feel that they are getting "second-class" representation since there is a certain stigma and disfavorable attitude toward Blacks within the United States.[92] Pettigrew states that the complexity and social psychological consequences of racial stereotypes may create a type of vicious circle with regard to race relations, which may proceed as follows:

> Both whites and Negroes can confuse their
> own roles as being an essential part of
> themselves. Whites can easily flatter
> themselves into believing that they are
> in fact "superior"; after all, does not
> the deferent behavior of the role-play-
> ing Negro confirm this "superiority?"
> And Negroes in turn often accept much
> of the mythology; for does not the
> imperious behavior of the role-playing
> white confirm this "inferiority?"...
> In short, racial roles have profound
> and direct psychological as well as
> behavioral effects upon their adopters.[93]

In the context of colonialism as a social process, what Fanon has referred to as "psychic injury" rather than just material exploitation, is at the heart of the foregoing discussion. For instance, one could argue that the "psychic injury" to Afro-Americans was even greater than that which occurred to Africans during colonial domination, for even though Africans, too, often emulated those who ruled over them, familial and tribal orientations remained intact except for the partitioning effect of colonialism which split up some tribes into different European territories. Curtin notes that in instances in which African culture was most cohesive, racism hurt the least and that the African's sense of identity and self-respect was directly related to the frequency of contact with Europeans.[94]

In this regard, Curtin argues that in North

America where Europeans were a majority there was probably greater psychic injury, to use Fanon's expression, than in South Africa. Euro-Americans so thoroughly dominated information and communication channels in the early decades of this century that Blacks indeed were led to the half-belief that they were inferior, especially since differences in language and communication patterns between the races were long since erased.[95]

If one is to propose that such psychic injury inflicted upon Blacks is, in fact, part of colonial domination, one could argue that racism was not merely a southern phenomenon involving de jure segregation, but also has been prominent in the North although it has come under a different term--de facto segregation. Hare's amusing yet penetrating analysis of the Black middle class, like Frazier's, bears out the idea that imitation of the dominant, White culture by Blacks was not merely a southern phenomenon as much as it is a class one among Blacks themselves, irrespective of geographic location.[96] In this sense, it could be argued, Blacks are not just segregated in a de facto manner along racial lines, but as noted above, they impose segregation among themselves along class lines.

On the other hand, the negative identity that Blacks have taken on has been coined as a "nowhere identity",[97] and in other psychological terms as a "surrendered identity",[98] the latter term suggesting that the Black male could never truly assert his manhood in an oppressive society in the face of danger, for to do so often meant instant death.[99] Pettigrew, too, suggests that for the Negro not to play his formal "role", he may be judged by Whites as "not knowing his place" and severe and oppressive sanctions could follow.[100] Friedman argues that from a historical and psychological perspective, no less than five elements are responsible for the negative identity that Blacks have taken on which include: systematic debasement, the role of missionaries in projecting Africans as savage and heathen, schools and elementary education which also projected such stereotypes, the mass media, and the peer groups of Black children which tended to reinforce such negative identity.[101]

If an important aspect of colonialism is the degree to which the colonized emulate the dominant and oppressive culture, then certain classes and lifestyles of Afro-Americans, past and present, should show indications of it in their speech patterns (Hare), social values (Frazier), class stratification (Dollard, Warner, Salamon), and physical appearances to "look White" (Emerson and Kilson). But if one is to interpret such phenomena as merely a reaction to being ruled over by others rather than a social process of domestic colonialism analogous to classic colonialism, a more objective, or at least a less semantic, concept for analytical purposes would be such sociological euphemisms as dominant-subordinate or majority-minority relations, in which the culture of the dominant group is superimposed on the subordinate one. Obviously, from the foregoing discussion, Afro-Americans have shared many similar experiences with other people who were subjected to colonial rule, but the analogy breaks down if one were to argue that Blacks are fighting for physical independence in the same sense as African states, which are separate geographical and political entities. In this vein, one could suggest that mental and cultural "decolonization" may be a more appropriate and realistic appraisal of the contemporary movement among Blacks in America, if one argues that Blacks are domestically colonized. Also, one could argue a position contrary to the one articulated upon here, and that is that Blacks do not display a negative identity or crisis of identity. McCarthy and Yancey, for instance, in a more elaborate summation of the literature reviewed here, not only present major theoretical statements concerning the negative identity of Blacks, but challenge such assumptions:

> ...to the degree that Negroes do not use biased white evaluators in developing a self-evaluation, the process of development of self-identity within the black community will parallel the development process in the white community, and to that degree, when social class is controlled, Negroes and whites should not differ in levels of self-esteem.[102]

Yet, the authors also conclude that middle class Blacks tend to show lower levels of self-esteem than middle class Whites, while lower class Blacks tend to show higher levels of self-esteem than lower class

Whites,[103] which, to say the least, appears somewhat
paradoxical yet bears witness to the dilemma of the
middle class Black noted earlier with our discussion
of Frazier. Finally, one other point to keep in mind
here is that the foregoing discussion does not attempt
to conclude that Blacks who do suffer from a negative
identity (if any do) as the result of domestic colonialism, are therefore "pathological" or "deviant" from
the mainstream of American culture, but rather that
cultural and psychological "misunderstanding" between
Whites and Blacks would tend to exacerbate the situation in this line of reasoning. Since the emphasis
here has been upon the dependent relationship analogous
to colonialism such indicators that follow should
suggest this as a competing thesis or model to understanding the social, economic and political conditions
of Blacks in America rather than an absolute one.
Furthermore, although stressing the colonial relationship, such indicators suggest that this dependency is
not just analogous to colonial nations, but may also
be analogous to developing ones, if one assumes that
Blacks are gaining political independence (not physical
separation), yet are still economically dependent and
politically manipulated.

Historical (Forced Entry) Indicator

1) Did the enslavement of Afro-Americans constitute a form of domestic colonialism analogous to
colonial domination in the Third World? (Cruse)[104]

Socio-Cultural Indicators

1) Is there an unusually high birth rate among
Blacks in the ghetto?

2) To what degree is "cultural imperalism"
ubiquitous in the ghetto in education and political
socialization? Do elementary textbooks and education
project positive images of the indigenous culture, or
teach the history of the Mother country only? (Kinloch)

3) To what degree has there been a destruction of
the indigenous Black culture? (Cruse)

4) Is there poor and inadequate health care and
facilities in the ghetto, based upon segregation and

race? (Kinloch)

5) Is there a high degree of social and family "disorganization" as a result of domestic colonialism, or does some other phenomena account for this?

Economic Indicators

1) Are the residents for the most part unskilled and technologically "backward?"

2) Do ghetto businesses lack capital and managerial or administrative know-how? (Tabb, Winegarden, Blauner)

3) Is there a "dual labor market" in the ghetto, one for Whites and one for Blacks? (Tabb)

4) Is there a limited amount of local markets in the ghetto? Do goods and services, for the most part, tend to be "imported" from the Mother country? (Blauner, Tabb)

5) Is there a high incidence of credit default, a small amount of capital and savings in the ghetto, and local investment of capital by ghetto merchants who profit from the economic sources in the Black community? (Tabb)

6) To what extent is the ghetto dependent upon one basic "export"--unskilled human labor power? (Tabb) Does the demand for this "export" increase enough to match the growth of the labor supply? (Tabb) Are the Black ghettoes dependent economically upon "foreign aid" from the Mother country? (Blauner)

Political Indicators

1) Are political structures in the Black ghetto dependent upon and subordinate to, dominant political structures of Whites? Are political structures that are now independent of "White" control in the ghetto still dependent upon "foreign" economic aid from the "outside?"

2) Is there continued exploitation and domination of administrative structures by "alien" rule and not in the interest of the indigenous population? (Sjoberg,

Brymer, Farris, Murphy)

3) Are political boundaries systematically manipulated in metropolitan areas through gerrymandering, annexation, consolidation and metropolitan reorganization in a manner to maintain White control and keep Blacks dependent? (Cloward and Piven)

Racial Indicators

1) To what extent do Blacks attempt to "look White" physically or emulate Whites by the use of skin bleaches, hair straighteners, and the like? (Hare, Emerson, Kilson, Frazier) Does this constitute a self-hatred of one's "blackness" or skin color, and is it the result of domestic colonialism? (Fanon)

2) To what extent is there still an intra-class cleavage among Blacks based upon feelings of superiority resulting from oppression? (Dollard, Warner, Salamon, Frazier) Do certain classes of Blacks strive to achieve and emulate social values prized by Whites? (Frazier, Hare)

Notes

1. This is a school of thought associated with the perspective that America represents the great "Melting Pot" for people of diverse ethnic and cultural backgrounds. For a comprehensive summary and the ideological implications of research on American race relations and assimilation, see John Pease, William H. Form, and John H. Rytina, "Ideological Currents in America Stratification Literature," American Sociologist, 5, (May, 1970), pp. 127-37.

2. The culture of poverty school of thought is one which suggest that if Afro-Americans have not, in fact, assimilated, it is due to something endemic to their own culture rather than structural and societal barriers that may prevent assimilation. One of the most ardent supporters of this view is Edward C. Banfield, The Unheavenly City, (Boston and Toronto: Brown, Little and Co., 1966). See also Daniel P. Moynihan and Paul Barton, The Negro Family: The Case for National Action, (United States Department of Labor, 1965), which came to be known in more precise terms as The Moynihan Report. For a look at critics of the culture of poverty school, see William Ryan, Blaming the Victim, (New York: Pantheon Books (Random House), 1979), and Charles Valentine, Culture and

Poverty: Critique and Counter-Proposals, (Chicago: University of Chicago Press, 1969).

3. Perry L. Weed, for one, contends that not only have ethnics not lost their cultural heritage, but that there is a "new" ethnic consciousness that has arisen among Whites in the face of Black gains and the Black protest in the 1960's, in The White Ethnic Movement and Ethnic Politics, (New York: Praeger, 1973).

4. Robert Blauner, "Internal Colonialism and Ghetto Revolt", p. 396.

5. Philip D. Curtin, "The Black Experience of Colonialism and Imperialism", Daedalus, 103, (Spring, 1974), p. 17. However, this is not to say that this is the first study to take this orientation emphasizing the behavior and impact upon the colonized, but to suggest that it is in the spirit of this school of thought that the analysis will be developed. Other studies that emphasize this point of view are Franz Fanon, The Wretched of the Earth, (New York: Grove Press, Inc., 1966); and Black Skin, White Mask, (New York: Grove Press, Inc., 1968); A. Memmi, The Colonizer and the Colonized, (Boston: Beacon Press, 1954); and Dominated Man, (Boston: Beacon Press, 1971); and O. Mannoni, Prospero and Caliban: The Psychology of Colonization, (New York: Praeger, 1964), to name but a few studies, although still in the minority, with this orientation.

6. Philip Curtin, op. cit., p. 17.

7. Ibid., pp. 22-23.

8. Robert Blauner, op. cit., p. 395.

9. Ibid., p. 398.

10. G. Balandier, "The Colonial Situation: A Theoretical Approach (1951)", in Social Change: The Colonial Situation, ed. by Immanuel Wallerstein, (New York: John Wiley and Sons, Inc., 1966).

11. Ibid., p. 45. The reference here is actually taken from Balandier's citation of Laurentie.

12. Harold Cruse, Rebellion or Revolution, p. 77.

13. Ibid., pp. 75-77, passim.

14. O. Mannoni, op. cit.

15. Frantz Fanon, Black Skin: White Mask, p. 87.

16. Albert Memmi, Dominated Man, pp. 85-86. Also, see Albert
    Memmi, The Colonizer and the Colonized, op. cit.

17. Ibid., p. 88.

18. Ibid., p. 86.

19. Nathan Glazer, "Blacks and Ethnic Groups: The Difference, and
    the Political Difference It Makes", Social Problems, 18,
    (Spring, 1971), pp. 444-61.

20. Ibid.

21. Robert Blauner, op. cit.

22. Nathan Glazer, op. cit., pp. 451-54, passim. The reference
    to Kantrowitz by Glazer is from Nathan Kantrowitz,
    "Segregation in New York, 1960", American Journal of
    Sociology, 74, (May, 1969), pp. 685-95.

23. Tom Hayden, "Colonialism and Liberation as American Problems",
    in Politics and the Ghetto, ed. by Roland Warren, (New York:
    Atherton Press, 1969), pp. 170-90.

24. A.A. Fatouros, "Sartre on Colonialism", World Politics, 17,
    (June, 1965), pp. 703-19.

25. Graham C. Kinloch, The Dynamics of Race Relations, (New York:
    McGraw-Hill, 1974), p. 138.

26. For an example of the school of thought in regard to Black
    inferiority, in a concise essay, see Rhett Jones, "Blacks
    in Colonial America", Black World, 21, (February, 1972),
    pp. 11-19.

27. David Apter, The Political Kingdom of Uganda, (Princeton:
    Princeton University Press, 1961), pp. 448-51. Others, such
    as Karenga, speaks of stages of colonialism which lead to
    subordination of the colonized and rationales to justify
    it, also arguing in three stages similar to Apter which are
    worth nothing: 1) missionaries, which came to "civilize" the
    "heathens", 2) mercenaries, which involved institutionaliza-
    tion and economic exploitation, and 3) military, which
    served as a coercive instrument to maintain order and

stability once an economic foothold was achieved. Op. cit.,
p. 25. Balandier, citing Julien, also notes three forces
leading to subordination: 1) governmental administration,
2) missionaries, and 3) a new economy. Op. cit., p. 39
In somewhat similar terms, Barth and Noel speak of a triad
that leads to ethnic stratification (assuming that stratification is an important aspect of colonialism) which
involves ethnocentrism, competition, and the relative power
of groups. See Earnest Barth and Donald Noel, "Conceptual
Frameworks for the Analysis of Race Relations: An Evaluation",
in Social Forces, 50, (March 1972). Erickson speaks of a
"dangerous combination" involving tehcnological specializa-
tion, moral righteousness, and the territoriality of iden-
tity--lethal weaponry, moral hypocrisy, and identity-panic,
Erik H. Erikson, "The Concept of Identity", in The Negro
American, op. cit., p. 235. A recurring theme in all of
these aspects of colonialism and imperialism appear to be
moral superiority, force, and economic exploitation.

28. Eric Williams, Capitalism and Slavery, (Chapel Hill: Univer-
    sity of North Carolina Press), 1944.

29. Graham C. Kinloch, op. cit., p. 137.

30. G. Balandier, op. cit., p. 37

31. Philip Curtin, op. cit., p. 21

32. Eric Williams, op. cit.

33. Harold Cruse, Rebellion or Revolution, p. 76.

34. Robert Blauner, op. cit.

35. L. Singer, "Ethnogenesis and Negro-Americans Today", Social
    Research, 29, (Winter, 1962), p. 423.

36. Rupert Emerson and Martin Kilson, "The Rise of Africa and
    the Negro American", in The Negro American, p. 638. Boggs
    contends that exploitation and cultural degradation worked
    hand in hand in America, and therefore you can not separate
    the two. James Boggs, Racism and the Class Struggle, (New
    York: Monthly Review Press, 1970).

37. E. Franklin Frazier, The Negro in The United States, (New
    York: The Macmillan Co., 1949). See especially pp. 6-21.

38. John Blasingame, The Slave Community, (New York: Oxford

University, 1972); check out especially pp. 17-21. Blasingame concedes, though, that the controversy is limited by inadequate research, that in analyzing primary sources one still must arrive at tentative conclusions. The reference here to Dalby is from "The African Element in American English", in Rappin' and Stylin' Out, ed. by Thomas Kochman, (Chicago: University of Illinois Press, 1972), pp. 170-186.

39. Kenneth Stampp, The Peculiar Institution, (New York: Alfred A. Knopf, 1956). Stampp elaborates particularly on this point in Chapter 5.

40. John W. Blasingame, op. cit., pp. 88-91, passim.

41. E. F. Frazier, The Negro Family in the United States, (Chicago: University of Chicago Press, 1939), taking note particularly of pp. 33-49.

42. Robert Staples, "Race and Ideology", Journal of Black Studies 3, (March, 1973), pp. 395-422.

43. Philip Curtin, op. cit., p. 27.

44. C.L.R. James, "Kwame Nkrumah: Founder of African Emancipation", Black World, 21, (July, 1972), pp. 4-11.

45. Quoted from Rupert Emerson, "Parties and National Integration in Africa", in Political Parties and Political Development, ed. by J. LaPalombara, (Princeton: Princeton University Press, 1963), p. 277.

46. Theodore Lowi, "Machine Politics--Old and New", in Black Politics, ed. by Edward S. Greenberg, Neal Milner, and David J. Olson, (New York: Holt, Rinehart and Winston, 1971), pp. 131-40.

47. Francis Fox Piven and Richard A. Cloward, "Black Control of Cities", in Black Politics, pp. 118-30.

48. Ibid.

49. Gideon Sjoberg, Richard A. Brymer, and Buford Farris, "Bureaucracy and the Lower Class", Sociology and Social Research, 50, (April, 1966), p. 325.

50. Russell D. Murphy, Political Entrepeneurs and Urban Poverty, (Lexington: Heath Lexington Books, 1971), p. 99. For a case study of this relationship of bureaucracy to public housing,

one may look at Jack Levin and Gerald Taube, "Bureaucracy and the Socially Handicapped: A Study of Lower-Status Tenants in Public Housing", Sociology and Social Research, 54, (January, 1970), pp. 209-19.

51. Richard A. Cloward and Francis Fox Piven, "Welfare for Whom?" in Black Politics, ed. by Greenberg, Milner and Olson, p. 152.

52. Roy Simon Bryce-Laporte, "The Slave Plantation: Background to Present Conditions of Urban Blacks", in Race Relations, ed. by Edgar G. Epps, (Cambridge: Winthrop Publishers, Inc., 1973), pp. 69-93.

53. Mfanya D. Tryman, "Black Mayoralty Campaigns: Running the 'Race'", Phylon, 35, (December, 1974), pp. 346-58; and Nathan Glazer, op. cit., A smiilar point is made by Boggs who argues that the election of "safe" Blacks is to keep the White power structure intact, op. cit.

54. Nathan Glazer, op. cit., p. 450.

55. Lester Salamon, "Leadership and Modernization: The Emerging Black Political Elite in the American South", Journal of Politics, 35, (August, 1973), pp. 615-46.

56. Ibid.

57. Mfanya D. Tryman, op. cit.

58. Christopher Fyfe, "The Legacy of Colonialism-Old Colony, New State", Phylon, 25 (September, 1964), pp. 247-53.

59. Paul Metzger, op. cit.

60. William K. Tabb, The Political Economy of the Black Ghetto, (New York: W.W. Norton, 1970), p. 21.

61. C.R. Winegarden, "Industrialization in the Black Economy: Industry Selection", Review of Black Political Economy, 1, (Autumn, 1970), p. 28. See, also, the previous reference to Cruse, Rebellion or Revolution, especially pp, 75-76. For a good discussion of the historical aspects of economics and internal colonialism, see Ron Bailey, "Economic Aspects of the Black Internal Colony", The Review of Black Political Economy, 3, (Summer, 1973), pp. 43-69.

62. Wilfred L. Davis, "Black America in Development Perspective,

Part I", The Review of Black Political Economy, 3, (Fall, 1972), pp. 91-96, passim.

63. Ibid., pp. 91-100, passim.

64. Ibid.

65. William K. Tabb, "Race Relations Models and Social Change", Social Problems, 18, (Spring, 1971), pp. 431-43. Also, see the former citation of Tabb, op. cit. Similar themes can be found in Harry Magdoff's "Problems of United States Capitalism", in The Socialist Register, ed. by Ralph Miliband and John Saville, (New York: Monthly Review Press, 1965); John C. Leggett, Class, Race and Labor, (New York: Oxford University Press, 1968); and Harold M. Baron, The Demand for Black Labor: Historical Notes on the Political Economy of Racism, (Cambridge: Radical America, 1971).

66. William K. Tabb, op. cit.

67. Samuel Yette, The Choice: The Issue of Black Survival in America, (New York: G.P. Putnams Sons, 1971); Sidney Wilhelm, Who Needs the Negro? (Cambridge: Schenkman Publishing Co., 1970); and Boggs, op. cit.

68. Ibid., pp. 172-73, passim.

69. Samuel Yette, op. cit., p. 18. Boggs makes much of the same argument, but argues later on that the non-utility of Black labor will not lead to extinction, but will provide the basis for revolution. See especially page 41., op. cit.

70. Most notable in this regard are the assimilationist and culture of poverty models mentioned in the beginning of the chapter.

71. There is an abundance of literature, nevertheless, which does take this position and discuss colonialism and racism and the advantages obtained through the continued practice of it. For example, one may look at some of the following: Carmichael and Hamilton, Black Power, op. cit., in which they argue that racism is both an institutional and individual phenomenon; L. Knowles and K. Prewitt, Institutional Racism in America, (Englewood Cliffs: Prentice-Hall, Inc., 1969); Edward S. Greenberg, who argues that neither the pluralist nor the elitest model is applicable to Blacks with regard to community power, since, according to Greenberg, both models fall into the category of institutional racism, in "Models of

the Political Process: Implications for the Black Community",
in Black Politics, op. cit., pp. 3-15; The Report of the
National Advisory Commission on Civil Disorders, (Washington:
U.S. Government Printing Office, 1967). Some studies dealing
more particularly with the psychological advantages of racism
in the domestic colonial sphere include Graham Kinloch, op.
cit.; Franz Fanon, op. cit.; Neal Friedman, "Africa and the
Afro-American: The Changing Negro Identity", Psychiatry, 33,
(May 1969), pp. 127-36; Robert Staples, op. cit.; William
Tabb, op. cit.; Blauner, op. cit.; Eric C. Erickson, who, like
Fanon, speaks in psychological terms of the "id" and "ego",
and the evil aspects of the id being cast upon an "inferior"
group of people, in "The Concept of Identity in Race Relations:
Notes and Queries", in The Negro American, ed. by Parsons and
Clark, pp. 227-53; and Thomas Pettigrew, op. cit.

72. Graham C. Kinloch, op. cit.

73. R. Blauner, op. cit.

74. R. Staples, op. cit. See especially Oliver C. Cox, who argues
that the role of prejudice must be related to exploitation
in a capitalist society, and that any study of prejudice which
fails to do so is inadequate, in Caste, Class, and Race, (New
York: Doubleday, 1948).

75. Stanley Elkins, Slavery, (Chicago: University of Chicago Press,
1968).

76. Leo Kuper, "On Theories of Race Relations", in Ethnicity and
Nation-Building, ed. by W. Bell and W.E. Freeman, (Beverly
Hills: Sage Publications, 1974), pp. 15-26.

77. For a good discussion that such doctrines played in colonialism
and slavery, see Ali A. Mazrui, "From Social Darwinism to
Current Theories of Modernization"; Rhett Jones, op. cit.;
Philip D. Curtin, op. cit.; Michael Banton, "1960: A Turning
Point in the Study of Race Relations", Daedalus, 103, (Spring,
1974), pp. 31-44; and Franz Fanon, op. cit.

78. Winthrop Jordan, White Over Black, (Chapel Hill: University
of North Carolina Press, 1968).

79. Leo Kuper, op. cit., pp. 25-26.

80. Thomas Pettigrew, op. cit.

81. Ibid. Pettigrew's definition is actually a citation of

E. Goffman, Stigma: Notes on the Management of Spoiled Identity, (Englewood Cliffs: Prentice-Hall, 1963).

82. C. Eric Lincoln, "Color and Group Identity in the United States", Daedalus, 96, (Spring, 1967), p. 527. The citation is from an unpublished manuscript by the same author entitled "Joe Jipson", The Autobiography of a Southern Town, (No further citation given).

83. This author personally remembers this saying while growing up. While it may suffer from academic documentation, it is to bring the absurdity associated with being Black into the "light."

84. Franz Fanon, op. cit.

85. C. Eric Lincoln, op. cit.

86. Rupert Emerson and Martin Kilson, op. cit.

87. Ibid.

88. John Dollard, Caste and Class in a Southern Town, (Garden City: Doubleday, 1957).

89. W. Lloyd Warner, "American Caste and Class", American Journal of Sociology, 32, (September, 1936), pp. 234-37.

90. E. Franklin Frazier, "The MacIver Award Lecture", Social Problems, 4, (April, 1957), pp. 291-301. The article was originally a speech given at the Annual Meeting of the Eastern Sociological Society held in New York, April 13-14, 1957. Frazier's more profound work is Black Bourgeoisie, (Glencoe: Free Press, 1957).

91. Ibid.

92. Rupert Emerson and Martin Kilson, op. cit.

93. Thomas Pettigrew, op. cit., p. 327.

94. Philip Curtin, op. cit, p. 27

95. Ibid. This does not contradict the earlier assertion that Blacks have maintained part of their linguistic and cultural heritage. The difference is that although Blacks may still maintain communication elements associated with Africa, they do not have a systematic language pattern that would isolate

them from the views and distorted images projected by the "dominant" English language and culture.

96. Nathan Hare, The Black Anglo-Saxons, (London: Collier-MacMillian Ltd., 1965).

97. Ralph Ellison, Shadow and Act, (New York: Random House, 1964).

98. Erik H. Erikson, op. cit.

99. Ibid., see especially p. 236 with regard to this point.

100. Thomas Pettigrew, op. cit.

101. Neil Friedman, "Africa and the Afro-American: The Changing Negro Identity."

102. John D. McCarthy and William L. Yancey, "Uncle Tom and Mr. Charlie: Metaphysical Pathos in the Study of Racism and Personal Disorganization", in Race Relations, ed. by Edgar G. Epps, (Cambridge: Winthrop Publishers, 1973), p. 60.

103. Ibid., p. 62.

104. Indicators followed by parentheses refer to the author in the foregoing discussion or a similar statement made by them.

CHAPTER III

AFRO-AMERICAN POLITICAL INTEGRATION:
METHOD FOR A MODEL

This work differs from most published studies in
the field of political science in that the methodological approach for the model constitutes the Third
Chapter of the work. The rationale for this is that
the methodology applies primarily to the Fourth and
Fifth Chapters of the study in a theoretical context
rather than in an empirical study. As a result, the
methodology provides for greater continuity in understanding the model and may be seen as an integral part
of the model than if it was placed in the beginning of
the overall work.

The classical approach to the study of politics is
one that stems at least partially from the Aristotelian
inquiry into the nature of the <u>polis</u>. As Graham notes,
the classical orientation in political science has come
to delete the term <u>polis</u> for the more contemporary one
of nation, enabling one to shift the approach to the
level of the nation-state as a political community.[1]
It is the classical method that will be used in this
part of the study, i.e., not only does this work examine
the nation as the basic unit of analysis, but speaks
as classical theorists in political science do, in
normative terms. Let us approach method in more fundamental terms by delineating the scope and its approach
in the model.

Definition of Method

The methodology of a scientific discipline, as
Rudner points out, is not just a matter of its tran-
sient techniques but of its logic of justification, the
rationale on which it bases its acceptance or rejection
of hypotheses or theories.[2] In this context, it is the
rules of interpretation and the criteria for admissible
explanations that the scientific method is concerned
with, rather than the proper use of techniques, with
which method is often confused as a synonym.[3] Thus,
method as defined and used here makes reference to rules
and justifications as pertinent criteria for interpreting political phenomena. In the following subsections
of this chapter, let us explicate how such rules
relate to the method in this study.

Rules of Interpretation

Rules, as Kuhn suggest, has to do with "established viewpoints" or "preconceptions" regarding the way one will proceed and interpret his or her research findings.[4]   Therefore, rules not only set up criteria for the admissibility and interpretation of data or relevant political phenomena, but also serves to legitimate one's findings in concrete terms. The rules of interpretation employed in the research here makes reference to a subjective and normative approach, i.e., selecting interpretations of political phenomena and events on the basis of a given preconceived orientation rather than on the basis of "objective" conditions. As a normative approach, such interpretations of political phenomena rest upon the basic assumption of "what is" or "what should be" as authoritative in translating a social event, or articulating how such an event "should" occur. Hence, this approach does not exclude value neutrality, but rather puts a special premium on values as an important aspect of one's method and findings. This emphasis should be taken note of without getting into the continuing debate in political science as to whether the study of human behavior can be value-free and objective, or whether value-preferences and subjective orientations enter into the investigator's research findings.[5]   Rather, it suggests that what Sibley terms "primary value judgements" are pertinent as an important rule for interpreting political phenomena and conducting research.[6]   In sum, to speak in normative and subjective terms does not preclude other avenues of investigation, but rather puts such an emphasis upon a particular orientation which is set forth initially in conducting the research.

Comparative Method

As noted, there appears to be a considerable debate over the proper methods of scientific investigation in political science, and this ambivalence has extended to comparative politics and political studies as well. Like the traditional approach to political science, comparative politics tended to be nothing more than the study of discrete foreign governments, in which more emphasis "was placed upon uniqueness than upon elements of commonality; any comparisons that were drawn were largely for pedagogical or rhetorical reasons."[7]   In more recent times, ironically, comparative politics has not referred to a method of comparison, but to the building of empirical political theory by scholars such as Apter, Pye, and Riggs and applying it to more than one political system.[8] Comparative methodology as utilized here makes reference to rules of interpretation for comparing similar and dissimilar elements and concepts in the model of political change. An important aspect of such a method is that it does not just pursue normative avenues, but employs nonculture bound concepts in doing so. Consequently, although one may speak and interpret phenomena in normative explanations, concepts such as political culture, political change, and political integration are ones that do not apply to any one particular political system or type, but may be operationalized in order to have meaning in different types of polities. A more practical articulation of such concepts and the comparative method may be subsumed under the phrase "dual partial systems approach."

This concept is a reference to what are considered here as essential political concepts within two such systems that are either dynamic in that they foster political change and integration, or static in deterring such a type of change. Dual in this regard merely refers to two systems and comparative concepts within them. But partial systems makes reference to only a segment of those systems considered significant for treating them on a comparative level, i.e., those concepts central to and dependent upon the overall explanation which is sought. The idea of partial also carries another intended meaning here. The one who is conducting the political inquiry is partial in considering such an investigation into the system under study as being a normative one. Therefore, the nomenclature of "dual partial systems approach" denotes not only the nature of method and comparison, but a significant aspect of the rules for justifying such claims.

On the other hand, speaking of a dual partial systems approach may be just the coining of a neologism to suggest that a middle range theory will be invoked in the methodology. Middle range makes reference to generalizations that attempt to explain only certain aspects in the political process and how they relate to the phenomena under study, rather than attempting to explain the entire political process.[9] Schematically, a dual partial systems approach or a middle range orientation may be shown as in Figure 3-1.

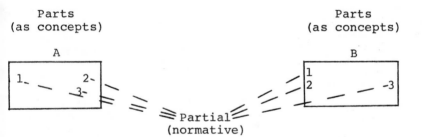

Fig. 3-1 Dual partial systems
approach

In which A and B represent the dual nature of the
comparative political systems under study, and 1,2 and
3 in each are symbolic of the parts (i.e., concepts)
of those systems to be explained. Partial, however,
as noted above, makes reference to a different type of
linkage with 1,2 and 3 in which they are related in
normative and subjective terms, thus denoting also a
means of reinforcing the rules for interpretation set
forth above.

Relationship of Method to Model

The relationship of the methodology to the model
can be perceived in several steps. One should, however,
not confuse this method with the actual steps in the
model-building, which will be outlined in appropriate
form in Chapter Four. First, deductive reasoning is
employed to arrive at the model. In this context, going from a general statement (axiom) on political
change and political integration to particular propositions or theorems seen as necessary for political change
to take place. This assumes that a theorem or what
constitutes the working hypothesis or hypotheses can be
deduced from an empirical law or axiom whose truth for
the moment is accepted. Second, the implementation of
political theory to arrive at such deductive theorems.
Although the term political theory may have a host of
different meanings to a particular political scientist
in question, here political theory makes reference to
the classical approach in political science which has
been partially resurrected in studying developing
nations. Just as Aristotle's inquiry into what constitutes a healthy polis, the significance of utilizing
political theory as the classical approach lies in

investigating the way the nation should be. Third, perhaps the most significant step involved in the relationship of the methodology to the model is the deductive
process in placing a greater emphasis upon dissimilarities rather than similarities that lead to a similar
political end. For example, the relationship of the
political capacity of the United States to maintain
"law and order" in America through physical oppression,
combined with the changing political culture of Afro-
Americans and their awareness of new political orientations toward the American political system, may lead to
an increase in nationalism and ethnic cohesiveness. We
can demonstrate this symbolically as in Figure 3-2, as
political concepts and variables.

Fig. 3-2 Deductive process and
dissimilarities

Where SN represents the sovereign nation of the
United States, CN represents the cultural nation of
Afro-Americans, A symbolically is the political capacity
to maintain order through oppression and violence, B
is the "new" political culture and consciousness among
Blacks, C is the resulting nationalism that arises from
the combination of A and B occurring simultaneously
over a period of time, and D is the ethnic and cultural
cohesiveness formed as a result of C. The relationship
could also be demonstrated as in Figure 3-3, using the
same symbols as changes in variables:

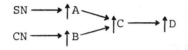

Fig. 3-3 Deductive process and
changes in variables

In which an increase in A in the sovereign nation
(SN) along with an increase in B in the cultural nation

(CN), leads to an increase in nationalism (C) and ethnic cohesiveness (D). What is illustrative here with regard to the methodology, and the foregoing discussion, is how disparate or uncommon political concepts and variables emanating from different sources leads to the same or common conclusion (ethnic cohesiveness).

Scope

Geographic. The concern here is with a mass model of Afro-American political change and integration, and the way it affects ideological orientations of Black groups. One of the problems of formulating some models of Black politics in the past has been their sectarian or status orientation. For example, their limitation to urban or southern areas, and/or the emphasis upon elitist Black organizations, such as the N.A.A.C.P. or the Urban League. Few, if any, empirical or theoretical studies have been done on the Black masses, and although the model proposed here does not close the gap between the vast empirical-theoretical dichotomy, it does attempt to move away from a secular or sectional orientation to a more general level and emphasize mass Black politics rather than what is termed here as elitist Black politics. Thus, the focus is upon the national level in which the United States serves as convenient geographic parameters for the model.

Basic unit of analysis. The basic unit is the nation, where two different types of "nations" will be defined, along with a consideration of how interaction of such nations with regard to certain variables affects political change. This may better be explained in our articulation of the relationship of the basic unit of analysis to the subunit of analysis, which deserves a cursory discussion.

Subunit of analysis. Many orientations to the study of politics include such approaches as "power" or "the authoritative allocation of values", as Lasswell terms it. While the basic unit of analysis is the "nation", the subunit involves that of "leadership groups", the latter part of this term perhaps best articulated upon by David Truman.[10] Many approaches to the study of politics involve either one of the above basic approaches, or a combination of them. The concern here is how group integration is affected

by changes in the polity or nation and by leaders
themselves, as we shall define them. The approach
subsumes group interaction under the more basic notion
of the nation. The two are inseparable in that elaboration upon one in the model is dependent upon changes
in the other. For example, there is little practical
interest in speaking of group integration among Afro-
Americans just for integration's sake. One may ask the
question: Why is political integration among Blacks
necessary, or why does nationalism continue to flourish
even during times of affluence? What is significant
is the relationship between policies emanating from
the sovereign (U.S.) nation that affects Afro-Americans
in different ways. This relationship between the
nation as the basic unit of analysis and groups as the
subunit of analysis is schematically shown in Figure 3-4

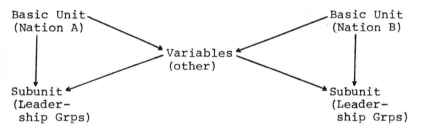

Fig. 3-4 The relationship between basic
unit(s) and subunit(s) of analysis

What is inferred in the above relationship is that
the interaction of Nation A and Nation B as the basic
unit(s) affect Black groups with different political
orientations in disparate ways as subunit(s). Of
course, there are other variables which provide the
linkage, but in the scheme they are merely designated
as (other), in order to keep the relationship between
basic units and subunits clear and simplified.
Although this is a rather rudimentary form, it attempts
only to illustrate the relationship between the units
of analysis under investigation.

Time period. The model reflects the initial time
period of the early sixties. Hypothetically, it is
suggested that it is during this period that an
embryonic and unique political culture was developing
among the younger, Black masses, based upon a "new"
political identity with Africa as such newly independent countries on that continent emerged from European

colonial domination.[11] It is inferred here that the emergence of such newly independent countries gave new implications for the emerging Black political culture on Afro-American political integration and political change. It should be pointed out, however, that the model is applicable at any time when you have an increase in political oppression or increased Black identity and racial pride.

Age Group. An assumption made in the model is that this emergent political culture had its greatest impact upon the age group of Blacks in the age range from 15-35 years old. Further, that the emerging leadership originating in the sixties with more of a nationalist orientation tended to be and continues to be younger than Black leaders in more conventional Black organizations.

Model-Type

Ideal. Although normative and subjective channels will be pursued in model-building, it does not suggest that the model is an ideal-type in that it does not explain empirical political phenomena or reality. Rather, it can be perceived as an ideal-tupe in that it sets certain priorities in its logical construction for unified political change and integration to take place. However, one must distinguish types of political concepts employed, because while it may be assumed that some concepts exist in actuality, others are ideal or value concepts, which will be elaborated upon in the model in Chapter Four. What may be asserted here is that the manner in which the concepts-variables are juxtaposed in the model, and the interrelationships inferred, are what makes the construction of the model ideal. Hence, a distinction should be made between a model and a theory. Graham states:

> The model is legitimate even if it does not conform to the complexities to which it is applied. Theory must approximate the reality and lead to further projections about the reality that support the validity of the theoretical structures. The model's test is a test of validity of conclusions and derivations-it is a test

of internal consistency; the theory's
test is whether it generates true
statements about the real world. The
difference, then, is both in the
intent and in the structures for testing and use.[12]

While some of the conceptualizations and variables
abstracted from reality are purported to have an
empirical base, the arrangement and model-building with
such concepts and variables, and the prerequisites
set forth, may not reflect actual political phenomena
in structure, but rather suggest how such phenomena
"should be" interpreted in normative terms. From this
perspective, the model can also be perceived as an
ideal-type.

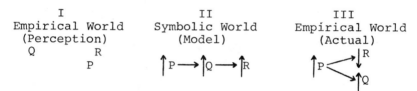

I	II	III
Empirical World	Symbolic World	Empirical World
(Perception)	(Model)	(Actual)

Fig. 3-5 Relation between variables
in the empirical world
and symbolic world or model

In one's perception of the empirical world (I),
empirical concepts P,Q, and R are assumed to exist.
In the model which represents a symbolic representation
of reality (II), the arrangement, sequence and construction of the concepts and variables (concepts and
variables are references to the same symbolic letters
here) represents the way it "should be" and stresses
internal consistency. In the actual empirical world
(III), a reflection of what is actually happening
between the variables is shown. For instance, whereas
in (II) it suggests that as variable Q increases, so
should variable R increase (in which the arrow (———➤)
represents an "If...then" relationship). But perhaps
in actuality, as P increases, R decreases and Q still
increases because of some intervening variable such as
cooptation. In other words, if we let P represent
for the moment, political oppression, Q represent
nationalism, and R represent political integration and
change, we see in the model (II) the way that as P
increases, so does Q and R, or at least the way that,

81

in a normative sense, they should. But in (III), as
there is an increase in P, Q goes up but R goes down.
In this sense, as nationalism increases, perhaps
political integration does not follow because "radical"
leaders are "coopted" in a way that slows down, or
decreases Afro-American political integration. Let it
suffice to say in the above, however, that while
empirical concepts are employed, they become utilized
in an "ideal" or normative fashion as one moves from
(I) to (II).

But the model is ideal in the stricter sense in
that ideal concepts, and value concepts are employed.
An ideal concept refers to the way that a kind of
political behavior or activity would look if other
variables did not affect its outcome,[13] and is somewhat
implicit in the above discussion of the difference
between (II) and (III). A value concept is one which
is assigned special worth in a political or social
context.[14] Thus, the three major types of concepts
in the model are empirical, ideal, and value ones.
This can be suggested in Figure 3-6 below.

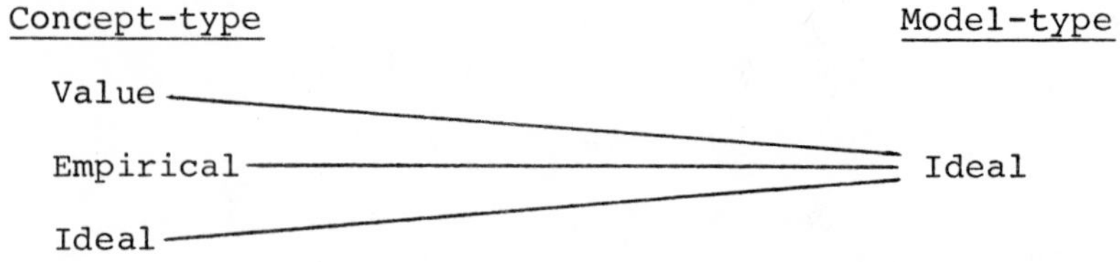

Concept-type   Model-type

   Value

   Empirical   Ideal

   Ideal

Fig. 3-6 Relation between concept-
types and model-type

In the above representation, the model becomes
an ideal one not just with regard to structure, but
also in the sense that ideal and value concept-types
are utilized. In summary, let us say that while the
model attempts to reflect reality in abstracting what
are considered the essential elements reflected in
the model, it is also ideal in the structure that it
follows and the other concept-types employed in a
normative manner.

Explanatory. A second major aspect of the model
is that it seeks partial explanations of certain types
of relationships between concepts and variables by
usage of the deductive method. Keeping in mind our

82

previous discussion of "partial systems analysis", here
we seek <u>partial rather than whole explanations of certain types of events</u>. Making a distinction between
partial and complete explanations is an important one
because it delineates the difference between a deductive explanation as opposed to predictive power based
upon variables one is able to account for. Brodbeck's
summary of this difference, though somewhat lengthy, is
worthy of note with regard to such a distinction:

> To say "The only cause of X is A" is at
> lease to affirm the law that X never
> occurs without A. In other words, A
> is a necessary condition for X, or
> "Whenever we have X, then we also have
> A." It is also, however, to say more,
> namely, that there is a complex of
> conditions, of which A is always one,
> under which X occurs; that is, certain
> other factors, B,C,D, and A are suffi-
> cient for X. In other words (sic), A
> is a necessary condition and also one
> of several jointly sufficient condi-
> tions...By hypothesis, we do not know
> the other sufficient conditions. If we
> knew them, then deductive explanation
> and prediction would follow directly
> from a statement of the necessary and
> sufficient conditions. However, since
> we do not know the sufficient con-
> ditions, how do we account for the fact
> that actually we would normally explain
> X by A? Our only justification, and
> in fact the only way anyone...does
> justify doing this, is by implicitly
> adding to our knowledge of the neces-
> sary-condition law, our "guess" about
> the sufficient-condition law. Knowing
> that both X and A have occurred, we
> assume the presence of the unspecifiable
> B,C, and D. The explanation of X then
> follows deductively. That is why we
> accept A as an explanation of X. In
> order to predict X from A, the unknown
> factors must also be specified and this
> we cannot do.[15]

Such a type of partial explanation differs from

the ideal form of explanation, which attempts to deduce
that the event was to be expected because universal
laws suggest that under the conditions in which it
occurred, its occurrence was predictable.[16] The type
of explanation sought here is similar to the one that
Hempel refers to as elliptically formulated, i.e.,
accounts of particular events which forego mention of
certain laws or variables that are tacitly taken for
granted, but whose explicit inclusion would yield a
complete deductive-nomological argument.[17] In the
context used here, these laws or variables are the ones
explicitly unaccounted for in formulating the explanatory model but are realized as still having an affect
on the event in question. Hempel refers to the deductive-nomological explanation as a part of the covering-
law model which consists of two basic parts, the explanandum or phenomena to be explained, and the explanan
or set of statements which provide an explanation.[18]
It is also fruitful in seeking explanations to make a
distinction between what Rudner refers to as retro-
dictive and pro-dictive explanations. Here we are
concerned with the former. Rudner defines a retro-
dictive explanatory argument as "one whose explanandum
describes an event that is temporally antecedent to any
events described by the particular-circumstance statements of its explanans."[19] A pro-dictive explanatory
argument is one whose explanandum suggests or describes
an event temporally posterior to at least one of the
particular-circumstance statements of the explanans.[20]
Thus, we are concerned with events of the past, and
more particularly the early 1960's, though our explanan
may attempt to explain such events through contemporary
political phenomena as well as phenomena in the past.

In summary, let us say that the explanations sought
do not attempt to account for a total explanation of
a particular event, but assumes that other variables
may account in part for the phenomena in question also,
as with Hempel's elliptical formulation. It is
implicitly understood that such other variables may
also affect the explanation of the event, although we
do not know just what variables they are, and this
should be understood from the outset. Although we
cannot account for these unknowns (variables), we can
still state that when a particular event occurs,
certain variables will be present. This does not
attempt to predict the event, as Brodbeck notes, but
only to explain that when X occurs, so will A, and as

such delineates the difference between explanation
and prediction. Hempel refers to this as explanatory
incompleteness in one's elliptical formulation in a
rather harmless way. With these precautions kept in
mind, let us suggest the limitations of the overall
methodology.

Limitations of Method

1) The method lacks first hand empirical or systematic data.

2) The method is based upon what is assumed to be
observable political phenomena.

3) The method seeks explanation only through normative and subjective orientations.

4) The method seeks internal consistency through
partial rather than total explanations of variables
that account for a particular phenomena. As such, the
emphasis is upon explaining rather than predicting.

Notes

1. George C. Graham, Methodological Foundations of Political
   Analysis, (Waltham: Ginn and Co., 1971).

2. Richard S. Rudner, Philosophy of Social Science, (Englewood:
   Prentice-Hall, Inc., 1966).

3. Robert T. Holt and John E. Turner, "The Methodology of
   Comparative Research", in The Methodology of Comparative
   Research, ed. by Robert T. Holt and John E. Turner, (New York:
   The Free Press, 1970), pp. 1-22.

4. Thomas Kuhn, The Structure of Scientific Revolutions, (Chicago:
   University of Chicago Press, 1970).

5. For a more comprehensive look at the polemices surrounding
   this point, which may also be termed the "traditional-
   behavioral-post-behavioral" trichotomy, one may look at
   David Easton's "The New Revolution in Political Science",
   and Haas and Becker, "The Behavioral Revolution and After",
   both of which can be found in Approaches to the Study of
   Political Science, ed. by Michael Haas and Henry Kariel,
   (Scranton: Chandler Publishing Co., 1970); Mulford Q. Sibley,
   "The Limitations of Behavioralism", in Contemporary Political

Analysis, ed. by James C. Charlesworth, (New York: The Free Press, 1967), pp. 51-71.

6. Mulford Sibley, op. cit.

7. Robert T. Holt and John E. Turner, op. cit., p. 5.

8. Ibid.

9. George C. Graham, op. cit., p. 126. See, also, Bruce M. Russett, "International Behavior Research: Case Studies and Cumulation", in Approaches to the Study of Political Science, op. cit.

10. David Truman, The Governmental Process: Political Interest and Public Opinion, (New York: Alfred A. Knopf, 1951).

11. On this point, see Harold Cruse, Rebellion, and Martin Kilson and Rupert Emerson, "The American Dilemma in a Changing World: The Rise of Africa and the Negro American", in The Negro American, pp. 626-55.

12. George C. Graham, op. cit., p. 124.

13. Ibid., p. 72.

14. Ibid., p. 72.

15. May Brodbeck, "Explanation, Prediction, and 'Imperfect' Knowledge", in Readings in the Philosophy of the Social Sciences, ed. by May Brodbeck, (London: Collier-MacMillan Limited, 1968), p. 380.

16. George C. Graham, op. cit.

17. Carl G. Hempel, "Explanatory Incompleteness", in Readings in the Philosophy of the Social Sciences, pp. 398-415.

18. For further explication of the covering-law model see Carl G. Hempel, "The Logic of Functional Analysis", in Symposium on Sociological Theory, edited by Llewellyn Gross, (New York: Harper and Row, 1959), pp. 271-307, and reprinted in Readings in the Philosophy of the Social Sciences, pp. 179-210.

19. Richard S. Rudner, op. cit., pp. 63-64.

20. Ibid., p. 64.

CHAPTER IV

AFRO-AMERICAN POLITICAL INTEGRATION:
A CONCEPTUAL APPROACH

In order to understand and explain a model of Afro-American political integration, important concepts related to the model must be defined and clarified. The purpose of this chapter is to outline the conceptual parameters of the model and explain and elaborate upon several of the steps involved in model-building applicable to Afro-American political integration.

The model of political integration proposed here is a combination of the political culture and social systems approaches to developing nations, which was discussed in an earlier chapter. In short, we are concerned with the role of identity and integration in political change. The idea of a social systems approach is one that involves bridging ideological, geographical, religious and other types of cleavages. One should not assume that because we are using the social systems approach to political change and integration, we should use functional analysis in terms of how the system adapts or adjusts as part of an ongoing system. In fact, we are not sure if the "system" spoken of here is a self-regulating one.

Rather, we are only concerned with certain aspects of political and social integration within the system which entails a causal explanation. As we shall see, it may be that the "system" spoken of here is at least partially regulated from the outside rather than from within. More will be said later on about the role of such functional statements in science when we offer some alternative scientific explanations. Let us begin by turning to some important concepts and aspects of scientific explanation.

Calculus

A calculus is a set of interrelated propositions that are stated in formal language. Such propositions of the calculus are networks of relations that allows one to move from one step to another in a certain sequence but are neither true nor false since it says nothing per se about the empirical world.[1] Meehan states that a calculus is a logical structure consisting of a set of symbols and the rules for manipulating them or relating changes in their values. Furthermore, Meehan goes on to state that it is the calculi that provides the grounds for justifying inferences and expectations, and that within a calculus inferences can be tested or justified perfectly.[2]

As such, the calculus provides the means for justifying inferences in no other way than to demonstrate in a formal manner that they result from a valid calculus by known rules from known premises.[3] In sum, a calculus is a logical construct in which one may deduce certain conclusions because they implicitly follow from the initial definitions and axioms. The calculus in deductive reasoning is similar to the concept of a scientific paradigm as elaborated upon by Kuhn in that it sets up useful guidelines and parameters within which one may work and research. It is from the calculus that one initially begins with axioms or postulates, and deduces from them by the use of a logical construct certain theorems or propositions that logically entail. Before actually outlining the steps that will be included in deducing from generic statements to particular conclusions, let us first clarify a few concepts with respect to the calculus.

Analytic and Synthetic Statements

Brecht states that an analytic statement is one that adds **nothing** to the meaning of a given term or proposition, but only makes explicit what is implicit or implied in the meaning. Although such a statement adds nothing that is not implied in the meaning, it may, however, be relevant for inquiry because implications of a statement are not immediately always seen, and if made explicit add considerable knowledge and may be surprising in character.[4] Graham, in somewhat more succinct terms, states that an analytic statement is one:

> ...that is neither true nor false in this sense. An analytic claim is a tautological statement that is true because it merely asserts a relationship contained within its definitions.[5]

It is analytic statements that we will be concerned with in constructing our axioms as opposed to synthetic statements. Such a statement of the latter type may be one that:

> ...asserts that a condition exists in the real world that can be tested and verified...The truth of a synthetic statement is contingent upon reality. It is true only if it accurately describes relationships observed in reality.[6]

Keeping such a distinction in mind is in agreement with the earlier assertion in the methods section which suggested that internal consistency involved in deductive reasoning is the primary concern. Thus, this model is not contingent upon whether or not there is an isomorphic relationship to reality. Although this may in fact be the case, it does not invalidate the analytic nature of the statements to be set forth.

The Context of Justification and Discovery

Diesing states that the context of justification, in a similar vein to analytic statements, is one that can be given a strict logical reconstruction, whereas discovery cannot. Discovery is a form of creativity which does not embody any logic and therefore is unknowable and unpredictable.[7] March states that the context of justification in all science is one that is reported and communicated in the form of a logical reconstruction which aims at providing justification for the inferences produced and that such justification involves the outlining of steps, i.e., assumptions, deductive processes, indicators or ways of testing. March notes, however, that such a procedure is often mistaken by the beginner as a description of the process of discovery.[8]

The context of discovery, as opposed to justification, is one that occurs either at the preconscious or intuitive level (a guess about some phenomena in reality) and at the empirical level by either answering in the affirmative by describing and reconstructing one or more such logics, or by disconfirming a proposed reconstruction.[9] Although we are concerned mainly with the context of justification, it is worthwhile to note as Diesing does that justification and verification are not treated as a set of formal procedures occurring after discovery, but are included within the process of discovery.[10]

The Context of Verification

The logic or context of verification is one concerned with the generality of the laws that one hypoth-
esizes. The major goal of verification is a statement
of the classes of events to which the theory applies
in a clear and precise manner. Verification as such
may be spread throughout one's method of logical reconstruction. Verification may also occur only at one
point in time, and there may be two or more kinds of
verification or only one. Nevertheless, such a process
is always, according to Diesing, subordinate to the
larger process of discovery.[11] The significance of
verification in logical constructs is that it provides
and constitutes one or more checkpoints in the process
of deductive reasoning. The usage of verification in
our model suggests that it may occur as a checkpoint
at more than one point in time in our deduction, and
that there may be more than one kind of such verification. An example of the latter is the final two
steps in deducing the model, the theorems and the
indices which constitute different types of verification as a result of deducing what is implicit in the
postulates.

Some Specific Rules and Explanation

As we suggested earlier in the methodology, the
overall guide for interpreting rules was to speak in
normative and subjective terms; however, while this
may be justified in general terms the logic of deductive reasoning begs that we implement more specific
rules. Rules located within the calculus attempts to
relate it to the empirical world by giving a verbal
translation of the terms of the calculus, telling us
what the calculus means empirically.[12] As Diesing
asserts, unlike an ordinary translation a rule never
gives a definite set of possible empirical meanings
since any calculus can have an indefinite number of
interpretations.[13] Meehan uses the term "priority
structure", a set of rules for ordering a set of outcomes, and that such rules are not absolute and fixed,
although it must be transitive at any given point in
time, i.e., one may use variable X first in one
instance and last in another without contradiction.[14]
In sum, rules may be used in a logical construct to

90

"force" particular outcomes by manipulating variables and concepts associated with reality. Let us suggest the following rules in particular for making our deductions in the calculus (other than the overall normative implication).

First, we will attempt to interpret concepts into variables by using symbolic letter variables closest in meaning to the concept. For example, if one were to attempt to interpret the concept of political participation into a symbolic variable, the closest relationship would be PP (for political participation). In this way, the closest relationship and clarity is maintained between the concept and variable in terms of isomorphism.

Second, if we should encounter two concepts that may have similar meaning when translated into symbolic terms, such as political culture and political capacity, which would be interpreted as PC and PC respectively, then one will arbitrarily be assigned a "1" in order to avoid confusion, therefore, the two aforementioned concepts would be translated as PC and PC^1.

A third rule that we want to keep in mind in our deduction is that which Greer refers to as the rule of identity. Greer states that the rule of identity is one in which the terms and concepts that a scientist uses should maintain their meaning throughout an argument.[15] Or else, as Greer states "empirical research will resemble verbal juggling: the rabbit mysteriously appears and disappears, 'groups' come and go at the will of the scientists."[16]

A fourth rule is that in our model of causality the starting point is an arbitrary one so that we are not attempting to regress to find an "initial" starting point. More will be stated with regard to this rule in our next subsection on explanation and causality.

Our final rule, though not as specific as the others, is one that will state an interpretation of a given phenomena as we proceed and may not always be foreseen from the start. This may occur in explaining causality or in manipulating the variables, or anywhere else in the steps of our deductive calculus. A more generic rule of this sort is to safeguard us from stating "all" possible rules in the beginning only to encounter later on in deducing some aspect of the model a situation for which we did not account through a rule. This may result from analytic statements in which all possible deductions cannot be forseen in advance.

Explanation and Causality

Earlier in the methods section we distinguished between the necessary and sufficient-condition law in attempting to show the difference between explanation and prediction; however, as with our rules for deduction, more stringent and specific conditions need to be set forth in the process of deductive reasoning for our explanatory model. To begin with, we are making the assumption that our explanatory model is not a closed system in the sense that no other external variables may affect conclusions that are drawn from deducing the axioms. By invoking the necessary-condition law, though, we can legitimize certain types of deductions made without attempting to account for unknown variables. Also, by recognizing that "unknowns" may affect our conclusions, we can say that with controlled boundary conditions of the variable we are considering, i.e., ceteris paribus, the propositions and conclusions are still valid. To say that one has a closed system or theory suggests that the values of any one variable at any given time can be computed by means of the laws from the values of all the others at any other time, which would constitute "perfect knowledge" that does not exist in the social sciences.[17]

Rudner outlines three different types of explanations in social science: functional, scientific, and teleological.[18] Our concern is with the second type, i.e., scientific, but, it is worthwhile to distinguish between empirical and theoretical science for our explanatory model. As noted earlier, we are concerned with theoretical deductions which can be validated for empirical science by the use of a logical construct and calculus through proper deductive reasoning. Although Meehan points out that the minimum requirement for explanation is any structure that can stipulate and define a set of interactions that will produce an event and suggest a means of controlling it,[19] we still must define what type of scientific explanation within the theoretical calculus we are seeking. What is

proposed here is a causal relationship between variables and events, the conventional phrase of "cause and
effect" in social science for the interrelationship
between two successive events where the occurrence of
of the earlier is regarded as a condition for that of
the latter, i.e., event A causes event B.[20] In a
cause-effect relationship, a pair of variables imply
that one is treated as the independent variable (cause)
and the other as the dependent variable (effect).[21]
The correlation that one finds between the two variables serves as the first approximation or ingredient
of some potential or respective law.[22] We should
stipulate, however, from the beginning that in part of
our explanatory model involving causality one cannot
infer a one to one relationship between event A and
event C because a covariable (B) is also effecting
the outcome. Therefore, a more complex relationship
is established which will become clear as we proceed
and engage in the deductive process. A final note is
in order for the role of causal explanation in model-
building. When one speaks of causality, there can be
no "first cause" or "initial" changes in any sequence
of events in the environment, the beginning or orgin
is always an arbitrary one.[23] If one were able to
account for every explanation by invoking a former one,
explanation itself would be complete in which there
would be nothing left to be explained, leaving a situation which Hempel refers to as explanatory closure.[24]
The problem with attempting this type of explanation
is similar to Dahl's critique of the elitist theory
of community power; it would involve an infinite
regression in explanations, which is impossible,
because for every explanation put forth there would
be a preceeding one, no matter how far one regressed.[25]
Hence, the arbitrariness of a starting point in causality achieves its legitimacy in our model, as a result
of the very nature of causal relationships. With these
precautions set forth in this discussion of explanation and the limits of causality, let us move to our
specific steps in model-building.

Steps in Model-Building

Let us suggest seven major components or steps in
model-building and the calculus with which we will be
working. Then we will develop each step fully and
elaborate upon each component in sequence. These components of the model will constitute the remainder of

Chapter Four and all of Chapter Five. In Chapter Five various causal relationships between the concept-variables will be examined as well. The first component involves putting forth a set of axioms or postulates that will allow for the initial stage from which we can deduce other events in symbolic and written terms. The terms "axiom" and "postulate" will be used interchangeably for the sake of convenience, but we will begin with a definition of them. The second phase involves the development of a blueprint of the structure of our model. This will entail showing a causal relationship between concepts and variables and their interrelated nature. Once we have established the causal structure of our model we move on to the third component which will involve defining the major concepts and variables that are related to the development of the model. These will be fundamental or operational definitions needed to proceed, but other definitions may be necessary as we move along. These three phases of model-building will close out the chapter and will provide the conceptual approach and framework for the various causal relationships that will be constructed in Chapter Five.

In Chapter Five, the fourth component of the model will involve the relationships between the variables and how a change in one variable affects a change in another. It will also establish which variable is dependent and independent in any given relationship. The fifth phase in deducing the model will be establishing rationales for the relationships given and how our rationales relate to the literature on political change and integration. In the sixth phase of the deductive process and model, we will define and build our theorems or propositions based upon conclusions that can be logically deduced from the other component steps and the initial axioms set forth. Finally, the seventh component of the model will attempt to relate our major concepts in the model to empirical indices or referents in the real world. While such indicators may not be precise enough for measurement per se, they provide useful guidelines for one if they were to try to measure such phenomena empirically. But such indices are included as an important part of the deductive process and stressing the internal consistency of the model, which takes priority over whether they are empirically valid. Let us now turn to our axioms as the initial phase of the model.

Axioms

In social science, and more particularly in logical constructs of a theoretical nature, there must be a significant "puzzle" to be solved. It is a puzzle that generates an important question about some event that the investigator wants to undertake in order to answer. In short, if there is no question, research cannot commence. Ashby asserts that in model-building the generating question of research must in turn generate many possible sets of variables since the relationship between the question and the set is almost never one to one. As a result, there are often many sets of variables that may satisfy the demand in various ways and degrees.[26] We are concerned with only one set of variables which satisfy the demand of the model here. Hence, it suggests that not only are we working with an open system (as opposed to a closed system) in the sense that other variables may affect our outcomes, but also an open system that could possibly account for other sets of variables in our model. As a result, we must stipulate here that we are only attempting to work with one set of such variables which, at a minimum in normative terms, best suits the needs of our deductive and causal explanations. Our question is twofold: What are the major, critical components and variables of political integration and change on both the community and national level among Afro-Americans, and how do such variables and components affect political integration in a causal manner when external variables not included in the explanation are accounted for by the necessary-condition law and ceteris paribus clause? It is from this question and "puzzle" that we may develop our axioms; but let us first define what we mean by an axiom. An axiom may be defined as a law whose truth is universally accepted for the moment in order to make certain deductions from it.[27] According to Blalock, such axioms and lawlike statements themselves must interrelate concepts two or more at a time in order to make deductive statements connecting the propositions.[28] Thus, axioms are translated as propositions involving variables that are taken to be linked causally and connecting statements that imply such direct causal links. The calculus, by usage of the axioms, can create warranted expectations in that if we accept the axioms within the calculus as true, then certain conclusions are inescapable and others are enjoined if we are to avoid self-contradiction.[29]

We may say, in summary, that axioms have at least three properties, according to Brown: 1) their truth is assumed, 2) their truth can be tested only by testing some of their logical consequences, and 3) their truth cannot be deduced from other statements within the system.[30]

Above we defined axioms as involving "lawlike generalizations", a term which itself deserves to be defined in order to maintain clarity. A law, according to Greer, may be defined as invariable associations, but one must limit that definition and state that laws describe those events which have already occurred, indicating patterns in past experiences with great fidelity.[31] It is such "lawlike generalizations", as part of the definition of axioms, that assumes an "If... then" or causal relationship related to axiomatic statements.[32] In its most simple terms, a law is some event that is assumed to occur with some degree of regularity. Furthermore, laws always link two or more concepts together.

Keeping the above discussion of axioms and laws in mind, let us suggest the following axioms that will allow us to deduce from them our theorems.

Axiom 1. Whenever there is an increase in the political capacity of the sovereign nation, there will be an increase in social mobilization among Afro-Americans.

Axiom 2. Given an increase in the "new" political culture among Afro-Americans, there will be an increase in social mobilization among Afro-Americans.

Axiom 3. An increase in social mobilization causes a corresponding increase in political authority (among Afro-Americans).

Axiom 4. An increase in political authority causes an increase in political integration.

Axiom 5. Therefore, whenever we have an increase in social mobilization we will have an increase in political integration.

It is important to note, however, that whereas
we are able to use a deductive syllogism in axioms
3-5, we are not able to do the same with axioms 1 and
2. In this respect, axioms 1 and 2 (and consequently
the model) represent an important break with the aforementioned discussion of axioms and laws and what they
logically entail. Axioms 3-5 represent what may be
termed a hypothetical syllogism, which means that when
you have two sets of implications, and they are
connected in a relationship in which one is the conclusion and the other the premise in the implication,
the other terms will be linked appropriately.[33] For
example, if A implies B and B implies C, then A implies
C. When establishing a causal chain, this is the ideal
connection or linkage that is sought. But such deductive logic cannot be employed with regard to the first
two axioms. To say that, as with the first axiom, whenever we have an increase in political capacity, we
will have an increase in social mobilization is a valid
statement. Also, we make a valid assertion by suggesting that an increase in political culture causes an
increase in social mobilization as in the second axiom.
These valid statements or rules of influence are called
modus ponens, which suggests that if political capacity
(PC^1) implies social mobilization (SM), and PC^1 (as an
axiom) is true, then it follows that SM is also true.[34]
The same deductive logic can be employed with political
culture and social mobilization. Nevertheless, it
would be faulty logic to attempt to apply the hypothetical syllogism to axioms 1 and 2 since they do not
represent a causal chain in relationship to axiom 3.
The fault of this logic can be argued in symbolic terms
as follows:

the greater the PC^1, the greater the SM
the greater the PC, the greater the SM
Therefore, the greater the PC^1, the greater the PC.

The logic is misleading here because it would have
to assume a causal chain, such as $PC^1 \longrightarrow PC \longrightarrow SM$,
which is not the case. While we could assume PC^1 and
SM to be related as part of a causal chain in our overall model, this is not the case in the above example
and axioms one and two. But there is no reason for us
to assume that PC^1 and PC are related merely because
they have the same effect upon SM. In a revised
version, we would not expect a causal chain between
the three variables merely because PC^1 and PC have the

same effect on SM. Rather, the relationship shown,
would be suggested as in Figure 4-1.

Fig. 4-1 Relationship between covariants
and social mobilization in which
PC^1 and PC are acting independently
on SM and have no causal relationship
between each other.

It may be stated that if two statements are linked
(i.e., PC^1 and SM) to form a true conjunction, then it
follows that either conjunct in the statement is true
by what Graham calls the "simplification" rule of inference.[35] In summary, a statement of the form "the
greater the PC^1, the greater the SM" does not really
permit one, as Blalock so aptly points out, to deduce
implications unless they are meant to be more than just
covariant statements.[36] When a statement of this type
is made, one cannot infer deductively that the statement has a relationship with some other covariant that
is not related. It is also worthwhile to take note of
here, as Brodbeck does, that in a model employing
deduction one does not have to assert an "exact truth"
for its premises, only an exact statement of a hypothesis about their truth. The hypothesis is then tested
by the "exact deduction" which means not only the
syllogistic deduction which critics sometime equate
it.[37] Graham makes such a similar distinction by
offering the following example:

        If it is green, it will rain
        It is green
        Therefore it will rain.[38]

Graham concludes that an argument can be validly drawn,
but does not have to follow empirically. As a result
a logical argument can still be valid even when a
false premise leads to a false conclusion. While this
type of deductive argument does not affect deducing
from our axioms, it might affect ideal concepts which
may be employed in developing the model, but this is
consistent with our discussion earlier in the methods
section in which we noted not only ideal concepts but

our argument for internal consistency and the logic of deduction. A final thought is in order here before moving on to the second step of our model which is the structural outline of the conceptual model and its interrelated parts, i.e., the continuing controversy over induction and deduction as part of the scientific method, which can be divided into two parts.

As early as 1959 Brecht noted that the scientific method (empirical) has not replaced analytical deduction with inductive reasoning. Rather, what has been replaced is not deductive reasoning but the acceptance in scientific procedure of a major premise (generalizing statements) as true and valid on some ultimate grounds other than inductive reasoning that is carefully checked, in which proponents of the scientific method object to the acceptance of a priori propositions; they do not object to a correct statement of the propositions logical implications.[39] Brecht goes on to reason that on the contrary, the method used to refute false propositions whether they be a priori or other, is to state deductively all their logical implications in order to produce them for test and compatibility with other propositions. The second point worth taking note of here is attempting to delineate between induction and deduction as completely different procedures in science, according to Rudner, which is a moot question. Rudner states that it is a vulgar notion to suggest that induction and deduction are opposites as well as the idea that one involves going from the specific to the general (induction), while the other involves going from the general to the specific (deduction). In rather precise terms, Rudner states that deduction is not restricted only to infer from the general to the particular, but also that induction which comprises the selection of a hypothesis, frequently involves, as one of its steps the making of a deduction.[40]

Although we have consistently spoken to this point of deductive reasoning in our overall model, it is agreed with Rudner here that induction is also taking place and we will not attempt to separate the two in any specific terms nor argue this point any further.

In the structural outline of the conceptual model below, part of the foregoing discussion with regard to our covariants and their relation to social mobilization

are presented. Let us now turn to the second component
or step two of the model and the formal structure.

The causal model of explanation can be outlined as
in Figure 4-2.

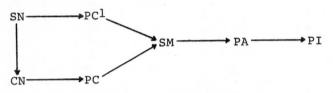

Fig.4-2 Model of causality and
political integration

The causal relationship originates from the concept of
a sovereign nation (SN) which will be defined in our
next step (as well as other germane concepts and terms).
A rule needs to be invoked, however, before we proceed
any further in our model. A horizontal, diagonal or
vertical arrow (——→) in the above model suggests an
"If...then" relationship of cause and effect. We may
say that SN for example, causes the effect PC^1, assuming that the arrow shows that if SN is accepted as
true, then the cause is PC^1. There is one exception
in our structural model that needs clarification with
regard to the cause and effect relationship. We are
not necessarily saying that SN causes CN (cultural
nation), but rather that the cultural nation emanates
from within the confines or borders of the sovereign
nation. This distinction is made because in many
states, such as Israel, the cultural nation is synonomous to that of the sovereign state for the most part.
On the other hand, in the United States the heterogeneous nature of many ethnic groups is witnessed by
expressions such as "Little Italy" and "Chinatown",
which are another way of speaking of a cultural nation.
Hence, the relationship between SN (sovereign nation)
and CN (cultural nation) in our theoretical structure
is merely a way of showing that the latter emanates
(although geographically speaking, it still exists
within the confines of SN) from the former.

Elaboration upon the causal chain of political

change and integration in the model is necessary at this point. As noted in the methods section, the time period under investigation is from 1965 onward. One should not infer that the model is unique only to this time period in Afro-American history, because one could also apply it, for example, to the period of the "Garvey Movement" in which there was a strong identification with Africa. In the above structure, the model suggest that the sovereign nation causes PC^1 (political capacity-effect) with a direct causal link. That is, public policies in the sovereign political system may involve political oppression as well as resistance to change. PC^1, in turn, causes social mobilization. On the other hand, the cultural nation (CN) causes PC (effect). In turn, PC causes SM (social mobilization-effect). The attempt to use a hypothetical deductive syllogism at this point, and the faulty logic involved, was revealed in the discussion of the first two axioms, and for the sake of avoiding redundancy, need not be repeated in tautological semantics here. It should be pointed out, though, as witnessed in our discussion of axioms 3-5 above, that a hypothetical or deductive syllogism sufficiently explains the causal connection between social mobilization (SM), political authority (PA), and political integration (PI). In cause-effect terms, it may be stated that social mobilization causes political authority (effect) and leadership to emerge among Blacks and political authority, by manipulating and recruiting the masses, causes political integration (effect), albeit it may take different forms. Let us reflect back for a moment on the statement that "the cultural nation (CN) causes PC (effect)." Obviously, there are no formal political structures of decision-making bodies that formulate public policies for Afro-Americans within the cultural nation that would be analogous to a sovereign political system. So that when we say that CN causes PC, it is important to make a stipulation of in what way, which will become self-evident in our definition of the cultural nation. It is argued here with regard to causality that the Pan-African emphasis, which grew out of the cultural nation as a result of African nations achieving independence and removing the yoke of colonialism in the period of 1960-65 gave rise to a new political culture among Afro-Americans, and it is in this sense that the cultural nation gave rise to and caused the embryonic political culture, as a result of the vicarious identification with African liberation movements.[41]

101

It is important, however, to be more specific by identifying what particular sources within the context of the cultural nation gave rise to a new political culture and identity. It is contended that Black leaders, intellectuals, and college students, for the most part, were largely responsible for the aroused racial identity with Africa. In this regard, we may state that the political culture and aroused identity was caused more specifically by leaders within the cultural nation, but that the political culture was still in its infant stage. It was mostly Black leaders, intellectuals, and Black college students adhering to this new identity at this point in time. It is this identity among the few that leads to, arouses, and causes social mobilization among the masses.

The structure of the model also suggests, for the most part, that the necessary-condition law is enforced. By this, as taken account of earlier, we may say that whenever we have X, we will also have B. It does not attempt to account for all conditions of external variables that may also cause X. It only states that whenever we have X, we will also have B. In the practical realm of our model, this means that when we have a rise in political authority, for instance, we will also have social mobilization (which may precede it or continue along with political authority once the latter has emerged). This does not attempt to account, however, for all the conditions or variables that cause or relate to political authority. An important distinction must be made, nevertheless, with regard to the necessary-condition law with respect to what causes social mobilization. One may witness in the model that social mobilization is likely to occur from two separate sources. As a result of the time period in question, it could be stated that PC^1 and PC are acting independently (vis-à-vis each other) upon social mobilization, and although acting simultaneously from time to time do not always occur together. If PC^1 and PC should act concurrently upon social mobilization, the sufficient-condition law can be stated as those variables sufficient to add to our knowledge those conditions that will cause social mobilization. If social mobilization should be effected at different times by PC^1 and PC acting independent of each other, it is proposed here that social mobilization may be effected by one variable acting independently or both variables acting concurrently, which effects the rate of social mobilization like the moon effects the high and low tides of the ocean. We will come back to this simile in the manipulation of our variables. When such variables occur together, we invoke the sufficient-condition law, when separate the necessary-condition law.

What then, does our causal model suggest other than the mere causal relationship? That is, what is the overall thesis? This is a question deserving some amount of explication at this point. Our model proposes that political change (integration) may be initiated from two separate and somewhat distinct political and cultural entities, and that its emanation generates (causes) social mobilization as the result of certain political phenomena. However, as social mobilization occurs, it causes different forms of political authority to emerge, compete for allegiance, and affects the speed of social mobilization which, in turn, allows political integration to take different forms. In a sense, it is suggested that authoritative leadership is quiescent, but that the process of social mobilization "arouses" it, so to speak. Nevertheless, this is not to say that such authority types are completely inactive, only that they reach their fullest leadership potential and political activity as the result of the process of social mobilization. Furthermore, the model implies that the crucial link in political integration is political authority. In a given Black community, one or more types of the political authority to be identified can be found, and the number of different types will determine the level and type of political integration. The problem of a lack of centralized political authority, and the problem in our model of political integration, stems directly from our conceptualization of a cultural nation which, by definition, does not have a central authoritative figure of a political nature or territorially defined land and border areas. Hence, the competitive and consequently divisive nature for political allegiance by leaders as social mobilization occurs.

Even if one were to argue Cruse's "Second Reconstruction Thesis", i.e., that Afro-American political gains and equality is of a cyclical nature,[42] the model proposed here would argue that even if this were so, the lack of a centralized political authority in the cultural nation of an institutional nature, is a major problem in breaking such a cycle. For example, an institutionalized, central authority among the Black masses could hold the allegiance of the people, sway their opinions and possibly attitudes, help to engrain political values (i.e., brotherhood, unity, etc.,), and promote programs to better their condition. This is not to say that Black institutions do not and have not existed, nor that Black leaders have not prevailed that could hold the allegiance of Blacks, but to say that such institutions (i.e., Black Church) and leaders are fragmentary rather than whole (centralized) and have competed for support rather than cooperated in the quest for it.

A final note is in order here before we move on. This is the idea of ceteris paribus with respect to the conceptual structure of our model. "All other factors remaining equal", as ceteris paribus implies, allows us to state this rule in conceiving abstractly a "structure" that stays the same in various temporal manifestations. In other words, one must assume that there is some empirical phenomena that allows us to hold it constant or stable while we examine it in various spatial-temporal dimensions. For if we could not perceive or visualize social and political phenomena without it being stable, one could not examine simple components, not to mention minute details of the phenomena under investigation. We will come back to the ceteris paribus (CP) clause in the next component of the model when we define our variables.

Definitions of Concepts and Variables

Concepts

A concept may be defined as a tool which allows the investigator to organize perceptions, classify events, and link changes in the pattern of one's perceptions.[43] A concept by definition, then, is not a statement but names or labels and consequently cannot be true or false; however, it is of value to take note of the fact that only sentences, never concepts, can serve as either premises or conclusions of a deduction. The idea of an "explanatory concept" is merely a confused way of speaking about significant concepts, those of which we know laws that permit explanation and prediction, depending upon what one is attempting to accomplish.[44] Before we begin to define our main concepts, it is vital that we also stipulate that any further concepts that should need defining or explaining will be done as we go along, in order to avoid confusion and maintain unambiguous analytic arguments. The concepts presented here provide us with some operational definitions necessary to provide clarity in the deductions we will make.

Cultural Nation. A cultural nation is a socio-cultural entity of people who are held together by a common emotional and historical cement that transcends territorial statehood. Connor states the essence of this definition: "The essence of the nation is not tangible. It is psychological, a matter of attitude rather than of fact."[45] The concept of a cultural nation does not suggest a physical abstraction or territory separate from the dominate nation-state (United States), but suggest that such ethnic and racial bonds represent a nation within a nation-state, so to speak. Similarly, the Irish Catholic Church was referred to as a "state" within a state because of its pervasive influence. Territorial borders are super-ficial in the cultural nation, being established by the sovereign entity within which it exist. Because of the implications of the concept of a cultural nation for our model, let us elaborate a little further.

Holden, in a somewhat similar definition (to ours) but more extended concept of what he terms the Black "nation", asserts:

> The term used here has nothing to do with the idea that separate "nations" are, as a matter of right, entitled to separate governments or judicial institutions. It is a way of describing the social and economic relationship of one group to another...If any two groups differ significantly as to physical places of residence, cultural styles and outlooks, levels of capital and income, political habits, legal rights, and habits of communication and exchange, then it may be quite reasonable to describe them as separate "nations."[46]

This conceptualization of a Black "nation" may be perceived as those Black communities which represent constituent parts. Again, Holden states the relevance of the "nation" as part of a more parochial concept:

> The politics of the black "nation" may
> be explained, at least partially, by
> reference to the local black communities
> out of which it is aggregated. Within
> each such community there is a political
> system, by which we mean a system of
> influence and control, based upon the wide
> variety of institutions that serve
> people's ordinary needs. These institu-
> tions are manifold as to their size,
> permanence, resources, degrees of social
> respectability, appeal to different
> social classes, and legal status.[47]

Therefore, when we speak of a cultural nation,
one may perceive it on the community or local level as
well as on the national level, and as a psychological
entity as well as other definable social and economic
characteristics.

Sovereign Nation. A state refers, as Weiner points
out, to a central authority with some ability to regulate political behavior.[48] A nation-state, by contrast,
refers "to a situation in which the borders of the
nation approximate those of the state."[49] The sovereign
nation, besides having a central authority which the
cultural nation lacks, also has the ability to implement public policies through legislation, the courts,
police, etc., which may affect the concept of political
capacity.

Political Integration/Change. Political change and
political integration will be used synonomously and
interchangeably in the model. It is contended here
that given the ambiguity and complexity of the literature on political development, the concept of political change is a more neutral one than political
development. Furthermore, given the limits of how far
we can go with the concept of political integration in
what is not an autonomous or independent cultural
nation, it is proposed here that political integration
is itself a significant form of political change and
this is our justification for using the two interchangeably. For the sake of precision, let us define this
somewhat amorphous term as symbolic and political
integration of political values among Blacks on the

community and national level. This should not be confused with our definition of a cultural nation in
which the people are held together by socio-psychological and cultural norms and values rather than political
ones. The difference in political values is witnessed
by the fact that in almost any nation or nation-state
a people of the same ethnic group (culture) may have
varying political and ideological orientations from
"left" to "right" on a liberal-conservative continuum.

When we speak of particular values in political
integration, such concepts as the legitimacy of political authority in the Black community as well as a
decline in violent conflict among various political
groups serve as indices or references to such values.
Others may include the bridging of intra-racial political cleavages based upon color, the ability of the
ethnic group or race to maximize their political power
by uniting in an operational as opposed to ideal sense,
the bridging of geographical cleavages (for example,
northern Blacks speaking of southern Blacks as "country"), and the ability of the ethnic group to vote
cohesively in local, state and federal elections.

Social Mobilization. Deutsch has defined social
mobilization as a "process in which major clusters of
old social, economic and psychological commitments
are eroded or broken and people become available for
new patterns of socialization and behavior."[50] Deutsch
discerns two stages in this process:

> 1) the stage of uprooting or breaking
> away from old settings, habits and
> commitments; and 2) the induction of
> the mobilized persons into some rela-
> tively stable new patterns of group
> membership, organization and committ-
> ment.[51]

We are concerned with three specific elements or
stages of the concept social mobilization: 1) breakdown, 2) transitional, and 3) the emergence stage.
There is a need to elaborate upon each one in order to
clarify their relation to the model. The breakdown
stage is best characterized by alienation which has a
double-entendre. We may speak of alienation in the
breakdown stage of social mobilization as directed
either toward the political system (sovereign nation)

107

as the result of police brutality, racial oppression and the like (political capacity), or alienation in this stage as the beginning of a changing Afro-American identity from negative to positive, in which old values, stereotypes, and a negative self-concept among the masses start to be redefined. As we see here, alienation in the breakdown stage has a <u>political</u> implication in the former instance and a <u>cultural</u> one in the latter case. This stage should be distinguished from our definition of political culture which concerns a new identity and values initially among only a few Black leaders.

In this stage of social mobilization we concern ourselves with the implications of identity and values toward the masses. The second stage of social mobilization is characterized by chaos and instability of one's previous values and attitudes as he begins to question them. In other words, this stage may be characterized by identities which are in transition in which allegiance and previous committments go through a metamorphasis. Finally, in the third stage, there is the clear emergence of new political orientations as well as cultural values toward the American political system, ethnic identity, and group solidarity. It is at this stage (and this is most important when the causal inferences in the model are examined) that the masses are most susceptible to particular types of political integration with the appearance on the political horizon of the authority types in the model who are instrumental to this end. Although at this stage there is a greater committment to in-group solidarity among the ethnic group generally, it is given more specific orientations which may be dogmatic in nature as political authority types compete for the allegiance of the masses.

Political Culture. Almond and Verba speak of culture as a "psychological orientation toward social objects", and political culture of a nation as "the particular distribution of patterns of orientation toward political objects among the members of the nation."[52] Pye and Verba define political culture as "the system of empirical beliefs, expressive symbols, and values which defines the situation in which political action takes place."[53] Finally, Kim speaks of two aspects of political culture which encompass both:

> 1) the political behavior patterns which
> have developed out of previous political
> systems, and 2) the national political
> mythology relating to political values
> and political legitimacy, on which the
> leaders may draw to reinforce his own
> legitimacy and to increase support for
> the new system.[54]

Political culture may be defined for our purposes as the establishment of a new identity and symbolism that may lead to the breakdown of old values and action toward the political system, and this identity is sometimes accompanied by a national cultural mythology. A national cultural mythology may be defined as new forms of social romanticism and the rebirth of myths and glorification of the African homeland by Blacks. At this point, however, political culture is in its embryonic stage, and is being formed, in part, by an "elite" cadre of Black political leaders, college students, and intellectuals. It is at this point that a positive identity among this cadre should be distinguished from the positive identity forming among the masses in the third stage of social mobilization. Initially, this elite cadre is an amorphous group ideologically, and is not necessarily the same political authority type that arises as the result of social mobilization. When social mobilization causes political authority to emerge, the latter is quite distinct with certain political characteristics that set the authority types apart from each other. The elite cadre, on the other hand, is not as distinguishable at this point with respect to political orientation and ideological commitment.

Political Capacity. Political capacity may be defined as the capability of the political system to implement "law and order" policies aimed at oppressing Blacks (such as incidences of police brutality in the ghetto which may spark racial hostilities) and a political inability or unwillingness to change and make concessions to Blacks when Blacks are expecting such change (i.e., an increase in policies or laws toward racial and socio-economic equality). Police repression and inflexibility on the part of the political system may both breed alienation which is the first stage of social mobilization. This alienation undoubtedly has increased as the result of high expectations of the

Carter administration which were never fulfilled and the repressive social and economic policies of the Reagan administration on the other. Such policies may occur at the national, state or local level. Consequently, such policies may affect Blacks nationally, state-wide, or on the local and community level.

Nation-Building. Nation-building does not assume the prior existence of a state, but may be defined as the process of building and integrating new loyalties on the basis of subjective ties while maintaining past ethnic ties which have given Afro-Americans a common (racial) identity in the first place.

Institutionalization. Talcott Parsons defines institutionalization as "the organization of action around sufficiently stable patterns so that they may be treated as structured from the point of view of the system."[55] Huntington states that "Institutions are stable, valued, recurring patterns of behavior", and "Institutionalization is the process by which organizations and procedures acquire value and stability."[56] Stability and recurring patterns of behavior appear to be the main components of this concept and suffice for our definition here.

Political Authority. Because our authority types are crucial to our model of political integration and needs to be distinguished from related concepts such as "power", "influence" and "force", an adequate discussion will be undertaken here to make certain clarifications. Furthermore, a summary of past classifications of leadership models on Afro-Americans appears in order to show their shortcomings vis-à-vis our typology. In discussing our authority types, and in the rest of the model, the terms authority and leadership will be used interchangeably as synonyms, with the following distinctions below between authority and related concepts kept in mind.

We concur with Bachrach and Baratz here, who reject authority defined as "formal power", and that which conceives it as "institutionalized power."[57] In the first instance, one is at a loss to know who has power when the agent who possesses "formal power" is actually powerless, (i.e., the assassination of a president) and few of our authority types as we will take note of below, have "formal power." In the latter instance it assumes the legitimacy of laws without warrant (e.g., Dr. King's rejection of southern "authorities" during the civil rights movement in the sixties).

Bachrach and Baratz's rejection of the above views on authority lead them to the following definition: "' a quality of communication'" that possesses "'the potentiality of reasoned elaboration.'"[58] This concept of authority, which we will use (contrary to the above), has both relational and rational attributes. Its relational quality, according to the authors, is found in the communicative aspect; it is not necessary that A possess authority, but that B regard A's communication as authoritative. The rationality of authority is found in that B finds A's command reasonable in terms of his own values which he can rationalize, rather than a fear of sanctions which is the case of power. In defining authority types in the model of political integration, it will be stipulated that their power is limited in the cultural nation. Bachrach and Baratz go on to define "false" authority as a situation in which effective communication cannot be elaborated upon by A in his command to B. In such an instance there is a shift in relationship from one initially involving authority to one ultimately involving power. When such an instance occurs there is a situation in which potential compliance becomes one of potential noncompliance. Authority in this sense can be looked upon as both a source of and restraint upon the exercise of power; it both justifies and limits the amount of power.[59]

On the other hand, authority is not seen as a special case of power, because power has been defined by Dahl as "A has power over B to the extent that he can get B to do something that B would not ordinarily do."[60] Rossi, in a similar manner, defines power as one "in which individual A affects the behavior of individual B because B wishes to avoid the sanctions which A would employ if B did not comply with his wishes."[61] The latter definition of Rossi more specifically points up the problem of power with regard to the political authority typology here. Except for special cases of the Traditional-Brokerage in which formal positions are held such as Black mayors, the authority types in the model do not have sanctions as a political resource to wield against the masses in the face of noncompliance. Institutional arrangements, by-and-large, are lacking among the authority types here as a base from which to impose sanctions against the masses who do not comply, although they may wield "power" among their own constituencies in an institutional sense. For example, a Muslim minister may yield power within the confines of his mosque and within the hierarchical sect, but this power is not extended to the Black community in general. By definition, the cultural nation has no centralized authority figure with ultimate power and authority over the masses in the sense that Eisenhower had when he called out the national guard in order to make local authorities desegregate public schools in Little Rock. Therefore, when we speak of authority it is pertinent to keep this distinction with power in mind, since authority types are viewed here in relation to their effect upon Blacks at-large in the process of political integration rather than upon a particular ideological following, although by definition they may be identified with a particular group.

Because the concept of authority is often related to influence, it is important to make some further distinctions between influence and its relation to authority. Lasswell and Kaplan see influence as value potential or the position a person or group is likely to occupy as the outcome of conflict. They state:

> It is important to take both potential
> and position into account. A group may
> be more and more influential even though
> its value position remains constant, if
> its potential is increasing...and con-
> versely a group may have little influence
> regardless of its value position, because
> of its low potential.[62]

This passage is extremely important with regard to the concept of influence because it is contended here that three of our four authorities (types) appeal to the Black masses without any hierarchical representation in the political stratum of the American system. At the same time, the fourth authority type, Traditional-Brokerage, from a hierarchical perspective, may have a high value position (as a mayor, congressperson, and so forth), yet little influence over the masses in political integration. Finally, the implication of the concept of force and its relationship to authority are worth explicating in outlining the limitations of the latter concept. Force, unlike authority and power, in which one party obtains another's compliance, is a situation in which one's objectives must be achieved, if possible, in the face of noncompliance.[63] In a force situation, a person's scope of decision-making is extremely curtailed since the intended victim is stripped of choice between compliance and noncompliance, whereas a choice is retained in an authority or power relationship. Force is not a valid concept with respect to our authority types. Although as with power and influence, there may be certain instances where force is significant, but it is not important in our leadership types because they are not in a position to force the masses of Afro-Americans in political integration. Blacks in America have many political choices that override one that may be defined by Black authority figures in the cultural nation. These authorities have no control since the position here is that the masses are restricted (in terms of compliance and noncompliance) more by the larger and more powerful sovereign political system that constitutes the United States then they are by a cultural national entity within those same confines.

In summary, the concept of authority and related components often used interchangably or confused with it may be further clarified here. While our authority types possess a communicative aspect that the masses may perceive as authoritative and reasonable with their own values which they can rationalize, they do not possess power or force over the masses in any absolute manner. Influence may be positively related to their authority, however, using Lasswell and Kaplan's definition, since it does not depend upon hierarchy and position. The authority types here not only lack (for the most part) formal positions outside of their own organization and following, but occupy a positional level most influential in mobilizing the masses (i.e., located in the same community they attempt to integrate). Now that such distinctions have been made a cursory discussion of past leadership types on Afro-Americans as well as the ones we find most appropiate in a model of political integration is in order.

Leadership Types

Many attempts have been made to characterize Black leadership and develop typologies with respect to race relations with Whites in the United States, some of

113

which have been regional case studies while others have been national in scope. Myrdal, for instance, developed an Accommodationist-Protest typology of Black leadership in the United States.[64] Wilson, in his classic work of 1960 speaks of the Moderate-Militant dichotomy in a case study of Chicago, in which the Moderate leader is one who does not attempt to aggregate complex problems in race relations under one heading (i.e., racism) whereas the Militant does.[65] Thompson, on the other hand, takes this dichotomous typology one step further in his case study of New Orleans in 1963, speaking of the Uncle Tom, Race Diplomat and Race Man as those most prevalent.[66] In a more recent case study by Ladd in 1969 of Greenville, South Carolina and Winston-Salem, North Carolina, he develops a similar typology to Thompson in his descriptions of the Conservative, Militant and Moderate styles.[67]

On the other hand, a study of Black leadership with much broader implications is that of Hamilton. Hamilton distinguishes four analytical types of Black leadership in the United States; the Political Bargainer, who operates within the two party system and receives the support of the Black and White middle-class; the Moral Crusader who introduces morality into the political arena not as a tool or strategy, but as a goal, often using nonviolence as a tactic, but is often accused of being a "sell-out" or "Uncle-Tom" once negotiations begin and compromise is inevitable; the Alienated Reformer who does not have faith in existing political structures as the Political Bargainer does, and speaks of creating alternative institutions while emphasizing group consciousness and Black pride, but is still amenable to electoral politics with a Black constituency but is caught between different approaches since he must use one approach with his constituency (language of alienation) and another (conciliation) with those whom he must deal with in the political arena; and the Alienated Revolutionary who feels that calulated violence is necessary for any significant change to take place, and speaks of establishing a Black nation.[68]

What all of the above leadership typologies have in common is their relationship with the American political system vis-à-vis Whites. Hamilton's typology goes further than the others, however, in the emphasis upon alienation and the establishment of a Black nation, although it is still based upon certain assumptions about race relations in the present political system. Another significant characteristic of the above typologies of leadership is that they appear easier to describe than to define, although definitions are implicit in the descriptions.

The leadership typology to be developed here is intended to describe the relationship of leadership styles to the Black masses and their role in political integration among Blacks as an ethnic and racial group. In other words, we are not concerned so much with the functions of these leaders in racial integration and in competing in the political arena with Whites, although this may be the ultimate strategy once integration among Blacks has taken place, as much as we are concerned with how they affect integration among the Black masses.

In this context, the leadership styles represent a sharp break with past studies mentioned here. Nevertheless, we may find part of Hamilton's classification useful in our typology, although it will be to serve different ends, since it may help to clarify our styles. What is important to keep in mind is that the authority and leadership types in a model of political integration are not absolutely distinct with no overlap. For example, the Traditional-Brokerage type is one who typically has engaged in conventional politicking such as lobbying, nonviolent protest, and as a go-between for the Black and White community. These leaders work within and accept the status quo with regard to the American political system. The Traditional-Brokerage type does not question the various structures and functions in the United States as a political entity, although they do realize that there are racial injustices. The Traditional-Brokerage is significantly different in that he is concerned with racial integration and nonviolent protest, while the Religious-Nationalist is dedicated more to in-group solidarity than racial integration, and self-determination and self-defense more than nonviolent protest.

In more recent years, however, some leaders in the Religious Nationalist category have become less militant, such as the Black Muslims who have become fragmented, with a large segment now referring to themselves as The World Community of Islam in the West. Similarly, leaders such as Richard Hatcher in the Traditional-Brokerage category have been perceived as a Black Power advocate by some, similar to the category of Cultural Nationalist.[69] Hatcher's politics, however, are still confined, for the most part, to the American political process while Cultural Nationalists tend to engage in this form of political activity only periodically while stressing culture and values as their main emphasis for guidance in political activities, which is not confined mainly to the type Hatcher participates in. As Maulana Karenga, a Cultural Nationalist states:

> Everything that we do, think, or learn
> is somehow interpreted as a culture
> expression. So when we discuss politics
> to us that is a sign of culture. When
> we discuss economics to us that is a
> sign of culture. In other words, we
> define culture as a complete value
> system and also means and ways of
> maintaining that value system.[70]

Thus, while there may be some overlap in our authority types, what is important to keep in mind is their role in Afro-American political integration, and for this purpose it is asserted here that we have captured the essence of those leadership styles most closely conforming to this end. It is important at this point to turn more specifically to each authority type in order to clarify their main characteristics, keeping the above stipulations in mind.

Traditional-Brokerage

Traditional-Brokerage consists of types of political authority and leadership which, for the most part, have traditionally characterized the Black community. They may serve a "peace-keeping" function, such as the typical Black minister in many communities during a racial crisis, a brokerage function between the Black community and the White power structure, in which certain concessions are made to them (leaders) in return for the allegiance of Blacks to a political machine, or legal, economic and civil rights functions, with organizations such as the NAACP and SCLC and the Urban League. One of the outstanding characteristics of the Traditional-Brokerage leadership type is that, for the most part, they work within the established American political system. This is what is meant by traditional here although it may take a multitude of

forms. One other stipulation that should be made with
regard to the above type, implicit in the foregoing
discussion, is that the term Traditional-Brokerage
does not mean that every type of such traditional
leadership defined serves a brokerage function. They
tend, generally speaking, not to be concerned with
Black self-determination and racial cohesion, but with
racial integration into the American political system
in order to achieve change. These leaders play by the
established "rules of the game" and do not question the
nature of the American political system. A somewhat
new form of this leadership type is the recent election
of Black mayors in relatively large, urban areas. It
should be kept in mind that this leadership type, as
well as the others to be defined are not absolute types
that encompass clear and distinct lines between them,
and thus there may be a tendency for overlap of some
forms. But it does propose that such types as defined
can be distinguished with some degree of certainty in
the empirical world. What types of leaders in the
empirical world constitute the Traditional-Brokerage?
Civil Rights leaders such as Roy Wilkins and Dr. Martin
Luther King, along with Benjamin Hooks and Vernon
Jordan, and more recently political leaders and elected
mayors such as Richard Hatcher, Kenneth Gibson, and the
Black Caucus in Congress, constitute this leadership
type. This authority type collapses the Political
Bargainer and Moral Crusader dimensions of Hamilton's
typology. As noted above, however, even though there
is some similarity in their descriptive definitions,
their functions serve quite different ends in our model.

Cultural Nationalist

Malcolm X and Maulana Ron Karenga are two of the
best prototypes of this leadership style. Such nationalist leaders appear somewhat dogmatic in terms of pro-
fessing political doctrine but are flexible enough to
achieve their goals "by any means necessary." They
tend to be charismatic and to "politicize" religion,
although they are distinguished from the Religious
Nationalists by the fact that culture rather than
religion is their main emphasis. The term Black Nationalist has a host of meanings, just as the term nationalism itself found in much of the literature on political development and change.[71] It often suggests one of
several orientations among Afro-Americans on a continuum from complete separation in an autonomous state

117

outside the United States, or an independent state within the United States, to mere calls for ethnic solidarity and group conscious among and between Afro-Americans. Here we are concerned with, and want to distinguish between, those nationalists whose appeal is directed only to a particular segment of the Afro-American population, and those nationalists who appeal for Black unity on a national level irrespective of class, age or pragmatic orientation. It is the latter type of nationalism that we are concerned with here. The emphasis upon culture as the basis for political action is manifested in an emphasis upon Black pride and a positive identity as a basis for other orientations. This leadership type is similar to Hamilton's Alienated Reformer, in which they may or may not pursue activities within the American political process to further their goals. In sum, we may state that charisma, political religion, culture and political flexibility are their fundamental attributes. It is these last two attributes, however, that distinctly set them apart from the Religious Nationalist. Groups which tend to be associated with this leadership type include US Organizations and CAP (Congress of African People).

Religious Nationalist

This leadership type attempts to politicize religion (a form of political religion) and use it as a dogma and rationale in order to promote self-determination and integration, i.e., the use of religion as a means to an end, while at the same time to promoting identity. Like the Cultural Nationalist, these leaders, too, tend to be charismatic. But they are also nationalist in that their appeal for solidarity is to a particular ethnic and racial group of people, and suggest that Afro-Americans must be strong, united and integrated among themselves while seeking full freedom and justice. In this sense, they do not represent a radical form of nationalism, i.e., advocating a violent revolution and separate nation-state. Their form of religious Black nationalism often takes the form of substituting a Black God for a White God or substituting the Arabic name, Allah, for God, a Black Jesus for a White Jesus, or the Prophet Muhammad instead of the Prophet Jesus, and Black Angels in lieu of White Angels in order to promote in-group solidarity as well as a positive self-concept. In short, they tend to be both Christian and Muslim Religious Nationalists.

Leadership of this type is best represented by the likes of the Reverend Jesse Jackson of PUSH (People United to Save Humanity) in Chicago, the Reverend Albert Cleage of Detroit, and Minister Farrakhan of the Black Muslims whose headquarters are in Chicago who have separated from The World Community of Islam in the West and have spread across the cultural nation. This leadership type is not new and took similar forms during the period of enslavement of Blacks in America with the likes of Henry Highland Garnet and David Walker.[72]

Some of the main attributes of this leadership type, then, are political religion, charisma, and inflexibility in their beliefs and attitudes and unwillingness to work within the American political process through such means as voting, lobbying, running for office and the like. Although these leaders put a great emphasis upon race pride and in-group solidarity like the Cultural Nationalists, religion and inflexibility of attitudes toward the political process are two attributes that distinctly set them apart from the Cultural Nationalists. Exceptions to this may be leaders such as Jesse Jackson, who from time to time engages in economic and political bargaining in the American political process.

Faddist-Rhetorical

The Faddist-Rhetorical authority type is the most radical of the forces. They tend to engage in the "revolution" because it is the "latest" thing to do; it is in vogue, so to speak. As nations in the Third World have achieved independence in the last two decades, they have attempted to initiate or duplicate this feat in America. Such a perception of revolution by this leadership type as being in vogue has often been characterized by rhetoric such as "off the pig", "power to the people", and other rhetorical philosophy denoting a political revolution. This authority type is closest to what Hamilton refers to as the Alienated Revolutionary:

> This...type of leadership feels that
> no substantial change can take place
> in this society without calculated
> acts of instrumental violence. The
> Alienated Revolutionary clearly is
> distrustful of the existing order...

119

> the Revolutionary is not unhappy with
> acts of expressive violence (riots) and
> uses these acts to forecast coming acts
> of instrumental violence (urban guerilla
> warfare). His heroes are Mao-Tse-Tung,
> Che Guevera and Robert Williams...the
> substance of any theories of nation-
> building is rarely absorbed.[73]

It is the last two lines of the above citation
that are worth taking note of here with regard to our
category of Faddist-Rhetorical. Rhetoric centers not
just around revolution, but slogans from Mao and Che,
and the absence of a goal centered around nation-building (which is an instrumental part of revolution) makes
one question whether they are in fact, faddist at best,
social romanticist at worse. What leaders in the
empirical world have been suggestive of this leadership type? This type includes people such as Huey P.
Newton, Eldridge Cleaver, and Bobby Seale (since the
beginning of the time period under discussion Cleaver
has become a born-again Christian and Seale has run
for public office), all of whom were past leaders of
the Black Panther Party. Such leaders tend not so
much to romanticize a national or African mythology as
suggested in our concept of political culture, as much
as they tend to romanticize violent revolution by
quotations from Mao-Tse-Tung, Lenin and Che Guevera
and slogans such as "pick up the gun." Other groups
with this orientation includes the RNA (Republic of
New Africa) and RAM (Revolutionary Action Movement).
It is a contention here that it is groups and leaders
with this type of political orientation that are either
almost extinct physically or have gone underground in
order to avoid physical annihilation, since by their
very actions they have represented an immediate, if
limited, threat to police departments across the country, and the political system at-large. This authority
type not only abhors any association with the American
political process which distinguishes them from the
Traditional-Brokerage, but does not even advocate
political participation in this context when it is
advantageous to them, like the Cultural Nationalist.
They do not put great emphasis upon Black pride and
identity in the manner of the Cultural and Religious
Nationalists. For the most part, they tend to emphasize politics over religion and culture in the most
extreme sense, i.e., a violent, political, revolutionary

upheaval.

Variables

A rule for defining our variables is that they constitute the same ones as our main concepts in the structure of the model, except for the notion of a cultural nation and sovereign nation, which represents our conceptual approach to model-building and as such, cannot be operationalized _per se_ as variables. As suggested earlier, in translating our concepts into symbolic or variable representation, we will use the same letters that begin words in the concepts as symbols for our variables.

In abstracting the variables from the concepts, and concepts from the real world, we are not attempting a complete truth claim or total isomorphism of the empirical world as part of the calculus. In fact, Meehan contends that no explanation can be a perfect isomorph for some part of the empirical world, and that the gap is filled only by the ceteris paribus (CP) clause which closes the structure of the calculus in order for one to deduce certain implications.[74] The CP clause also allows one to lump together all of the external influences on the selected set of variables which allows the investigator to calculate the reliability of the explanation in terms of the influence of all external factors without having to identify or specify them (variables) and their particular impact.[75] The CP clause, then, is similar to our necessary-condition law in that it takes into account all external factors by lumping them together, yet still allowing one to propose certain explanations working within the formal calculus. However, the ceteris paribus clause goes one step further in that it closes the structure of the calculus formally in the process of seeking explanations.

For clarification and simplification of our variables, let us delineate them by using the translations in Figure 4-3, although the sovereign and cultural nations should not be viewed so much in terms of variables as political and cultural entities.

In the written translation in Figure 4-3, in which the variables are represented in symbolic terms, the correspondence between the symbols and the concepts is

Sovereign Nation	=SN
Cultural Nation	=CN
Political Culture	=PC
Political Capacity	$=PC^1$
Social Mobilization	=SM
Political Authority	=PA
Political Integration	=PI

Fig. 4-3 Translation of concepts
to variables

done in such a way that allows us to maintain clarity
in manipulating our variables. It is suggested here
that such symbols are more appropriate than letter
representations such as a,b,c,d...etc., since it allows
one to follow the arguments without having to continuously fall back upon the prior translations. Now
that the concepts and variables have been defined and
translated, this chapter may be summarized.

The purpose here has been to delineate the conceptual parameters of the model. This involved the discussion of important aspects of scientific explanation
and the way in which these concepts relate to the model
of political integration. Several components were also
discussed as an integral part of model-building and a
model of Afro-American political integration. This
included certain axioms or postulates, the actual
structure of the model, and definitions of the major
concepts and variables that will be utilized in an
operational context. At this point, we turn to Chapter
Five which involves other important components of model-
building and various causal relationships in the model
of political integration.

Notes

1. Paul Diesing, Patterns of Discovery in the Social Sciences,
   (Chicago and New York: Aldine-Atherton, Inc., 1971), p. 35.

2. Eugene E. Meehan, The Foundations of Political Analysis,
   (Homewood: The Dorsey Press, 1971), p. 9.

3. Ibid., p. 10.

4. Arnold Brecht, Political Theory, (Princeton: Princeton
   University Press, 1959), p. 55-57, passim.

5. George J. Graham, op. cit., p. 117.

6. Ibid., p. 119.

7. Paul Diesing, op. cit., p. 306.

8. James March, "Model-Building", in The Process of Model-Building in the Behavioral Sciences, edited by Ralph M. Stodgill, (Columbus: Ohio State University Press, 1970), p. 77.

9. Paul Diesing, op. cit., p. 14.

10. Ibid.

11. Ibid.

12. Ibid.

13. Ibid.

14. Eugene J. Meehan, The Foundations of Political Analysis, p. 202.

15. Scott Greer, The Logic of Social Inquiry, (Chicago: Aldine Publishing Co., 1969), pp. 85-86.

16. Ibid., p. 86.

17. May Brodbeck, "Explanation, Prediction, and 'Imperfect' Knowledge."

18. Richard S. Rudner, op. cit.

19. Eugene Meehan, op. cit.

20. Arnold Brecht, op. cit.

21. Paul Diesing, op. cit., p. 3.

22. Ibid., p. 3.

23. Eugene Meehan, op. cit., p. 67.

24. Carl G. Hempel, "Explanatory Incompleteness" in Readings in the Philosophy of Social Science, p. 410.

25. Ibid., See Robert Dahl, "Critique of the Ruling Elite Model", American Political Science Review, 52, (June, 1958), pp.

463-69

26. W. Ross Ashby, "Analysis of the System to be Modeled", in The Process of Model-Building in the Behavioral Sciences, p. 106.

27. Herbert M. Blalock, Jr., Theory Construction, (Englewood Cliffs: Prentice-Hall, 1969), p. 10.

28. Ibid.

29. Eugene J. Meehan, op. cit., p. 84.

30. Robert Brown, Explanation in Social Science, (Chicago: Aldine Publishing Co., 1963), p. 174.

31. Scott Greer, op. cit., p. 117.

32. Scott Greer, op. cit., p. 120.

33. George J. Graham, op. cit., p. 154-55.

34. Ibid., p. 154.

35. Ibid., p. 15.

36. Herbert M. Blalock, op. cit., p. 15.

37. May Brodbeck, "Explanation, Prediction, and 'Imperfect' Knowledge", p. 373.

38. George C. Graham, op. cit., p. 151.

39. Arnold Brecht, op. cit., p. 92.

40. Richard S. Rudner, op. cit.

41. Harold Cruse, Rebellion or ·Revolution.

42. Harold Cruse, "Black and White: Outlines for the Next Stage", Black World, 20, (January, 1971), pp. 19-41.

43. Eugene J. Meehan, op. cit., p. 9.

44. May Brodbeck, "Introduction" to Readings in the Philosophy of the Social Sciences.

45. Walker Connor, "Nation-Building or Nation-Destroying", World

Politics, 1, (April, 1972), p. 337.

46. Matthew Holden Jr., The Politics of the Black "Nation", (New York: Chandler Publishing Co., 1973), p. 1.

47. Ibid., p. 3.

48. Myron Weiner, "Political Integration and Political Development", Annals of the American Academy of Political and Social Science, 358, (March, 1965), p. 57.

49. Walker Connors, op. cit., p. 334.

50. Kark Deutsch, "Social Mobilization and Political Development", American Political Science Review, 55, (September, 1961), p. 494.

51. Ibid., p. 494.

52. Gabriel Almond and Sidney Verba, op. cit., pp. 12-13.

53. Lucian Pye and Sidney Verba, Political Culture and Political Development, (Princeton: Princeton University Press, 1965), p. 513.

54. Joungwon Alexander Kim, "The Politics of Predevelopment", Comparative Politics, 5, (January, 1973), p. 224.

55. Talcott Parsons, "The Position of Sociological Theory", American Sociological Review, 13, (April, 1948), pp. 156-64.

56. Samuel P. Huntington, "Political Development and Political Decay", p. 394.

57. Peter Bachrach and Morton S. Baratz, "Decisions and Non-Decisions: An Analytical Framework", American Political Science Review, 57, (September, 1963), pp. 632-42.

58. Ibid., p. 638.

59. Robert A. Dahl, "The Concept of Power" in Politics and Social Life, edited by Dentler, Polsby and Smith, Boston Houghton Mifflin Co., 1963.

60. Ibid., p. 639.

61. Peter H. Rossi, "Community Decision-Making", in Administrative Science Quarterly, 1, (March 1957), pp. 2, 415-43.

62. Harold Lasswell and Abraham Kaplan, Power and Society, (New Haven: Yale University Press, 1950), p. 58.

63. Bachrach and Baratz, op. cit., p. 636.

64. Gunnar Myrdal, An American Dilemma, (New York: Harper and Row, 1944).

65. James Q. Wilson, Negro Politics: The Search for Leadership, (Glencoe: Free Press, 1960).

66. Daniel C. Thompson, The Negro Leadership Class, (Englewood Cliffs: Prentice-Hall, 1963).

67. Everett C. Ladd, Jr., Negro Political Leadership in the South (Ithaca: Cornell University Press, 1969).

68. Charles V. Hamilton, "Conflict, Race, and System-Transformation in the United States", in Readings on the American Political System, ed. by L. Earl Shaw and John C. Pierce, (Lexington: D.C. Heath and Co., 1970), pp. 609-18.

69. Hedley Donavan, "Real Black Power", Time Magazine, November, 17, 1967, pp. 22-24.

70. The Quotable Karenga, p. 17.

71. See the article by Walker Conner, "Nation-Building or Nation-Destroying?" in World Politics, 24, (April 1972), pp. 319-355.

72. One of the best collections of works to-date on this form of religion and Black leadership during slavery is that of Sterling Stuckey, The Ideological Origins of Black Nationalism, (Boston: Beacon Press, 1972).

73. Charles V. Hamilton, op. cit., pp. 615-616.

74. Eugene J. Meehan, op. cit., p. 114.

75. Ibid., p. 65.

CHAPTER V

AFRO-AMERICAN POLITICAL INTEGRATION:
CAUSAL RELATIONSHIPS

The purpose of this chapter is to establish
various causal relationships between variables in the
model, develop rationales, build theorems or propositions, and construct empirical indices that relate
to the major concepts in the model. Once this task is
accomplished the model of Afro-American political
integration will be complete. A simple one-by-one
matrix will be utilized in several instances to show
the relationship between social mobilization and political authority. The role of these political authority
(leadership) types is considered crucial in understanding and explaining Black political integration. Various
deductions will be utilized in order to explain certain
causal relationships among the variables. Let us now
turn to the relationships between the variables in the
model.

Relationships Between Variables

In defining the relationships of our variables,
perhaps it is best to begin with an equation that
would be tantamount to political integration, and then
deduce the implications of the equation in a systematic
fashion. Our equation for political integration may
be written:

$$PI = P(PC + PC^1 + SM \times PA^t)$$

It can be stated that political integration (PI)
is equal to the probability (P) of an increase in
political culture (PC, i.e., political identity and
mythology) and/or an increase in political capacity
(PC^1, i.e., oppression, resistance to change), plus
an increase in social mobilization (SM) times the type
of political authority (PA) in which (t) represents
the types that may emerge in any given community. Two
reservations should be stipulated in the equation of
political integration. First, we are still assuming a
causal relationship between the variables, and political culture and political capacity are treated as
covariants in their relationship to social mobilization
in which either or both can trigger SM independently of
the other. They are both represented in the equation,

however, in order to fulfill the requirements of the total equation of political integration suggested in the model. Secondly, the part of the equation, social mobilization "times" political authority, means that the number of political authority types (t) that arises when social mobilization occurs may be multiplied. For example, if we were to say that in community X social mobilization takes place, and two authority types emerge, it would be noted as social mobilization "times" two (PA), or SM x 2(PA).

If three leadership types should arise at that point in time, we would say SM x 3(PA). Thus, one may also infer from the equation that political integration is multiplied by the number and types of political authority that arise in a given community. For instance, if three authority types emerge in a given instance, it could be stated symbolically that, 3 PA x PI would mean that political integration is multiplied by three, although with three different ideas of what political integration should constitute. In short, that all three authority types contribute to political integration, but not necessarily in the same way. One exception should be taken note of here. The definition of the Traditional-Brokerage authority type suggests that racial integration rather than political integration is their main objective, and as we move along this will become self-evident with the variables.

While the political equation suggests the ingredients or formula for political integration, it does not tell us much in the logic of deduction in its present form. For this purpose, let us propose the following syllogism:

1) When we have political culture and political capacity effecting social mobilization, and social mobilization effecting political authority, we will have political integration.

2) Political culture and political capacity are effecting social mobilization, and social mobilization is effecting political authority.

3) Therefore, whenever we have political culture and political capacity effecting social mobilization, we will have political integration.

128

The above represents a translation of our probability statement into the language of deduction, which
is an alternative way of viewing the overall relationship of the variables in the model.

It should be kept in mind that the authoritative
types of leaders identified may differ from community
to community across the national spectrum both in the
type and number to be found there. In other words,
in any given community where social mobilization takes
place among Afro-Americans for political integration,
one may find a variety of such leadership types, one or
more of such in terms of numbers. We may find just one
political authority type in a small community, for
example, in the South, of those identified in the
model. This authority type most likely would be the
Traditional-Brokerage. On the other hand, two or more
competing leadership types would most likely be found
in northern urban areas of larger size, as well as
urban areas in the South. The rationale for suggesting
that leadership types may prevail on the basis of rural
and urban areas is that in southern and rural areas
there have been established patterns of relations among
Blacks as well as between Black and Whites, although
such patterns are undoubtedly changing as Afro-Americans have achieved the voting franchise, broken down
segregation barriers, became more militant, and elected
Black officials. In terms of leadership types, however,
we would argue that in such areas they would still fall
within our definition of the Traditional-Brokerage.

On the other hand, we would argue that new forms
of leadership are emerging in urban areas, particularly
in the North, since social relations and patterns are
not as established, and in this sense Blacks are relatively new to the areas. It should not be implied, as
noted in our conceptualization of leadership types,
that all such leaders engage in or attempt to influence
their followers to engage in conventional politicking
such as running for office, voting and the like.
Rather, they have a constituency of followers who perceive them as authoritative. In this respect one may
concur to some extent with Edelman on the masses perception of leadership and authority, who states:

> Leadership, then, is not to be under-
> stood as something an individual does or
> does not have, at all times and places.

> It is always defined by a specific
> situation and is recognized in the
> response of followers to individual
> acts and speeches. If they respond
> favorably and follow, there is leader-
> ship; if they do not, there is not.[1]

Edelman goes on to state that what determines
whether leadership is politically effective is based
not upon the good or bad effects flowing from political
acts as much as whether the leader can indefinitely
convey an impression of knowing what is to be done.[2]
The rationale for not applying the model to any particular community or geographic area was presented in
the earlier discussion, i.e., we are dealing with the
cultural nation as a national political entity. This
is not to say, however, that one could not investigate
a particular Black community with the model.

The relationship between social mobilization and
political authority could also be included in a simple
one-to-one matrix in order to determine how each
authority type affects social mobilization in relationship to political culture and political capacity.
Let us first suggest this relation with political
culture as the causal variable. In the matrix below
in Figure 5-1, social mobilization is used as a dichotomous variable between high and low with regard to inten-
sity.

What the matrix suggests is that when political
culture is used as the causal variable (rather than as
a covariant), and political capacity is held constant,
i.e., when political culture is defined as a positive
(racial) identity and cultural awareness among Afro-
Americans, social mobilization would tend to be high-
est among the masses in any Black community where
authoritative leadership types C and D are present,
and social mobilization would tend to be lowest where
authoritative types A and B are present. Our explanation for this phenomena is that generally speaking
(and we must speak in general terms in the model since
we are not dealing with a specific community), leadership types A and B do not appeal to race pride and
cultural identity (political culture) in the manner of
C and D and consequently do not effect social mobilization in the same way.

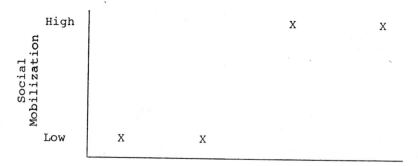

Fig. 5-1 Relationship between social
mobilization and political
authority with political culture
(identity) as the causal or independent variable

As a result, one may also surmise that political
integration would proceed at a slower (and lower) level
where leadership types A and B are present, given that
these leadership types do not put a big emphasis upon
political integration vis-à-vis the political culture
route. For example, the Traditional-Brokerage type
(which admittedly covers a broad range of sub-leader-
ship styles) is concerned more with racial integration
with Whites rather than intraracial or political integration among Blacks per se. The Traditional-Brokerage
may perceive integration of the latter type as a threat
to both his own authority as well as Whites. This
would apply to southern rural communities where such
leaders are "propped up" by the local political structure as being "their" man, although this phenomena is
surely changing.

Ironic as it may seem, it is interesting to note
that at this point we encounter an anomaly with regard
to the traditional leadership style. Even though such
leaders may not value political and intra-integration
as much as racial integration, such activities as
campaigning and running for political office may
effectively mobilize and consolidate the Black vote as

an effective form of political integration, which
nationalist leaders such as Baraka have suggested
doing, although perhaps with different ends in mind
than traditional leaders who may be primarily concerned with being elected.[3] This has surely happened
in large cities such as New Orleans, Atlanta, and
Birmingham, to name but a few such cities.

It is hypothesized here that the Faddist-Rhetorical leaders would achieve only a low rate of social
mobilization with regard to political culture because
they do not attempt to identify so much with racial
identity and cultural pride as much as with "picking
up the gun" and "world revolution", to use common
expressions of former Black Panther leaders such as
Huey Newton. In fact, this leadership type tends to
scoff at and ridicule what may be termed cultural
nationalism which is an important aspect of political
culture, and for that matter the concept of a cultural
nation.[4]

In order to view political culture, social mobilization and political authority in a causal relationship as a change in variables, may be viewed as

$$\uparrow PC \longrightarrow \uparrow SM \longrightarrow \uparrow PA^t \longrightarrow \uparrow PI$$

in which, as there is an increase in political culture
(identity), there is an increase in political authority,
with types C and D identified in the matrix above
exerting more influence on social mobilization and
political integration than types A and B. In sum, to
say that there is an increase in PA (political authority) in this causal chain implicitly recognizes only
the two authority types suggested above as having the
greatest influence on social mobilization. Hence, if
we were to further deduce from t(PA) in terms of its
relationship to social mobilization with political
culture as the initial causal variable, we would find
the pattern shown in Figure 5-2. Figure 5-2 constitutes
a pattern of authority types C and D having the most
influence on political integration. We would expect
Afro-Americans to find new rationales, and hence turn
to new forms of religion which may reinforce such a
positive identity instilled as part of the political
culture. Religious Nationalist such as Minister
Farrakhan and the Reverend Jesse Jackson tend to "push"
such programs using religion, racial pride and identity.

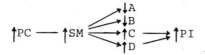

Fig. 5-2 The relationship between
          political culture, social
          mobilization and their effect
          upon political authority variables
          in political integration

Jackson, in fact, is the leader of an organization
entitled PUSH (People United to Save Humanity).

It is at this point that Apter's concept of political religion is vital to an analysis of the religious
character of our authority types because politicized
religion is crucial to the masses perception of these
leaders (types C and D). Apter states this religious
character of political leaders, and their role in
social mobilization and political integration:

> There are similarities with church
> and religion. There are saints and
> villians. There are prophets and
> missionaries. For each individual,
> the possibility of a political
> calling replaces the possibility
> of a religious calling. There is
> mysticism and authority. Justice is
> phrased less in terms of equity than
> in terms of purpose, with purpose
> directed toward collective ends.
> The search for meaning and identity
> results in such concepts as "African
> personality", Nkrumaism, or Sukarno's
> five principles. An earnest effort
> is made to ascribe new meaning to
> group life.[5]

The poor and forgotten Black masses, who may
perceive themselves as having been discriminated
against and oppressed all their lives and born with
"two strikes", are highly susceptible to the mobilizing
effects of political religion. As Apter points out,
the masses are given a feeling in political religion
of "rebirth", of being without sin, as a political
entity rising out of the shackles of colonialism (if

one accepts this analog with respect to Afro-Americans)
and independence with all the purity of the newborn.[6]
Of course, one would have to apply certain limitations
and reservations in suggesting that Afro-Americans are
attempting a break with colonialism and achieving independence, as noted earlier.

In an earlier chapter, the colonial analogy of
domestic colonialism with Afro-Americans was discussed
in detail, but an important limitation would be suggesting cultural decolonization and independence, since it
is unrealistic to argue that Blacks in America might
form or constitute a sovereign political entity. On
the other hand, it is no wonder that Apter's concept
takes on added significance in our model in the relationship between social mobilization, political
authority, and political integration. "Religious"
preachings of a political character from a Malcolm X,
Minister Farrakhan, or Maulana Karenga, in their denunciations of Whites as the "Devil" who has
enslaved and oppressed Blacks, and consequently their
"uplifting" of Blacks as the origin of "true man",[7]
has the affect of "legitimizing" Apter's concept of the
notion of a "rebirth", of people who can do no wrong,
and of "fingering" who are the saints and who are the
villains. Karenga, in a rather fiery passage, states
the essence of the foregoing discussion:

> The Christian is our worse enemy. Quiet
> as it's kept it was a Christian who
> enslaved us. Quiet as it's kept it's
> the Christian that burns us. Quiet
> as it's kept it's a Christian that
> beats us down on the street; and
> quiet as it's kept, when the thing goes
> down it'll be a Christian that's shooting
> us down. You have to face the fact that
> if the Christian is doing all this there
> must be something wrong with Christianity.[8]

Mysticism in Apter's concept of political religion
also rings true with these authority types (Religious
and Cultural Nationalists) in which "rebirth" may be
based upon the past in which to influence the present,
as the Black Muslims and their leaders have done in the
past with regard to rationalizing the origin of Whites
and Blacks and the mysticism surrounding the "creation"
of Whites. This, in turn, justifies their position for

134

the superiority of the Black man, which is also related
to a positive identity.[9] The idea of the Black masses
as "Brothers" and "Sisters" is related to the idea of
justice being related to equity and collective goals
in the concept of political religion; and finally, just
as Apter points out that the search for meaning and
identity results in such neologisms as Nkrumaism and
Sukarno's five principles, political religion has its
equivalent in our authority types with Maulana's
"Seven Principles" and Muhammad's "Ten Demands."[10]
Such meaning and identity, along with the concept of
"rebirth" among the masses, has arisen in slogan's
such as "Black is Beautiful", "Soul", and "Black
Pride."

Our concept of political religion as conceptualized by Apter is similar to what Holden terms "The
Hope for Deliverance." Holden states:

> Perhaps the single most common theme
> in all Afro-American culture is the
> hope for deliverance some day. For
> years and years (and perhaps even now),
> older people looked at their captivity
> and said "God will deliver us some day."
> At times, the hope took a more concrete
> form...[11]

Karenga carries the hope for deliverance one step
further and sees the Black masses as their own savior.
He states:

> We are God ourselves, therefore it is
> not good to be atheistic or agnostic.
> To be an atheist is to deny our exis-
> tence and to be an agnostic is to doubt
> it...If you can't change, it shows a
> lack in you and not in the other person.
> God is God who moves in power; God is
> God who moves in change and creates
> something out of nothing. If you want
> to be God just think about that.[12]

"Dieties" and "prophets" who appear in such concrete form and have come to save the masses, may themselves possess a special quality. In the above relationship in which we state that there is an increase
in authority types C and D (Religious and Cultural

Nationalists) and a decline in A and B when political culture is the independent variable, it could be argued that charisma is an important quality for types C and D in causing their authority to increase. Weber defines charisma as the:

> ...quality of an individual personality by virtue of which he is set apart from ordinary men and treated as endowed with supernatural, superhuman, or at least specifically exceptional powers or qualities. These are such as are not accessible to the ordinary person, but are regarded as of divine origin or as exemplary, and on the basis of them the individual is treated as a leader.[13]

Let us point out first of all that we do not necessarily see Weber's definition of charisma as conflicting with our earlier mention of Edelman's definition of authority, but rather as a special attribute of it. Specifically, the perception of such leaders by the masses may be enhanced on the basis of the way that they act publicly as the result of such charismatic attributes. In short, their public acts are given additional meaning when they tend to be charismatic. Charisma, as defined by Weber, is similar to Apter's concept of political religion, in that "supernatural" or "superhuman" qualities are the equivalent of Apter's prophets and missionaries. In this context, charisma is an important aspect of political religion. Leaders such as the late Malcolm X, Elijah Muhammad, and Martin Luther King (although the latter does not fit in our authority type under discussion), Jesse Jackson, Louis Farrakhan, Albert Cleage and Maulana Karenga are all leaders in types C and D in the above scheme who have or have had that special quality of charisma and missionary zeal, and Elijah Muhammad in particular as being the "last prophet of Allah."[14]

It does not appear to be an accident that our characterization of political religion, and the authority types associated with it in the model have an institutional base, namely the Black church. That is, a structural arrangement characterized by stable and recurring authority types who employ political religion with such an institutional arrangement may be more

successful in long-run political integration since
they have a more or less permanent base from which to
recruit and "politicize" their religious cause. In
this regard, the Black church (which historically has
had a political role), takes more than one form when
we speak of it and its relation to our authority types.
For example, Religious Nationalists such as the Black
Muslims make reference to the Black church as temples;
on the other hand, some Cultural Nationalists make
reference to their sacred shrines as the Temple of
Kawaida. What is similar in both of them, however,
is that which may be referred to as the Black church,
(a generic phrase), has particularistic institutional
forms. Hence, such institutional arrangements because
of their stability and longevity, may be instrumental
in political integration. Many authority type leaders
C and D combine charisma (within the leader) and racial
pride and identity (within the leader and the group or
organization they represent) to identify with the
masses and as political culture tends to go up, social
mobilization and political authority will also go up
as a result.

One further note with respect to the technical
aspects in the causal chain mentioned earlier, we
invoke the necessary-condition law and ceteris paribus
clause in order to validate the relationship between
political culture, social mobilization, political
authority, and political integration. In realizing
that the variable of political culture is just a
covariant in the overall model, we justify its usage
with the necessary-condition law by stating that in
this particular instance when social mobilization is
occurring in the absence of political capacity or state
oppression (or holding it constant), we can expect to
find PC (political culture) with SM. Further, we
assume that there is a direct causal link between the
variables, and this is all we can say without specifying what other variables or factors may be involved in
the causal chain, that is, without stating the sufficient-condition law. In other words, while other
variables may affect the causal connection, we can
still justify the relationship by use of the necessary-
condition law.

At this point, a discussion of political capacity
as the independent or causal variable, and establishing
the relationship between social mobilization and

political authority, and how the different authority types effect social mobilization is in order. When political capacity is the causal variable and political culture is held constant, we would expect social mobilization to be high among authority types B, C, and D, with respect to the masses. Social mobilization would remain low with type A, but with an increase from low in the first matrix in Figure 5-1, to high in Figure 5-3 for type B. It is necessary, however, to explicate upon all four types for our rationalization when oppression, resistance to change, police violence, and the like (PC^1) are the cause of social mobilization. Authority type A may in fact attempt to "keep the peace" even during political oppression by the sovereign nation. This is because such leaders ultimately see their role as an integrative one into the mainstream of society, and see such activities as police violence as merely an aberration of the normal political process rather than as an integral part of the American political system. Witness was served to this by the Black revolts during the "long hot summer" of 1967 in which, even in the midst of the killings of many Blacks (most of whom were innocent of any wrong-doing)[15] by local police and national guardsmen in the Black ghetto, local civil rights leaders were sent in to help restore calm during the upheaval.

It would be suspected that authority type C and D would remain high in social mobilization when political capacity is used as the causal variable since violence on the part of White police would have a prophetical ring to it, and since such leaders have labeled Whites as the "Devil" who, by definition, can only do evil according to these leaders. Police violence or other forms of oppression against Blacks, in essence would be a way of such leaders saying, "I told you so." It is contended here that charisma on the part of authority types C and D provide a sense of urgency among the masses, a feeling that the result of such charisma (i.e., supernatural powers) will somehow result in their grievances being vindicated when political capacity results in social mobilization.

Needless to say, the Faddist-Rhetorical leadership type would be expected to thrive on state oppression, since this is the heart and soul of their rhetoric. Social mobilization among the masses would be high, because the Faddist-Rhetorical leadership has

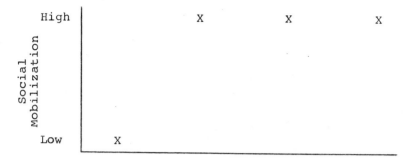

Fig. 5-3 Relationship between social
mobilization and political
authority with political
capacity (oppression) as the
causal or independent variable

a direct appeal to the young, Black masses with their
emphasis upon revolutionary romanticism, and slogans
which suggest rebelling against such imperalist
tactics. Again, we may represent this causal phenomena between political capacity, social mobilization,
political authority, and political integration in the
following manner:

$$\uparrow PC^1 \longrightarrow \uparrow SM \longrightarrow \uparrow PA^t \longrightarrow \uparrow PI$$

in which an increase in political capacity (oppression)
leads to an increase in social mobilization, which
causes an increase in political authority which, in
turn, causes political integration to increase. Of
course, again this is a generalized symbolic statement
which must take into account the foregoing discussion
as to what specific groups and authority types affect
social mobilization and consequently political integration, and to what different degrees. If we are to
deduce from this the specific authority types (t) that
have the greatest effect on social mobilization and
hence political integration, it would display its form
as in Figure 5-4.

Fig. 5-4 The relationship between
political capacity, social
mobilization and their affect
upon political authority in
political integration

This schema should be self-explanatory if one has followed the preceeding argument closely except to say
that authority types A, B, and C, have the greatest
cause-effect and increase in political integration when
PC^1 is the initial causal variable and political culture
is held constant. Again, the necessary-condition law
and ceteris paribus apply in the causal chain. It is
germane to understand, as noted earlier, that since
political culture (PC) is a covariant in the overall
model, we are stating that whenever we have PC^1, we
will also have social mobilization (SM) and not the
reverse; i.e., it could not be stated that whenever we
have SM, we will also have PC^1. This constitutes an
illogical deduction since PC^1 is a covariant and may
occur independently of, or jointly with PC (political
culture - i.e., racial pride) and social mobilization
may be caused with either or both of the variables. In
sum, the variables of oppression (political capacity)
and identity (political culture) do not necessarily
occur continuously together, but reach high and low
tides as a result of other political phenomena that may
not be accounted for in the model. This relationship can
be suggested hypothetically in the matrix in Figure 5-5.

Using 1965 as the origin for our model, the illustration suggest that PC and PC^1 were constantly on the
rise until 1967 when massive, urban rebellions began,
and occurred again in 1968 with the assasination of
Martin Luther King, and began to remain constant in the
latter sixties with its institutionalization taking
varying forms among competitive leadership groups.
Political violence by forces within the sovereign nation
(political capacity) against Blacks appears to have
reached its peak during the urban rebellion of 1967-
1968, and it has occurred sporadically since then with
recurring incidents of oppression and police violence
against Blacks.[16] This has probably been due more to the

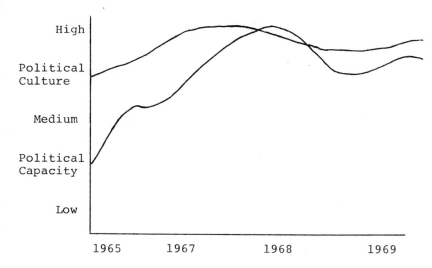

Fig. 5-5 Hypothetical relation between
the variables political capacity
and political culture from 1965
onward

successful oppression of militant Black leaders than
as a mere aberration of the political system.   In
short, political culture and political capacity from
this hypothetical illustration may effect social
mobilization at different time periods or occur in a
simultaneous manner.

Finally, it is the last part of this statement
that warrants attention in manipulating the variables
to determine their relationship, i.e., deducing what
type of relation we can expect between the variables
when political culture and political capacity are
occurring simultaneously in the model and the effect
that they have upon social mobilization.   It could be
expected that the relationship obtained between social
mobilization and political authority (in Figure 5-6)
when political culture and political capacity are both
causal covariants would be the same as when just political capacity is causing social mobilization, albeit not
for the same reasons.   Even though we obtain the same
end result of high social mobilization among the
authority types, it is from different causal phenomena
which are worth distinguishing from each other with
our leadership types.

141

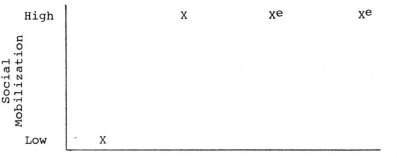

| | A.
Traditional
Brokerage | B.
Faddist
Rhetorical | C.
Religious
Nationalist | D.
Cultural
Nationalist |

Political Authority

Fig. 5-6 Relatiohship between social
mobilization and political
authority with political culture
and political capacity as
causal covariants

In Figure 5-6, authority type A remains low when
either causal variable is effecting social mobilization, or they interact simultaneously as covariants.
By and large (although there are exceptions), this
authority type appeals neither to racial identity and
pride or political capacity on the part of the sovereign
nation (i.e., police violence, oppression, etc. to
mobilize the masses) in order to effect social mobilization. Rather, these leaders are concerned with
maintaining the social order as it presently exists,
although as it was noted earlier some may ironically
mobilize and unite Blacks by running for office.
Authority type B would obtain a high degree of social
mobilization as a result of the political capacity
covariant, in which they constantly emphasize and use
rhetoric related to "oppression", "imperialism", and
the like. As noted earlier, however, the high rating
would not be the result of racial identity and pride
(political culture). Authoritative leadership type C
would remain high in social mobilization as a result of
both of the covariants, as would authority type D. It
may be stated that in the case of both of these leadership types, variables political culture and political
capacity are effecting the high rate of social

142

mobilization, and the previous discussion of them independently with each variable will suffice here.

An analytic statement may be proposed here in our logic of deduction since the high rate of social mobilization would be expected to maintain itself with greater longevity, because two variables are effecting it rather than one. The letter (e) attached to the X in authority types C and D, therefore, symbolizes that the high degree of social mobilization is likely to endure longer as a result of the effect of the covariants acting simultaneously upon social mobilization. The rationale for this is that such acts emanating from the variable of political capacity are likely to sustain internal group cohesion. This cohesion may be reinforced by the political culture variable which also promotes group identity and may lead to perceptions on the part of Blacks that such individual or collective acts are aimed at them because they are a distinct racial group, with one variable reinforcing the other when they appear concomitantly. This is an important assumption with regard to endurance that we will come back to in a later discussion on some empirical studies of political socialization.

In order to witness the overall picture of this phenomena in a causal chain, and in what manner the variables are effected, we can express it generically in Figure 5-7. In Figure 5-7 the same letters A-D are used to represent the same leadership types: Traditional-Brokerage (A), Faddist-Rhetorical (B), Religious-Nationalist (C), and Cultural Nationalist (D) respectively. In the past illustration and diagrams we have not suggested that authority type A effects an increase in political integration, although we attempted to show some exceptions. The justification for not relating this authority type in an "if...then" relation with political integration is because it is minimal at best, although we would not deny that it may take place, and since it is minimal or low in regard to social mobilization, its inclusion in such a type of linkage in which one infers an increase in political integration would not be proper. Since authority type A, unlike B, C, or D, does not increase with the advent of social mobilization which results in an increase in political integration, this deviant case can be represented in Figure 5-8.

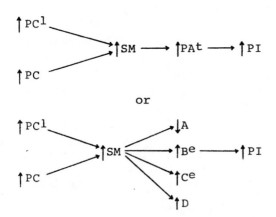

or

Fig. 5-7 The relationship between <u>political capacity</u> and <u>political culture</u> as covariants and their effect upon social mobilization and political authority variables in political integration

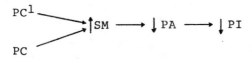

Fig. 5-8 The relationship between <u>political capacity</u> and <u>political culture</u> as covariants and their effect upon social mobilization and the Traditional-Brokerage political authority type in political integration

Again the causal relationship obtained in Figure 5-8 should warrant no further explanation if one has followed the inference made between political culture and political capacity and traditional political authority in treating the covariant separately. In short, when the covariants occur concomitantly, causing social mobilization, this authority type would still decline as well as the probability for political integration for this leadership type.

Ultimately, it is on the basis of an increase in social mobilization causing an increase in authority types B, C, and D, that effects a significant increase in political integration in any given Black community. At this point, the sufficient-condition law may be invoked with respect to covariants PC^1 and PC. This allows one to predict the occurrence of social mobilization by stating that whenever we have political capacity (i.e., oppression, as well as the hope for Black socio-economic gains which are denied by the political system), and political culture (positive) identity) simultaneously, we can expect rather than just suggest the occurrence of SM. We can do more than just "guess" about those other variables effecting social mobilization, we can specify them, which is enough to explain the outcome.[17]

A few words are in order here with respect to the concept and variable of political capacity, which is implicit in the definition, especially since the sufficient-condition law is proposed at this junction. The history of Afro-Americans in America has shown that it has been time periods when Blacks are expecting socio-economic and egalitarian advances in society, and when the political system refuses to grant or make such concessions, that the masses are most likely and most susceptible to turn to nationalism as an important form and expression of their discontent.[18] In our definition, this means that the capacity of the political system to maintain an equilibrium state by denying social, political, and economic advances, outruns the demands of the masses for equality or the political system's "capacity for equality." Related to this thesis is Cruse's assertion in an earlier chapter that economic exploitation of Blacks in America is perpetrated by, and related to, the unwillingness to make such concessions and advances for Afro-Americans.[19] In applying the sufficient-condition law to our covariants, this cursory discussion may be summarized to this point with respect to the variable of political capacity, by stating that it has been both the historical component of resistance to gains on the part of the American political system as well as the "exploitative" aspect that Cruse mentions which continues to foster nationalism and, in this model, contributes to social mobilization and eventually integration.

Guttenberg, in a rather elaborate summary of important sociological and psychological literature regarding factors that influence in-group cohesion among a people, suggest much of the foregoing in listing the following factors: 1) the ethnic groups perception of group solidarity, 2) a common threat toward the ethnic group from the outside, 3) the realization that cooperative behavior among the group may reduce the threat, 4) the realization that for Blacks as individuals upward mobility is limited, and 5) a moderate anxiety arousing condition.[20] From Guttentag's summary, it could be inferred in our model that elements 2, 4, and 5 are those similar to the definition here of political capacity, and 1 and 3 are related to the concept of political culture in satisfying the sufficient-condition law in this part of the calculus. Since the sufficient-condition law provides a crucial link, let us explicate briefly upon them, beginning with political capacity. We would argue that number two is the equivalent of violence and oppression on the part of the state which constitutes a common threat toward Blacks. The fourth factor that Guttentag asserts is similar to the historical reference we made to Blacks that rising expectations may be blunted or frustrated by the political system although we do not mean to imply this as part of the culture of poverty school, and the subsequent realization that upward mobility is limited. The fifth factor Guttentag mentions which one may relate to the variable of political capacity is that a moderate, anxiety arousing condition leads to nationalism. This may be the result, for example, of number two in which there is a common threat, (i.e., racial oppression, police brutality, etc.) toward an ethnic or racial group which arouses anxiety. On the other hand, we would contend that number one, the ethnic groups perceptions of group solidarity, goes along with our notion of political culture which arose out of the Black cultural awareness movement of the middle sixties that advocated group solidarity and cultural pride on the basis of racial identification. Finally, number three is related to our covariants in a more hypothetical manner than the other factors in the model (although all of them ultimately are hypothetical unless and until empirically tested), although some of our authority types may preach such slogans as "strength in unity."

In summary, we may state that "external" violence, historical explanations, and the resulting perpetration of nationalism (elements 2,4 and 5) are related to and subsumed under the concept of political capacity as an

important aspect of the sufficient-condition law.
Cultural pride and identity in ethnic unity (number 1),
and cooperation among the group (number 3) are related
to our variable and concept of political culture. This
conceptual model of political integration suggests
that these five factors are proper requisites for fulfilling the sufficient-condition law, although the
comparison is not a completely isomorphic one. Further,
the model here explicitly recongnizes that social
mobilization and political authority are important
variables in political integration, showing more specifically a process through which Guttentag's summation
of factors may be involved.

Let us relate the aspect between political authority and political integration of this last illustration
in Figure 5-9. It may not add anything new to our
knowledge by allowing new deductions from our axioms
and manipulation of our variables to this point, but
it may clarify this vital link by merely representing
it in another form.

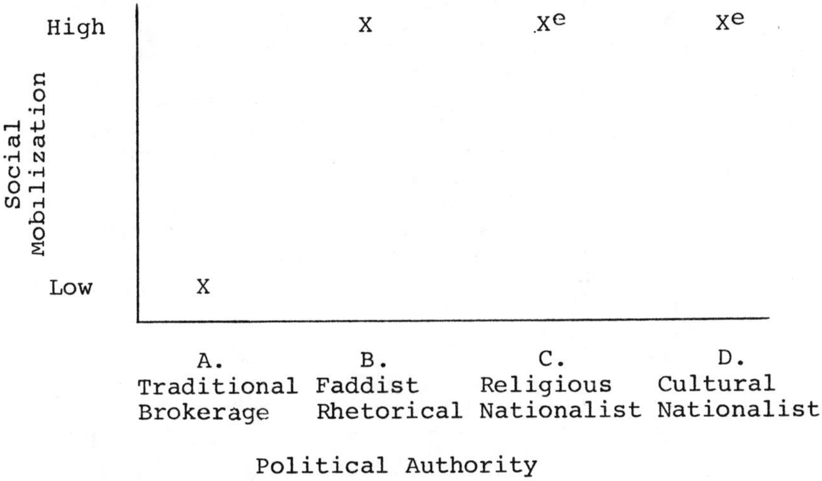

Fig. 5-9 The relationship between
         political integration and
         political authority when
         political capacity and
         political culture are
         covariants

Since it has been argued that one would expect
social mobilization to endure for a longer period of
time when the covariants are causing the phenomena,
we would also deduce from this argument that political
integration is likely to endure (e) for a longer
period of time, because the leadership types that
effect social mobilization (types C and D), it is
reasoned, will also be those likely to endure the longest in converting social mobilization into political
integration. Since, as social mobilization occurs,
its longevity is at least partially the result of the
forms of leadership that arise and their institutional
base.

To wit, it is not difficult to logically deduce
that past leaders such as Eldridge Cleaver (political
authority type B above), and an entity such as the
Black Panther Party, will not play an instrumental role
in long range or enduring political integration. This
is because Cleaver was absent and a "fugitive" from
the political scene (in Algeria) and the Panthers lack
an institutional base due simply to their political
extinction as a force in the Black community. A strong
argument could be made that both the fad and the
rhetoric with a political revolution in America has
passed. Political authority type A would not achieve
a high degree of political integration or have any
longevity (endurance) since these leaders not only do
not appeal to political culture and political capacity,
but their institutional base (which we have extrapo-
lated upon as prolonging political integration) is
oriented more toward racial integration than Black or
political integration.

Let us return to our axioms for a moment in order
to clarify a point and use a deductive syllogism. We
stated that an increase in social mobilization causes
an increase in political authority, an increase in
political authority causes an increase in political
integration and that, therefore, an increase in
social mobilization leads to an increase in political
integration; however, as a result of the deductive
process and assuming that the covariants are occurring
simultaneously, we can propose a deductive syllogism
in more specific and precise terms with respect to
duration. We may say that:

the greater the endurance (e) of SM, the greater

the endurance of PA^t
the greater the endurance of PA^t, the greater the
endurance of PI,
Therefore, the greater the endurance of SM, the
greater the endurance of PI^t

Thus, we would expect political integration to be
more enduring in the short run when social mobilization
is more enduring. And, in turn, social mobilization
may be more enduring when the covariants are acting
concurrently upon it (SM). However, this is only in
the short run. One would not hope, or for that matter
to expect, that the endurance of Afro-American political integration is dependent solely upon such elements
as police brutality and oppression (political capacity),
and other hostile acts toward them in order to maintain
political integration in the long run!

Rather, it suggest that in the short run such
events, along with the emerging political culture, are
likely to achieve the maximum amount of political integration in a community. Such a positive identity
instilled in the emerging political culture could become
self-perpetuating in the long run which could reinforce
political and intraracial integration based upon ethnic
group solidarity and pride. Here it could be assumed
that a model with a circular path of causality without
coercive measures on the part of the state (sovereign
nation) responsible for continued integration and
cohesiveness would explain this event. This may take
the form in Figure 5-10.

On the basis of the model, in semantic terms, we
may extrapolate that if we were to began at the end,
we could then assume that PI leads to a reinforcement
of PC. In turn, PC initiates SM anew. SM causes a
re-emergence or consolidation of PA, which causes and
reinforces PI in any given community. To some extent,
one could argue that such circular causality has taken
place in the past, but not with the impetus or momentum
of the middle sixties when the renewed "Black is
Beautiful" movement was at its peak; and therefore is
not as visible since it is proceeding at incremental
rates.

It should also be understood in explaining such
circular causality that it could not take place in a
vacuum. Rather, it would only suggest that if the

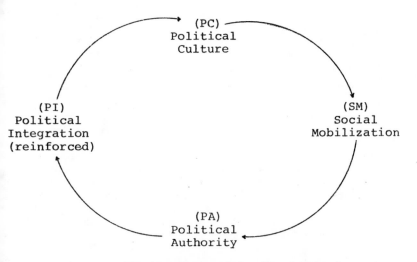

Fig. 5-10 A circular model of political
integration with political
culture as the causal variable

calculus one worked in assumed <u>ceteris paribus</u>, that
this would be the relationship established, assuming
other factors remained equal. And, of course, the
relationships that we established in our causal model,
while undoubtedly being affected by other elements,
assumes <u>ceteris paribus</u>. One should keep in mind,
however, the distinction that was made between an open
and closed system with respect to a theory or calculus.
Working within a closed system, it would suggest that
all deductive arguments could be accounted for on the
basis of all variables that account for the theory. In
our calculus the reasoning is that the deductive
process is based upon an open system, but that we may
invoke the CP clause which allows us to close the
structure formally in order to make such deductions.
In the above model, we would also invoke the necessary-
condition law which needs no further elaboration here.

On the other hand, ideology might be another
significant variable to look at in such a circular chain
of causality which might reinforce political integration
by attempting to instill particular values and attitudes
into the people on the part of the leadership or
authority in a community. One may suspect the Traditional-Brokerage type to be the weakest in reinforcing

political and symbolic values in the process of political-cal integration, since their appeal is not an ideological one. At the same time, it could be expected that the Religious Nationalists and Cultural Nationalists have the strongest ideological appeal since, by definition, they tend to be much more dogmatic, relatively speaking, to the Traditional-Brokerage.

Finally, we would assert that the Faddist-Rhetorical would fall somewhere in the middle of a trichotomy between the three above-mentioned types. Although they also are somewhat dogmatic, their doctrine is lose and not well structured, their discipline is lacking, and by their very title in our typology the rhetoric overshadows their actions. Slogans by the Faddist-Rhetorical such as "Off the pig" are only part of the fad of engaging in revolution, which is really a form of social romanticism that is not necessarily in harmony with reality. At this point, let us now offer some other types of explanation for the model before discussing the next component of the model-building process and Afro-American political integration.

Functional Explanation

At least three alternative explanations to the one represented in our model deserve mention at this point before we go on to the relationship between the model and other literature on political integration and development which will provide the foundation of the next component in the model.

A functional explanation would appear to be much more complex in what it would entail than the causal one we have established. Furthermore, words such as function, functional and functionalism or structural-functionalism appear to be amorphous concepts with no clear-cut meaning in the social sciences. Rudner states the complexity and magnitude of attempting such a functional explanation, as well as his doubt that social scientists have in fact provided one, in his example of precisely what would be required in order to explain cultural item X:

> 1) Specify X through some accurate description of it
> 2) Specify the constituents comprising the functional system Y

3) Show that X is one of the constituents of Y
4) Specify the state-variables of Y
5) Show that some state-properties
   are properties of X and of other
   constituents of Y, as well, so
   that state-descriptions can be
   given
6) Specify precisely what would constitute the set of E-states for the
   total system
7) Specify precisely an N subset of the
   E-states
8) Specify precisely the G subset of
   the E-states
9) Specify a set of state-descriptions
   of Y, some of which are temporally
   prior (or posterior) to the one in
   which X is characterized by the relevant property (i.e., the property
   that "makes it functional")
10) (And most difficult of all) produce a
    body of well-articulated theory which,
    as the theory of Y, contains at least
    laws connecting: (a) antecedent state-
    descriptions with the state-description
    in which Y has the relevant property;
    (b) the state-description, in which
    Y has the relevant property, with the
    specified N-state(s) of the total
    system; (c) the N-state (s) of Y with
    the specified G-state(s) of Y.[21]

Such an explanation would only be for one variable
in a model involving functional explanation! Hempel
claims that a functional explanation is one that seeks
to understand a behavior pattern or some socio-cultural
institution by determining the role it plays in keeping the system in proper working order or maintaining
it as an ongoing concern.[22] Not only are functional
explanations complex, as noted, but we are not sure
that in the model suggested here there is such a
"system" in the same broad context that has such particular functions, which are "self-regulating" and
"adaptive" to an ongoing process of political integration.

Other criticisms of functional explanation include

those by Runciman, who claims that it is incapable of accounting for historical change as well as the question of whether functionalism can provide an explanatory theory at all.[23] Levy also criticizes the functional approach on the grounds that in the absence of empirical criteria, terms such as "adjustment" and "adaptation" leave the danger of the researcher projecting into such concepts his own moral standards of what constitutes a "proper" or "good" adjustment of a given system.[24] Of course, Levy's criticism of functional explanation in this context conflicts with our own normative and subjective orientation, and it is not offered here as a valid criticism of functional explanation in offering a causal one as superior. It is only offered on an objective basis to suggest some of the problems of functional explanation vis-à-vis a causal one.

There are two concerns with regard to functional explanations, nevertheless, which need to be spoken of here that do have relevance to the model. The first concern of interest is that functional statements, apart from a functional explanation, have been asserted with our variables in order to justify our usage of the necessary-condition law. For example, to claim that the function of X is Y is merely to claim that in the majority of cases X, but not only X, produces or helps to produce Y.[25] In this context functional statements are indispensable since it is implicitly understood that they are fundamentally the same as stating an effect. In a broader perspective, the second concern here with regard to functional explanations is to what extent it is interrelated with causality. Should one provide functional explanations in order to find law-like ones, or is it that functional explanations are more easily obtained after law-like (causal) generalizations have been discovered? Durkheim argues that one must first look for causes, and that once such causes are established their discovery will help in determining the functions, or effects.[26] In this respect, our "If...then" statements of cause-effect are the equivalent of the functional requisite needed to establish the relationship between two events.

Let us summarize the discussion of functional explanations as an alternative to a causal one by making four major distinctions offered by Frohock. Frohock proposes that causality entails the establishment of precedence, while in functional analysis both the event and the system exist at the same time; causality suggests forcing, e.g., A bringing into being or changing B, whereas a functional state may vary concurrently with no apparent direction of force; a causal explanation necessitates separate independent and dependent variables, in a functional one the unit is part of the system; and in a causal relationship the variables are asymmetrical from one moment to the next (for example, if A causes B, B does not cause A), in a functional analysis the concept of feedback is essential.[27] Frohock's distinctions are self-explanatory and need no further clarification at this point.

Teleological Explanation

A second alternative "scientific" explanation to our causal model would be a teleological one in which the events that take place are the result of some future event or phenomenon. In this respect, there is an inverse relationship between cause and effect, or what may be termed "effecting a cause", in two ways: 1) future events often influence the present, and 2) the future seems to be incorporated in the very nature of many contemporary elements.[28] A teleological explanation collapses the temporal dimension of empirical causality in the notion of potentiality.[29] Teleological explanations are similar to functional ones from a historical viewpoint in that the latter are modifications of the former, not by reference to causes which might "bring about" the event in question but by reference to ends which determine its cause.[30]

However, Bergmann states that teleological explanations fail to meet the minimum requirements of scientific explanation because empirically such an explanation is impossible.[31] Rudner states the contradiction of proponents using teleological explanations most aptly:

> ...we are not forced to conclude,
> despite the misleading possibilities
> or ordinary usage, that the realm of
> teleological events is inhabited by
> ghostlike states of affairs-nonexis-
> tent, yet somehow causally efficacious.[32]

In our model of political change and integration,

it would seem irrational at best to propose such a
teleological explanation that would assert that political integration (our end result) as a future event, is
effecting a changing political identity in the present.
Of course, even if one were to accept such an assumption as true one could never test it empirically, or
for that matter, find the isomorph. It is no wonder
then, that the school of philosophy which arose in the
twenties and thirties which came to be known as
logical positivism attempted to cleanse science of
metaphysical abstractions and teleological inquiry
which advocates dismissed as vague, emotionally laden,
and having only a spurious claim to being scientific,
since they were immune to correction by facts.[33] As
with our previous discussion on functional explanations, it is felt that this cursory overview of teleological explanation does not beg further elaboration,
because what is implied appears to be self-evident.

Holism vs. Reductionism

      A third and final type of explanation that could
have been posed in opposition to the one we attempt to
account for does not distinguish between different
types of scientific explanations, but rather with respect
to our concepts would attempt to distinguish the
appropriateness of them in regard to the political
phenomena under scrutiny. In addition to choosing
concepts that satisfy one's basic unit of analysis
(i.e., groups and nations), one must also decide
whether the concepts chosen are reducible to more primary concepts that are more applicable to the phenomena
one is investigating. This may be labeled the reductionist argument. On the other hand, the counter argument to the reductionist approach attempts to justify
the usage of the concepts employed by stating that the
components of such entities cannot be understood unless
one looks at the whole, since it is more than the sum
of its parts. Graham states that:

                This claim is usually labeled an
                holistic argument. The group (or
                society) possesses some emergent
                qualities which are the result of
                its components, but which cannot be
                understood in terms less than those
                of the entire unit. This argument,
                obviously, is a counter to the

argument in favor of reduction.[34]

Our approach has, for the most part, been one
which has emphasized the holistic approach. What is
most important in the holistic-reductionist dichotomy
is that we chose such concepts for their simplicity
and analytical value in seeking particular laws, axioms
and theorems. Hence, the concept of political culture
could have been broken down into component parts such
as identity, culture, and particular attitudes (toward
the political system) and utilized these components
separately rather than subsuming them under the notion
of political culture. As a result, one could have
sought a similar or alternative explanation of the
model through the process of reductionism, which may
or may not have clarified the holistic approach taken
here. Our rationale for employing holistic concepts
such as political culture and social mobilization is
that we are inducing from their usage generalizations
about the whole nation and find them most applicable
to this end. In more practical terms, the analog
would be that such mass holistic concepts are most
appropriate since we are dealing with a mass theory of
Afro-American political integration. Furthermore, we
would concur with Hempel that such reduction to the
familiar does not in itself guarantee more precision,
conciseness and clarity. Hempel argues that Bridgeman's
assertion that explanation should consist of reducing
elements to a level we are familiar with, so that our
curiosity rests is not sufficient, and offers the following reasons why, which are worthy of note here:

1) What is familiar to one person
   may not be to another,
2) it suggests that what is familiar
   requires no explanation, Hempel
   appropriately notes that scientists
   have gone to great lengths to explain
   the familiar, such as thunder, light-
   ning, and darkness,
3) scientists often do the opposite by
   calling upon theoretical conceptions
   that are unfamiliar, yet account for
   certain generalizations and supports
   the results of scientific tests,
4) what is widely regarded as familiar
   "facts" in some scientific disciplines
   are not facts but regular stereotypes,

and such low-level generalizations
of such stereotypes is still false
even though it is a "reduction to the
familiar", and finally
5) such reduction may not fulfill
the necessary or sufficient law and
give one a sense of familiarity or
"at-homeness" with a puzzle without
conveying a scientifically acceptable
explanation, in which such familiarity
breeds content, but no insight.[35]

We would not, however, argue that reductionism of
empirical phenomena has no value simply because we
have chosen the holistic route, but rather that reduction does not, in and of itself, guarantee more conciseness of concepts, whether they be ideal, value or
empirical types. Further, since our primary concern
is internal consistency of the concepts and variables
used, they still meet this functional criteria. It is
worthwhile to point out, however, that the holistic
approach we have taken with regard to our concepts is
similar to concept types employed in studying developing nations and whole political systems, both of which
are involved in our model of political integration.
The concept of nation-building and political integration, as well as the study of whole political systems
are germane in research on developing as well as
developed nations. In sum, the selection of such
holistic concepts in our approach is to give the model
the same quality often applied to developing nations
and political systems. Let us now turn to the aspect
of model-building and the model here of political integration of rationales and relationships to other literature on political integration and political development.

Rationales and Relationships to the Literature

Our previous discussion of the holistic-reductionist argument provides an important rationale for the
manner in which we have chosen our concepts and variables, and it needs no further elaboration here.
Nevertheless, our definitions of the concepts are
inclusive of particular subconcepts which tend to
support the causal relationships that we have drawn
and as such can be identified with certain empirical
and theoretical studies. These empirical studies

would tend to help collapse the spatial-temporal dimension between our theoretical formulation and empirical phenomena, although as stated this is not our primary concern. Citations of some important theoretical literature, on the other hand, would tend to ground our model in the context of a body of literature.

These arguments, and the relationship they have to the literature, can be developed in two stages. In the first stage, we will analyze our covariants in the context of literature on American politics, and more particularly political socialization and identity studies. This route is selected here, rather than citing specific literature on political integration in comparative politics, because this literature is more germane in providing direct linkages to the causal chain in this part of the model and the implications of the findings. The second stage will relate the causal links between social mobilization, political authority, and political integration to the literature in the field of comparative politics that is more directly associated with the phenomenon of political integration and change. This route is taken for the second part of the model for two reasons. Firstly, the paucity of literature in American politics which views Afro-Americans in the context of a developing society (with the exception of a few studies); and secondly, to see in what respect our model is analogous to, or divergent from, other theories of political integration within a nation-state.

In our initial definition of social mobilization we asserted that alienation was an important aspect of the concept, especially with respect to the political capacity of the sovereign nation to inflict violence and oppression. What is implicit in the definition is that political capacity causes alienation as part of the breakdown stage of social mobilization as a result of oppression. There appears to be direct empirical evidence in political socialization studies for this phenomenon which would substantiate the causal correlation between political capacity and social mobilization. Greenberg, in an empirical study of Black and White children in Philadelphia and Pittsburgh in 1968, hypothesized that unpleasant life experiences may erode attachment to the polity gained early in life.[36] The latter part of this statement is the typical hypothesis in most socialization studies of the past, although it has been questioned as the result of some divergent findings.[37] Greenberg found what he termed a small but significant difference between Black-White support for the political system, and notes that this difference is broadened as Blacks grow older. Greenberg argues that if such divergence occurs as children grow older one cannot attribute it to differences in childhood and family socialization, and consequently one must look at later experiences in the life of Black children to account for the differences.[38] More direct empirical evidence for our causal inferences between political capacity and social mobilization, or racial oppression and alienation, can be drawn from another study of Greenberg's. He argues that support for the police by young Blacks decreases as early as the third grade when brought into line with police brutality, even though the police are a more potent figure, according to Greenberg, than the President since there is more direct contact.[39] Hence, Greenberg questions whether such political attachment can be transferred to the rest of the political system if it does not remain stable for these authority figures. In a similar view, Easton and Dennis argue that if children have negative feelings toward the police it will affect the acceptance of all political authority, since the policeman is seen as an important symbol of the political system throughout the child's pre-adult years.[40] In a study that reached similar conclusions to those of Greenberg, Engstrom found that Black children see the police as having less power than White children, but they tend to be more sensitive to such power out of fear of punishment without compliance.[41] Engstrom goes on to state that although White sensitivity to power is instrumental in the development of benevolent attitudes, such a benevolent basis for compliance is lacking for Blacks which constitutes a warning for the political system. Rodgers and Taylor, like Engstrom and Greenberg, state that Blacks have a negative attitude toward the police but interpret the consequences of their data in a different light, hypothesizing that such a negative attitude is an exception to what otherwise is a viable political system, and that such positive support may be transferred to other parts of the political system as a result.[42]

The results of such empirical findings, especially those of Engstrom and Greenberg, suggest that the causal connection between political capacity and social mobilization in our model and working calculus is a valid one. In effect, we have stated in several different ways that police violence, racial oppression and law and order policies lead to alienation as the initial or breakdown stage of social mobilization in the overall process of forming new orientations toward the political system. Bullough has argued that alienation among Blacks is due to their very isolation in the ghetto, rather than such elements as police brutality per se, in which this alienation is displayed through such concepts as anomie and powerlessness. Once Blacks had moved out of Black communities, Bullough argues, and severed ties with the ghetto "subculture", there was less alienation and greater expectation for control of events than Blacks in segregated communities.[43] Emerson and Kilson capture the gist of Bullough's findings in the following statement: "Failure to integrate the Negro into the total American society surely must intensify his alienation from that society..."[44]

Lyons, in a paper and pencil questionnaire to 2,868 students ranging from grades five through twelve in the Toledo Public School System, obtained 78% Black in an urban sample and 91% White in a surburban area. He found that a low sense of political efficacy and greater cynicism was a stronger predictor among Blacks as compared to Whites, regardless of where they lived.[45]

While the studies of Bullough and Lyons do not directly state that political capacity (i.e., police brutality and oppression) might lead to alienation and social mobilization as suggested by our model, it might be hypothesized that such cynicism and feelings of powerlessness might at least be partially the result of coercive behavior on the part of the police. It might also be stated that the isolation of Blacks in the ghetto might make them more susceptible to racial oppression and violence, since crime rates tend to be disproportionately higher, and police attitudes are more hostile and stereotyped than in other communities.[46] Consequently, this still may result in social mobilization.

There is a much more hypothetical causal relationship established in our model that cannot be substantiated in the same manner empirically as the alienation and political socialization studies cited. This is the relationship between a changing political identity and what we have termed political culture, and social mobilization or alienation from the political system and old ways, beliefs, and attitudes which carried negative connotations in many ways with regard to skin color and stigma.

Emerson and Kilson state the significance of this new emergent political culture, identity and cultural pride of the middle sixties among Afro-Americans in the following passages which are worthy of quotation for the causal relation we assert:

> ...the emergence of sovereign states in Africa has changed the Negro American's image of himself and of his place in the world...For the Negro in particular it has been a unique and stirring experience to see whole societies and political systems come into existence in which from top to bottom,...all posts are occupied by black men, not because of the sufferance of white superiors but because it is their sovereign right...It is one thing to be the descendant of a slave born in a colonial country of an allegedly barbaric continent, and another to be linked racially to a continent suddenly peopled with independent states making a strident and impressive entry into the world's affairs...47

The idea of a common bond with Africa, vicarious in nature in the early and middle sixties which increased racial pride and self-esteem, has also been related to the colonial heritage of subordination of both Africans and Afro-Americans. Weisbord, a frequent contributor of writings on African politics, states:

> The desirability of Africans and Afro-Americans making common cause has also been expressed by Killens. He has observed that non-whites throughout the world and blacks in the United States have shared a common experience of

                    subjugation by whites. They have all
                    been niggerized: "And all of us are
                    determined to 'deniggerize' the earth."[48]

     Hence, the term Pan-Africanism, with all of its
many denotations, seems to have the common element:
the same cultural basis for Africans and Afro-Americans.
Furthermore, the term suggest a political solution for
these people of color, based upon this recognition.[49]

     Cross, in a psychological explanation of tran-
sitional identity levels has proposed five specific
stages in what he terms the "Negro-to-Black" conversion
experience. In relationship to our model, this transition could originate either with political capacity or
political culture in causing social mobilization, and
for that matter may extend into the three stages of
social mobilization we identify. Let us briefly summarize each stage that Cross proposes: 1) pre-encounter, in
which one still maintains a negative identity and evalu-
ates and judges the world by the dominant, White culture; 2) encounter, in which there is a particular
experience, information or event that causes a person
functioning at the pre-encounter level to challenge such
assumptions, which, in turn, entails two steps: a)
experiencing the actual encounter, and b) beginning to
reinterpret the world as a consequence of the encounter;
3) immerson-emersion, a stage highlighted by one
actively participating in some form of Black politics,
Black art, Black culture and social programs, etc., in
which he or she "emerges" by unleashing talents that
have been inhibited as the result of stage one; 4)
internalization, in which one of three consequences may
affect the individual: a) disappointment and rejection,
in which one's expectations are rejected, b) continu-
ation and fixation at stage three in which one relent-
lessly focuses upon hostilities toward Whites, particularly because of their inability to move out of the
Black ghetto as opposed to Black college students and
researchers, who are at the middle class socio-economic
level, and c) internalization, in which one achieves a
feeling of inner security that may or may not lead to
further commitments that are political in nature; and
finally 5) internalization-commitment, the last stage in
which one does not focus so much upon being anti-White
as he is pro-Black, there is not so much anger and
rhetoric toward and about Whites as there is an emphasis
upon dedication and long-term commitment to cultural

and political aspects of development and change.[50]

While such stages as delineated by Cross are generalized in that they do not specifically relate what is termed an emergent political culture in our model as the result of certain factors in the foregoing discussion, step two does provide a particular point of departure that could be related to our notion of identity. Here, a particular experience, piece of information or certain event in the encounter stage could be part of our foregoing discussion of the new Black identity with African independence movements. Since Cross's five stages have implications for social mobilization, we will return to them shortly. For now, let it suffice to say in regard to them that the encounter stage could be related to identity in our definition of political culture.

On the other hand, it is no wonder that such neologisms to express this new identity and political culture in the foregoing discussion have found themselves in exhortations such as "Black is Beautiful" (cultural and racial pride), "Soul" (cultural ethos), "Negritude" (positive political and cultural identity), and "Black Power" (political self-determination). These terms emerged in rhetorical and doctrinaire form in the middle sixties, and also became manifested in the form of political religion which political leaders used to arouse the masses, which we took note of earlier. We have contended, however, that in our causal model in which the concept of political culture (cause) brings about social mobilization (effect), this political culture was only shared by a few intellectuals, scholars, college students, and some political leaders (specifically the Religious Nationalist and Cultural Nationalist). There is no significant political and cultural identity among the masses until the social mobilization stage, which may be negatively or positively reinforced by our leadership types who tend to emerge and become politically activated as social mobilization proceeds.

Let us now compare our concept of social mobilization, and the stages we outlined in our initial definition of it, with Cross's socio-psychological stages of converting one from Negro-to-Black, as he terms it. We stated that the encounter stage is one in which there is a particular experience, communication or event that may be related to our concept of political culture. Let us further suggest that Cross's encounter stage extends into our initial stage of social mobilization in which we find alienation and breakdown of old orientations toward the political system (sovereign nation) and/or values concerning identity among the masses (depending upon whether mobilization emanates from political capacity or political culture). Stages three and four of Cross's conversion thesis is the equivalent of stage two in our concept of social mobilization, i.e., his emphasis upon taking part in some form of Black art, culture, politics or social activity in step three, and either frustration of expectations, continued hostility toward Whites, or a feeling of internal security achieved in step four, is the equivalent of chaos and "movement" in step two of our concept of social mobilization. To speak of chaos and movement suggest that there still may be confusion among the masses because different alternatives are still open as the result of the essentially disruptive nature of social mobilization itself. We only suggest that this second stage is chaotic in that the political identity of the masses is in transition as new orientations take form. Identity may be confusing, however, as we noted with Pye in an earlier chapter since it can be with either the elites or masses, or oriented toward either tradition or modernization.[51]

In this middle stage of social mobilization, the masses are still not sure what road to take but may be influenced by environmental as well as personality factors, i.e., authoritative leadership. In Cross's fifth and final stage we find an equivalent in the third stage of social mobilization as we have defined it, internalization-commitment, being similar to new, albeit vague, political and social orientations among the masses. It is at this point in time that the acceleration and emergence of political authority gives such vague political orientations a definitive form in their ability to recruit and indoctrinate the masses into their fold and group goals.

We now turn more specifically to some of the literature on political integration in developing nations, as well as American politics, and suggest how it is related to our model. One of the crucial links in our model, stated earlier in step two of the model-building process, was that the competing authority types, rather than a centralized political authority, affects social mobilization which is already fragmentary by its very nature in different forms and, consequently, political integration will also take different forms. In short, social mobilization, which is disruptive by the very essence of what it entails, is further divisive because of the divided forms of authority types which compete for the allegiance of the masses whom they hope to recruit and integrate into their fold.

Ake's theory, on the other hand, argues that the political system and leadership undertaking social mobilization maximizes its capacity for carrying out the process and remaining stable even with the potential short-run effects of social mobilization which are disruptive of the system if such political authority is authoritarian, paternal, "identific" and consensual.[52] To put it in more succinct terms, social mobilization is maximized if governmental power is large, concentrated, easily mobilized and has the power to carry out its policies (authoritarian), dominated by a political class that is willing and able to lead (paternal), if the political system is characterized by mutual identity between the political class and the governed ("identific"), if the political class is solidary and if the hegemony of the political class is not threatened by a counter-elite (consensual).[53]

Deutsch, in a 1961 work, argued that a stage of rapid social mobilization may either consolidate or fragment cultural unity. He argues, on the one hand, that social mobilization may consolidate those states whose people already share the same language, culture, and major social institutions, and on the other hand that the same process may tend to either strain or destroy the unity of states in which the population is already divided into several groups with different languages, culture and lifestyles.[54] We would argue, in comparing this thesis of Deutsch's with our own, that in our model it is not so much a question of the homogeneity of the people within a state that determines assimilation (in our case political integration), as much as it is a question of how political authority affects social mobilization once the process has begun.

In a later work, Deutsch appears to be no closer

to our model of political integration in that he
suggests that assimilation and social mobilization
are causally isolated phenomena, in which the major
question is one of which process, from a chronological
point of view, precedes the other. Deutsch contends
that if assimilation stays ahead of mobilization or
at least stays abreast of it, the government is likely
not only to remain stable but to eventually integrate
the people into a whole; however, if social mobilization is fast and assimilation tends to be slow, there
will be the opposite effect.[55] Nevertheless, Deutsch's
thesis can be questioned not so much from the standpoint of our model, since these are significantly
different conceptual approaches to begin with, as from
the very idea that assimilation and ethnic integration
have taken place in the so-called "developed" societies.
Connors states:

> ...the doctrine that modernization
> dissolves ethnic loyalties can be
> challenged on purely empirical grounds.
> If the processes that comprise modern-
> ization led to a lessening of ethnic
> consciousness in favor of identification
> with the state, then the number of states
> troubled by ethnic disharmony would be
> on the decrease. To the contrary, how-
> ever, a global survey illustrates that
> ethnic consciousness is definitely in
> the ascendancy as a political force,
> and that state borders, as presently
> delimited, are being increasingly
> challenged by this trend.[56]

One has only to look at the continuing controversy over Russian Jews and their religious and ethnic
disharmony with the Soviet Union, Black and White
(racial and ethnic) conflicts in the United States,
and Connor's acknowledgement of Franco-Canadian movements, to bear witness to the fact that what Connors
terms a lengthy history as a state and a high degree
of technological and economic integration does not
guarantee ethnic assimilation.[57] Connors goes on to
argue that one of the major shortcomings of political
integration studies has been the potentially disruptive
force of ethnicity, and proposes twelve possible
reasons for such negligence of ethnicity in studies on
political integration.[58]

Again making reference to our model, we do not perceive the problem of integration between different ethnic groups or races as a major problem as much as closing the ranks within the ethnic group itself in political terms. Further, the state is defined not so much in terms of separate territorial entities with competing ethnic groups in our model, but as a single ethnic group, and the problem of intra-integration, within a single territorial entity (i.e., United States).

Weiner speaks of five different types of political integration which include the following: national integration, territorial integration, value integration, elite-mass integration, and "integrative behavior", each of which deserves a comment.[59] National integration involves overall loyalty to the state which either overshadows or eliminates subordinate parochial loyalties. Territorial integration, unlike national integration which involves subjective loyalties, is more objective in that it seeks control through central authority over the whole territory claimed under its jurisdiction. The elite-mass gap attempts to link the government with the governed as a result of marked differences in values, goals, aspirations and the like. The desire to maintain desirable conduct and social order, while sharing certain elements such as goals, symbols and history, constitutes what is known as value integration. Last but not least, "integrative behavior", according to Weiner, makes reference to the capacity of a people in a nation to organize for some common purpose.[60]

With respect to these five types of political integration as stated by Weiner in comparing our causal model of integration, we would contend that only national integration, value integration, and "integrative bahavior" are relevant, and the reasons why deserve to be articulated upon here. National integration is important not only on the basis of our notion of a cultural nation, but also because it involves subjective loyalties among Afro-Americans as an ethnic and racial group which would cut across caste and class within the Black social stratum. Value integration is important in solidifying national integration since it involves symbolic and tangible elements that give the masses a sense of peoplehood. This value integration has been attempted and continues to flourish in such things as Black history courses, the "Black American Flag", the clenched fist (or what has come to be known as the "Black Power" sign or salute), and the Black National Anthem. "Integrative behavior" would refer to our last aspect of the causal model in which, ideally, Afro-Americans would become politically integrated to achieve common goals and purposes within the realm of American politics.

In this respect, political integration is an ideal concept since it is not found anywhere in reality. Furthermore, it tends to take on greater complexity since our four authority types have different norms concerning what integration should entail. The question of the plausibility of territorial integration needs no elaboration here since its limitations are established in our earlier definition of a cultural nation. Finally, the notion of an elite-mass gap in Afro-American political integration appears unrealistic for two reasons. One, it is questionable if there is such a thing as a Black elite in the sense that they are not ultimately subordinate to White elites (and more specifically the social and political structure in a community). Two, the idea of an elite-mass gap may be subsumed under the concept of national integration, since collapsing the subjective loyalty dimension would ultimately involve closing the elite-mass gap (assuming that such an elite of this type existed). Weiner's typology of political integration, in sum, does not provide us with a thesis so much as it suggests fruitful parameters for one who engages in researching particular aspects of political integration.

The discussion earlier of Cross's psychological explanations for the transitional identity that many Afro-Americans go through is helpful in understanding our model of integration as well as providing stages of identity transition comparable to the political culture and social mobilization stages. Another psychological explanation involving the political integration of Afro-Americans is that of the psychiatrist Poussaint; however, Poussaint discusses psychological barriers involved in the lack of integration and authoritative leadership among Blacks which include: 1) a deficit in organizational and leadership skills, in which they have been denied the experience in successful enterprises; 2) the lack of such successful Black leadership models in the past; 3) the basic distrust and lack of confidence the masses have in Black leadership because of projected feelings of self-hatred and inferiority, in which Blacks have seen White success and Black failure all their lives; 4) the inferiority many Blacks have associated with "all-Black" organized and led organizations, as well as the fact that many Blacks have fought against such segregation, whether it be voluntary or forced, all their lives; 5) contradictory and cathartic needs of many Black leaders (although by no means confined to Blacks) who may "talk tough" within the confines of an all-Black group, although such talk is from repressed rage, pent-up and unexpressed anger that has resulted from being in the presence of Whites, which in turn leads them to dominate and intimidate other Blacks which becomes an end in itself, preventing constructive programs from being developed; and 6) certain status needs which many members and leaders have which result in personality cults, glorification ceremonies and the like which stem from the leaders' own basic feelings of worthlessness and inferiority, which also affects programs and operations within an organization since it creates cleavages and puts more emphasis upon such "cult" activities.[61]

Of course, many of the assumptions that we have made in developing the model would tend to contradict much of the above with respect to psychological explanations of Black identity. One may, however, speak in generalizations without being contradictory. For example, although we stated that many Blacks have taken on a positive identity when we suggest a relationship between political culture and social mobilization, there are, of course, exceptions to the rule. This is especially true, as has been contended, in the age groups over 35 years old (this is an arbitrary figure and not based upon empirical evidence) whom we would hypothesize would not place such a great emphasis upon this new identity, (with some exceptions). We would argue that it is the age group from 15-35 years old who would be most susceptible to social mobilization based upon this type of positive identity. Generally speaking, we would assert that the age categories of 35 and over would most closely relate to Poussaint's discussion, although his statements would have some validity in the context of leadership. Like political leadership in any political system, our authority types may suffer from some of these same contradictory and status ends.

Salamon's study of leadership and modernization among Blacks in Mississippi as the result of the 1965 Voting Rights Act fits our mold of the Traditional-Brokerage leadership type and would tend to contradict two of Poussaint's statements, since Poussaint does not specifically speak of what income level or age group that he is making reference to. Salamon, in analyzing Black leadership in Mississippi as being comparable to a developing nation, finds that traditional leadership groups tend to fill political roles created by modernization. He also found that the electoral process acts as a screening mechanism which systematically filters out Black candidates with less political and economic resources, lower status jobs and leaders who did not serve some type of brokerage role in the old caste system of segregation, in which the traditional leaders enjoyed a certain amount of prestige as well as the support of Whites.[62]

In this respect, Poussaint's statements of Blacks having a deficit of organizational and leadership skills, and of having a lack of successful Black leadership models in the past, would have to be examined under closer scrutiny and specificity because of the unique position these traditional leaders served in the class and caste system of the Old South. Therefore, one would have to question whether Poussaint is speaking of successful Black leaders only in the North, since one could argue that such Black leaders were highly successful within the position of the caste system that they occupied in the South, and hence, had no deficit of leadership skills.

Other than the conclusion that such traditional leaders tended to maintain their hierarchical position vis-à-vis the Black masses in an open democratic election in which the Black masses who held the voting franchise were allowed to vote, Salamon's study would tend to support our earlier assumption. In rural and small communities located especially in the South, one could assume that the Traditional-Brokerage authority type would be able to mobilize the masses in the absence of the other three leadership types we identified. Further, it would tend to support our earlier statements that the electoral vote may be effective in mobilizing and consolidating the Black vote, especially in bi-racial campaigns for electoral office. It does not necessarily mean, however, that it entails social mobilization in the manner that we have defined it, or that it will lead to symbolic and political integration of values as we have defined it, even though it was stated earlier that there is such a possibility.

Conversely, it may represent an empirical indicator of measuring political integration, although by itself it would be too simplified an analysis since we know that people may vote for a given candidate for a variety of reasons which might entail more than political values per se.[63] From this authors point of view, this is one of the weaknesses of Salamon's work. He focuses upon the attitudes and roles of the Black elites in maintaining this power, rather than upon the masses or the role that the leaders should have in integrating them within the polity.

A final work that we want to look at here with respect to political leadership and political integration is Kim's work on what he terms the "politics of predevelopment." Kim states that a political leaders short-run success is dependent upon two elements: 1) the leader's ability to claim legitimacy, and 2) the leaders capability for handling the tools of politics.[64] According to Kim, the tools of politics are guns, funds, organization, and ideas.[65] This is similar to Lasswell's identification of political tools which include symbols, violence, goods, and practices.[66] Kim's tools of politics are of interest to us with respect to our notion of authoritative leadership types. Although we would argue that each type has been able to legitimize authority, none command all four of the tools Kim speaks of that are needed to be successful.

On the other hand, legitimate authority, as Weber has pointed out, can be obtained by either traditionalism, charisma, or legal-rationalism.[67] In our model we would add a fourth category---rhetoric. The Traditional-Brokerage tends to legitimize authority through traditionalism or legal means or both. We would state that the Religious-Nationalist and Cultural Nationalist legitimize their authority through charisma and the religious tradition in the first instance, and through charisma, and in a smaller degree religion in

171

the second instance. Our fourth authority type is self-explanatory in its name Faddist-Rhetorical, the latter, a reference to the addendum we have added to Weber's authority types.

Coming back to Kim's idea of the tools of politics, it is interesting to ask that if none of our leadership types possess all four tools, can they still engage in short-run success? Further, if they should have success over long periods of time, what would explain the longevity in the absence of such tools? And finally, what may be the relevance of such tools to political integration? Let us develop tentative answers to these questions by looking at our authority types and looking at the extent to which they possess these tools or leadership resources. The Traditional-Brokerage type lacks guns as well as innovative ideas. Their short-run success is based upon their organization, funds and established tradition of working within the system, which also accounts for their long-run success because of their subsequent institutionalization. Their tools are not relevant so much with respect to our conceptualization of political integration as they are to racial integration, governing polities (cities and towns) and the like.

The Faddist-Rhetorical tend to emphasize guns and funds, with a lack of organizational discipline and ideas. They tend to possess funds, especially past groups such as the Black Panthers, because their Marxist orientation emphasizes class rather than race, and as a result often receive White, middle-class financial support. Their success, however, over long periods of time is doubtful since their emphasis on guns and revolution have made them the targets of police raids, investigations and shootouts which has, to say the least, minimized their longevity and raises questions about their own strategy. Hence, they also tend to be weak in political integration (of the Black masses) since this is not their primary goal. Furthermore, since they are faddist (i.e., whatever is "fashionable" and in vogue at the time) they are liable to appear and disappear on the political scene at any given time in history, like a magician performing a "now you see it--now you do not" act with a rabbit.

Religious Nationalists tend to have three of the four types of tools discussed by Kim, i.e., funds, organizations, and ideas and have had short-run success as well as longevity over a period of time precisely because of the handling and acquisition of these tools in the absence of the fourth tool (guns). In this regard, they do not represent a threat to external authority (in the sovereign political system) while consolidating their resources to build their own programs. One of the best examples of this type is the Black Muslims who have not only achieved funds through their own economic self-determination; but they have well disciplined and tightly knit organizations, and they have used innovative ideas to buy farmland as well as recruit segments of the Black masses which constitutes an important aspect of political integration.

Our nationalist authority type (that is, our Cultural Nationalist) tends to have organization and ideas as well as economic and political self-determination, but do not actually have abundant funds to implement many of their ideas, even though they may have viable programs acceptable to the masses over time to achieve political integration. The use of guns tends to occur only sporadically, and they do not preach violence in the manner of the Faddist-Rhetorical, so their longevity is relatively secured. At the same time, since their emphasis upon culture is such an important aspect of cementing values in any given political system, their chances for integrating the masses have a higher probability. However, their competitive squabbles among various nationalists groups, as well as some of the other factors we mentioned in our discussion of social mobilization, tend to minimize this end.

An important distinction, which should be kept in mind with regard to our authority types in relation to Kim's tools of politics, is that Kim speaks of such tools in an independent and sovereign nation, whereas our discussion is limited to a cultural nation vis-à-vis a sovereign nation. Consequently, while in the latter type of nation-state there is a centralized political leadership often with all four such tools at its disposal and with all challenges to its authority arising from below, our conceptualization of authority types are decentralized, and all exist subordinate to ultimate power and authority from above (the United States government).

Let us attempt to briefly summarize this component of the model-building process in which we have attempted to ground our causal model and concepts in theoretical and empirical data and then move on to some specific theorems or propositions that may be deduced from steps (components) one through five in the calculus. We began with a discussion of the covariants which are causal in relation to social mobilization. One of the most important conclusions with respect to political capacity was that there is a significant difference between White and Black children with regard to alienation, expecially toward the police and police brutality, political efficacy and political cynicism toward the political system. The findings of Greenberg, Lyons and Engstrom are all relevant in reaching this conclusion. Bullough argues that the alienation of Blacks in the ghetto is due not so much to police brutality per se as it is to the spatial isolation of Blacks. On the other hand, Rodgers and Taylor find that Black children also tend to become alienated toward the policeman as an agent of regime legitimation. They maintain, however, that unlike the assumptions of Greenberg, Lyons and Engstrom who maintain that such alienation may lead to diminishing support for the political system, the lack of such support may be transferred to other parts of the political system. In this part of our causal model, we concur with Greenberg that such acts of police brutality (even if only alledged) lead to alienation which is part of our definition of social mobilization.

Our proposition that identity and racial pride among the few (political culture) using an arbitrary date beginning in 1965, leads to social mobilization among the many is based more upon hypothetical assumptions than empirical evidence. In this light, we argued that a positive identity resulting from a combination of factors, correlated with African nations achieving independence, has brought about vicarious cultural and political rewards among Afro-Americans which, in turn, has effected social mobilization among the masses. Kilson, Emerson, and Cruse have argued this point in some detail, although not necessarily equating it conceptually and theoretically with social mobilization. Cross argues five particular stages in a conversion process that Blacks go through as a psychological explanation, which we compared to political culture and social mobilization as part of a causal chain. Further, we compared particular aspects of this conversion process to our stages of social mobilization, suggesting some degree of isomorphism. From this point on we compared our model of political integration and parochial concepts related to it including social mobilization, political authority, and political integration, with literature germane to the idea of a "developing nation." In short, we compared our model with literature in comparative and American politics on these last three concepts and their relevance to political integration.

Ake has proposed that the more authoritarian, paternal, identific and consensual political leadership is, the greater its chances for carrying out its policies and remaining stable even with the short-run disruptive effects of social mobilization. Deutsch's thesis is that political integration will be more successful in developing polities as long as there is a balance between social mobilization and assimilation, which will, in turn, diminish ethnic loyalties. This is questionable since ethnic loyalties have not diminished in "developed" nations, and for that matter appear to be on the upswing, which Conners so aptly points out. Weiner discusses five types of political integration phenomena associated with political development which are fruitful in delineating those aspects most relevant to our model. Poussaint's psychological explanations attempt to suggest why Black leaders have not been successful in recruiting or integrating the masses, but the shortcomings in his explanation would not apply to Salamon's study since Poussaint does not specifically point out what age group or class of political orientations he is making reference to. In fact, Poussaint's study is probably more appropriate for the prior discussion on domestic colonialism as an alternative way of looking at Black politics, since much of his discussion concerns negative identity and stigma associated with Blacks, which could be viewed as part of the colonial mentality. Poussaint's assertions still serve a useful function, however, since many of the concepts he discusses carry over into the "decolonial" or independence stage of a nation, which our model is more closely related to (than the domestic colonialism model), with certain restrictions. For example, our concept of a new identity among Afro-Americans is comparable to the identity found in "developing nations", one which involves moving from a traditional to a modern society.

Our approach to political integration is one
similar in nature to nations in the Third World who
are attempting to integrate their polities. Salamon's
study, in turn, shows that traditional leaders can be
effective in mobilizing the masses through the vote,
but it is questionable whether such leaders can precipitate social mobilization. Further, Salamon's study
is based upon elites, rather than the masses, which,
as noted in an earlier chapter, is a shortcoming of
political development and integration studies since it
emphasizes their own stability rather than provides
for upheaval and change among the masses. Finally,
Kim's conception of the tools of politics allowed us
to compare our authority types, with the chances for
short-run and long-run success of our authority types,
as well as their chances for political integration
of the masses based upon such tools. Let us now turn
to the theorems that can be deduced from the axioms
and the model-building components one through five.

Theorems Deduced From the Axioms

Theorems are assertions that are derived by
reasoning, or logical deductions from axioms whose
empirical truth is accepted for the moment in order
to make such deductions.[68] Blalock argues that such
axioms used to arrive at theorems should be causal
assertions that will be untestable, strictly speaking,
because of the fact that the investigator will never
be able to control for all relevant variables.[69] At
the same time, theorems attempt to explain lawlike
statements of the axioms by the implementation of rules,
which convert the axioms into logical lawlike statements. Brown states that this conversion process
gives one an interpreted calculus which, if revealed,
can be laid out in terms of definitions, axioms and
theorems. This does not suggest, however, that the
order of development has been from an uninterpreted
calculus to an interpreted calculus.[70]

With these reservations in mind, let us develop
the theorems that can be deduced from our initial
axioms. It should also be stated, nevertheless, that
these theorems can be deduced either directly or
indirectly, and are explicit or implicit in nature.
For instance, in our causal model we stated that the

political authority types that arise from social mobilization play an important role in political integration. What is not explicit in this causal statement is our definition of the authority types or their character and qualities. However, once defined and described, the implicit character of these political authorities may be instrumental in political integration. That is, in the manner of a syllogism, if one states, that charisma is instrumental in political integration, and that some of our political authority types possess charisma, then we may deduce from this argument that charismatic political authority is instrumental in political integration. This would be a correct deduction even though the concept of charisma was not initially explicit in our causal inference that political authority leads to political integration. These latent rather than manifest assumptions are worth noting in the explication of our theorems, but such assumptions can still correctly be deduced from our axioms once our major concepts have been explored and defined. In this vein, the following theorems are deduced.

Theorems

1) Political integration is likely to take different forms and obtain disparate levels in a given community and on the national level, depending upon the political authority types that emerge and compete.

    Corollary. Social mobilization, which is already a disruptive phenomena by the very nature of what it entails in developing nations, is likely to be further fragmented as the result of competing political authority types in a cultural nation.

2) Political integration is likely to be more enduring when political capacity and political culture occur simultaneously as covariants.

    Corollary. The greater the political capacity of the political system (sovereign nation), the greater will be the political integration in the "subpolitical" system (cultural nation).

    Corollary. The greater the level of political

culture obtained among Afro-Americans, the greater the level of political integration that will take place.

3) Charismatic political authorities using political religion, and with an institutional base, will play an important role in political integration.

Now that we have established our deductions in a formal manner in the above statements from the axioms that we initially stated in the first component of the model, we can proceed to the final component of the model and the relationship that our major concepts have to empirical indicators.

Relationships of Concepts to Indicators

Indicators allow one to explicate concepts in a manner that makes them conceptually and empirically clearer. By empirical we mean in the sense of political or social phenomena in the real world that may guide one if he were to attempt to make the model more complex or attempt to measure certain properties of it. It is also in this sense that such indices make the terms conceptually more distinct and clarify their meaning theoretically. As Toscano points out, even if we speak of ideal types (for example, a high level of political integration between our competing leadership groups) as concepts that have no empirical instances, they still must have empirical referents in order to have meaning. In short, concepts must in principle have empirical referents, if not in fact empirical instances.[71] The indices we establish for the concept of political integration are crucial to an adequate understanding of our model. Therefore, let us state that the indices proposed for this concept apply to our group leadership types, as well as the Black masses in general, rather than to a particular leadership type or segment of the population. In other words, they attempt to indicate the degree of political integration in the cultural nation or "subpolity" as a whole, even though we stated that the competing authority types divides allegiance, because the ultimate test is the degree to which the complete polity (cultural nation) is integrated.

With these thoughts in mind, let us briefly

summarize this chapter and then turn to the major
concepts and empirical indicators one may look at if
they were to attempt to operationalize the model. This
chapter concludes the model-building process and the
model of Afro-American political integration. Various
causal relationships were established between the
variables in the model. Deductive logic and the use
of syllogisms were used as well in establishing causal
relations. Rationales were constructed and theorems
built as a part of the model-building process. The
relationships between the variables were shown in
matrixes and illustrations (Figures). The major conclusions related to the model of Afro-American political integration may be found in the theorems above.
We now turn to indices related to the model.

Cultural Nation Indicators

1) Is there a common identity and emotional
cement holding an ethnic or racial group of
people together within the confines of a
sovereign nation?

2) Is there a common feeling of "oneness", of "us"
versus "them" ethnic (and in this case racial)
identity which separates them from other
ethnic groups?

3) Are ethnic loyalties (rather than state) reinforced through political leadership, the
intelligentsia, academia, social and community
ties?

4) Is there a centralized head of state (authoritative political figure) lacking among the
ethnic group?

5) Can the ethnic group in question send ambassadors, receive diplomats, make and break treaties
irrespective of the larger nation-state?

6) Does the ethnic group perceive itself as a
cultural entity operating as a "subsystem"
politically within the larger confines of a
territorially defined sovereign state?

7) Do calls on the part of political leaders for
ethnic and racial unity arouse the masses?

Political Integration/Change Indicators

1) Do the leadership types and their followers see "rival" organizations and groups as legitimate, i.e., accept them? Do the masses perceive a given political authority type as legitimate, or are their political orientation more secular and parochial?

2) Is there an increase or decrease in the amount of violence promoted between such leaders, groups, and their attempts to gain the allegiance of the masses?

3) Can Black groups overcome the "stigma" of color, or do they still tend to denigrate one another on the basis of being "light" and "dark"?

4) Can Black groups and political organizations come together to promote certain goals, irrespective of their diversified ideological and political orientations?

5) Do such leadership groups tend to "put down" other groups and people from different regions, territories, and areas, whether it be from across town in a given community, or the regions of the "nation", i.e., North "versus" South?

6) Do Blacks as an ethnic and racial group tend to vote cohesively in a community at election time, or are there sharp voting cleavages?

7) Do Blacks tend to identify with each other as "brothers" and "sisters" regardless of their social and economic status?

Social Mobilization Indicators

1) Is there greater alienation toward the American political system as the result of its political capacity, and greater in-group solidarity as a result?

2) Is there greater emphasis upon a positive identity, and a move away from the stigma and stereotypes associated with Blacks in the past?

3) Are there new political and cultural orientations developing to fill the vacuum created by
the breakdown of old cultural and political
values?

4) Does there appear to be a period of instability,
chaos, and indecisiveness in segments of the
Black community concerning new political and
cultural committments?

5) Have the older, traditional forms of political
activities and protest begun to breakdown in
the Black community?

olitical Culture Indicators

1) Is there racial pride and identity in being
Black among an elite cadre initially, which
moves away from the taboos and stigma of the
Black race in the past?

2) Is there a glorification and social romanticism
among college students, political leaders and
other Black elites identifying Afro-Americans
with Africa and African mythology?

3) Are symbolic gestures such as the clenched fist,
"Black Power" handshake, and "Black Liberation
Flag" used by the elite cadre to arouse and
cause social mobilization and ethnic solidarity
among the masses?

4) Is this elite cadre initially a generic group,
without distinct and specific political and
ideological commitments which separate them
from each other?

'olitical Capacity Indicators

1) Are there law and order and oppressive policies
initiated through bureaucracies (local, state,
and national) which are disproportionately aimed
at the Black masses?

2) Is there an official position advocating law
and order policies on the part of the incumbent
federal administration?

3) Are there racial incidents involving oppression and police brutality toward Blacks at the local or community level which are perceived by the Black masses as having hostile and racial overtones?

4) Are public policies implemented on a discriminatory basis in order to keep Blacks in a position of social and political powerlessness?

Political Authority Indicators

1) Is there an absence of a coherent or centralized political authority in the cultural nation?

2) Is there the absence of a leader who can command the support of the masses with an allegiance that is unquestioned?

3) Is there further fragmentation of social mobilization and political integration caused by the nature of political authority?

4) Do different leadership and political authority forms emerge as social mobilization occurs?

5) Do leadership forms possessing charismatic qualities (political religion) further the ability to mobilize (move) segments of the masses in an unquestioning manner, emerge as the result of social mobilization?

6) Are there leaders with the ability to mobilize segments of the masses as a result of their rhetoric and faddist (rather than fanatic) zeal for violent revolution?

7) Do traditional forms of leadership who often serve "peace-keeping" functions arise when political capacity causes social mobilization in the Black community, and do they tend to engage in moderate forms of politicking?

8) Do the political leadership styles wield authority and influence over the masses, as opposed to power and force?

Sovereign Nation-State Indicators

1) Is the nation-state distinctly defined geographically and physically by territorial borders?

2) Is there a centralized political figure who wields authority, power, and influence?

3) Does the sovereignty of the nation-state allow it to send and receive ambassadors, make treaties, and bound by international laws?

4) Is the sovereignty of the political system characterized by political autonomy and independence?

5) Can formal governmental structures be located and identified at the local, state, and federal level?

6) Are there formal laws and norms that maintain and regulate the social and political system?

Notes

1. Murray Edelman, The Symbolic Uses of Politics, (Urbana and Chicago: University of Illinois Press, 1980), p. 75.

2. Ibid.

3. Imamu Amiri Baraka, "Toward the Creation of Political Institutions for All African Peoples", Black World, 21, (October, 1972), pp. 54-78.

4. For a look at the polemics around this, see Eldridge Cleaver, "The Crisis of the Black Burgeoisie", The Black Scholar, 4, (January, 1973), pp. 2-11.

5. David Apter, The Politics of Modernization, p. 303.

6. Ibid.

7. The Quotable Karenga, p. 36.

8. The Quotable Karenga, p. 36.

9. See the former reference to C. Eric Lincoln, op, cit.

10. The <u>Quotable Karenga</u>, <u>op. cit.</u>; and see also the newspaper <u>Muhammad Speaks</u>, January, 21, 1972, p. 32.

11. Matthew Holden, <u>Black</u> "<u>Nation</u>", p. 16.

12. <u>The Quotable Karenga</u>, pp. 35-36, <u>passim</u>.

13. Max Weber, <u>The Theory of Social and Economic Organization</u>, (New York: The Free Press of Glencoe, Inc., 1957).

14. For a good reference on this particular idea as the "last prophet", see Margary Hassein, "'This Is the Way': Muhammed", <u>Muhammed Speaks,</u> September 6, 1974, p. 12.

15. Robert E. Conot, <u>Rivers of Blood, Years of Darkness</u>, (Toronto and New York: Bantam Books, 1967).

16. For instance, see "Fascist Police Repression: So. Bend, Ind.", <u>Unity and Struggle</u>, September, 1974, p. 8.

17. Arnold Brecht, <u>op. cit.</u>, p. 31; and May Brodbeck, "Explanation, Prediction and 'Imperfect' Knowledge", p. 380.

18. Rupert Emerson and Martin L. Kilson, <u>op. cit.</u>, p. 639.

19. Harold Cruse, <u>op. cit.</u>

20. Marcia Guttentag, "Group Cohesiveness, Ethnic Organization and Poverty", <u>Journal of Social Issues</u>, 26, (Spring, 1970), pp. 105-33.

21. Richard Rudner, <u>op. cit.</u>, pp. 108-09

22. Carl Hempel, "The Logic of Functional Analysis", in <u>Readings in the Philosophy of the Social Sciences</u>, p. 186.

23. W.G. Runciman, <u>Social Science and Political Theory</u>, (Cambridge: Cambridge University Press, 1963).

24. Marion Levy, <u>The Structure of Society</u>, (Princeton: Princeton University Press, 1952).

25. Robert Brown, <u>op. cit.</u>, p. 123

26. The citation is from Robert Brown, <u>Ibid</u>.

27. Fred Frohock, <u>The Nature of Political Inquiry</u>, (Homewood: The Dorsey Press, 1967), pp. 77-78.

28. Arnold Brecht, op. cit., p. 82.

29. Fred Frohock, op. cit., p. 61.

30. Carl G. Hempel, "The Logic of Functional Analysis", op. cit., p. 185.

31. Gustav Bergmann, "Purpose, Function and Scientific Explanation", in Readings in the Philosophy of the Social Sciences, p. 223.

32. Richard S. Rudner, op. cit., p. 85.

33. Paul Diesing, op. cit., p. 304.

34. George C. Graham, op. cit., p. 60-61.

35. Carl G. Hempel, "Explanatory Incompleteness", p. 412-13.

36. For example, Kenneth P. Langton and David A. Karns found that of three socialization agents, the family, the school and peer group, the family had the greatest impact on the development of political efficacy at all levels ranging from low to medium to high, in "The Relative Influence of the Family, Peer Group, and School in the Development of Political Efficacy", Western Political Quarterly, 22, (December, 1969), pp. 813-22. Similar conclusions have been reached by Robert Lane and David O. Sears, Public Opinion, (Englewood Cliffs: Prentice-Hall, 1964); Herbert Hyman, Political Socialization, (Glencoe: Free Press, 1959); and James C. Davies, "The Families Role in Political Socialization", Annals of the American Academy of Political and Social Science, 361, (September, 1965); in which all the authors conclude that the family is the primary agent of democratic socialization.

37. Contrary to the notion that the family is the basic unit of socialization, M. Jennings and R. Niemi argue that if the child is not a carbon copy image of one of the parents by the age of 18, through the value-acquisition process, other socio-technological changes enhance the possibility of differences in the acquisition of values. M. Jennings and R. Niemi, "The Transmission of Political Values From Parent to Child", American Political Science Review, 62, (March, 1968), pp. 169-84. Hess and Torney reach the major conclusion that public schools are the most important and effective "basic" agent of political socialization in the U.S. and that the role of the family is primarily responsible for socializing party preference and political involvement, but relatively

little else. R.D. Hess and J.V. Torney, <u>The Development of Political Attitudes in Children</u>, (Chicago: Aldine Publishing Co., 1967).

38. Edward S. Greenberg, "Black Children and the Political System", <u>Public Opinion Quarterly</u>, 34, (Fall, 1970), pp. 333-345.

39. Edward S. Greenberg, "Orientations of Black and White Children to Political Authority Figures", in <u>Black Political Attitudes</u> edited by C.S. Bullock and H.R. Rodgers, (Chicago: Markham Publishing Company, 1972), pp. 9-19.

40. David Easton, and Jack Dennis, <u>Children in the Political System</u>.

41. Richard L. Engstrom, "Race and Compliance: Differential Political Socialization", in <u>Black Political Attitudes</u>, pp. 35-45.

42. H.R. Rodgers and G. Taylor, "The Policeman as an Agent of Regime Legitimation", in <u>Black Political Attitudes</u>, pp. 20-33.

43. Bonnie Bullough, "Alienation in the Ghetto", in <u>Black Political Attitudes</u>, pp. 83-96.

44. Rupert Emerson and Martin Kilson, <u>op. cit.</u>, p. 650.

45. Schley R. Lyons, "The Political Socialization of Ghetto Children: Efficacy and Cynicism", <u>in Black Political Attitudes</u>, pp. 46-56.

46. <u>National Advisory Commission on Civil Disorders</u>, Supplemental Studies for the <u>National Advisory Commission on Civil Disorders</u>, (Washington: Government Printing Office, 1969).

47. Rupert Emerson and Martin Kilson, "The Rise of Africa and the Negro American", <u>op. cit.</u>, pp. 37-42, <u>passim</u>.

48. R. Weisbord, "Africa, Africans and the Afro-American: Images and Identities in Transition", <u>Race</u>, 10, (January, 1969), p. 314. Weisbord's reference to Killens is that found in <u>Black Man's Burden</u>, (New York: Trident, 1965).

49. Maulana Ron Karenga, "Which Road: Nationalism, Pan-Africanism, Socialism?", <u>The Black Scholar</u>, 6, (October, 1974), pp. 21-30. Karenga presents some definitive views on Pan-Africanism and

the inclusiveness of the concept.

50. William E. Cross, "The Negro-To-Black Conversion Experience", _Black World_, 20, (July, 1971), pp. 13-27.

51. Lucian Pye, _Political Culture and Political Development_

52. Claude Ake, _A Theory of Political Integration_, (Homewood: The Dorsey Press, 1970).

53. _Ibid._, pp. 101-11, _passim_.

54. Karl Deutsch, "Social Mobilization and Political Development", _American Political Science Review_, 55, (September, 1961), pp. 493-509.

55. Karl Deutsch, _Nationalism and Its Alternatives_, (New York: Knopf, distributed by Random House, 1969).

56. Walker Connor, _op. cit._, p. 327.

57. _Ibid._, See also the reference to Weed in footnote three of Chapter Two as to the causes of ethnic re-emergence and identity in America.

58. _Ibid._

59. Myron Weiner, _op. cit_.

60. _Ibid._

61. Alvin F. Poussaint and Linda R. McLean, "Black Roadblocks to Black Unity", _Black World_, 18, (November, 1968), pp. 11-18.

62. Lester M. Salamon, "Leadership and Modernization: The Emerging Black Political Elite in the American South", _Journal of Politics_, 35, (August, 1973), pp. 615-46.

63. For a sampling of some of these factors, one may look at Lester Milbrath, _Political Participation_, (Chicago: Rand McNally, 1965); and Dan Nimmo, _The Political Persuaders_, (Englewood Cliffs: Prentice-Hall, 1970).

64. Joungwon Alexander Kim, "The Politics of Predevelopment", _Comparative Politics_, 5, (January, 1973), pp. 224-35.

65. _Ibid._

66. Harold Lasswell, <u>Politics</u>: <u>Who Gets What, When, How</u>, (Cleveland: Meridian Books, 1958).

67. Citation of Max Weber is from Irving Louis Horowitz, "Party Charisma", <u>Studies in Comparative International Development</u>, 1 (March, 1965), p. 95.

68. Hubert M. Blalock, <u>op. cit</u>.

69. <u>Ibid</u>., p. 11.

70. Robert Brown, <u>op. cit</u>., p. 174.

71. James V. Toscano, "Models in the Study of Political Integration", in <u>The Integration of Political Communities</u>, ed. by Philip E. Jacobs and James V. Toscano, (Philadelphia and New York: J.B. Lippincott, 1964).

CHAPTER VI

THE LOGIC OF POLITICAL INTEGRATION

Overview

Initially, we began this study with a brief survey of the five approaches to the study of political development and change, especially in Third World nations. This was done in order to establish some degree of familiarity with the literature and to highlight some of the shortcomings of these approaches. In Chapter Two, we presented an alternative way of looking at Black politics in relation to the American political system, which suggested the colonial model of racial subordination. From this perspective, Afro-Americans may be viewed in the same light as other nations that have experienced a period of colonialism. If one were to begin with the initial period of Black slavery in America, however, it could be argued that the duration of colonialism was (and is) much longer with Afro-Americans than with Africans. Colonialism, as Fanon so aptly pointed out, generally creates a negative identity and stigma among the subordinated masses who are subjected to it. In this respect, it could be argued that, if one accepts the colonial analog, an inferiority complex among the Black masses is based, to a large extent, on their racial characteristics and color. In this context, race and three other components of domestic colonialism were analyzed as a social process, and the ways and means that these components work in order to keep Afro-Americans in a subordinate and dependent position. One of the major functional components to this end is the manipulation and management of political and economic structures, such as annexation and consolidation (where Blacks have achieved a numerical majority in many urban areas) in order to maintain a dependent relationship and political powerlessness. This is also true with regard to economic structures such as welfare and dependence upon the federal government for aid even though in some instances Afro-Americans are beginning to control political structures in some cities with the election of Black mayors. Hence, we encounter a paradox in that there may be political control with no economic base, but without the latter there is really no meaningful political "control."

189

The model of domestic colonialism may not be questioned so much today from the structural arrangements that keep Blacks dependent, but from the psychological notion of an inferiority complex among a colonized people, namely Afro-Americans, especially since the rise of Black consciousness and a positive racial identity in the sixties. This would constitute a serious psychological break with the proponents of colonialism since cultural decolonization is the first step toward political independence and has implications for the political integration model developed in Chapter Four and Chapter Five. Nevertheless, the model of domestic colonialism a la Cruse, Blauner and others is outlined in a manner to suggest one way of viewing Blacks in the American political process. Not only does the model have substantial differences with what we termed classical colonialism, but the empirical indicators offered at the end of the chapter may be open to other interpretations. On the other hand, if one utilizes the domestic colonial model for studying Afro-Americans in the political system, it could be argued that the treatment of them has been harsher and longer in duration than the colonial period in Africa under White rule. Blacks in America were stripped much more totally of their culture and social structure under White domination and slavery than Africans who remained in Africa, although we took note that this does not mean that cultural artifacts do not remain among Afro-Americans. In sum, perhaps the most pertinent statement to make about the colonial model here is not only that it provides one way of viewing Afro-Americans realistically in American society, but that it provides the stage for the offspring of a decolonial model or model of political integration. A model of this nature was elaborated upon and analyzed in Chapter Four and Five. Before we turn to this model let us say a few words about the methodology in Chapter Three.

The justification for putting the methodology in the third chapter was not only to first provide an overview of the literature on political development and competing model (domestic colonial) of Black politics but, more importantly, because the method is an integral part of the model. Chapter Three only constitutes an operational or general outline of the method, and more specific details are incorporated in the calculus and rules in the following chapter. The ideal, empirical and value concepts mentioned in the methodology are

elaborated on in the calculus and particularly the
fifth component of model-building in which we discuss
these concept types in relation to empirical and
theoretical literature pertinent to them. Besides
the discussion of empirical studies related to the
concept of political capacity (i.e., alienation and
political socialization studies) which we would propose as an empirical concept, the other concepts are
used as ideal and value types with some concepts fulfilling both criteria. For example, one could maintain
that political integration is both an ideal and value
concept if it is suggested on the national level, since
it is found nowhere in reality, (Afro-Americans fully
integrated on the national level), but is still valued
as a result of the normative and overall subjective
approach of our study. Other concepts, such as
political culture, may indeed be utilized. as an
empirical concept if tested, but our reasoning for
determining empirical and ideal concepts was on the
basis of whether our literature support was empirical
or normative. Because of this approach, we decided
that delineating or developing a typology of our concepts employed in the model any further in terms of
whether they were ideal, value or empirical ones was
unwarranted and unecessary.

With these reservations kept in mind concerning
the approach and method, the model of Afro-American
political integration was developed in detail in Chapter
Four and Five. Based upon the discussion in the first
chapter, we based our integrative model upon two
approaches to the study of political development and
change. This is the social system and political
culture approach. In turn, these two approaches are
most significant to the model because they involve
the integration of social and political cleavages
(social systems approach) and political actors'
identities and attitudes toward the political system
(political culture approach). It should be kept in
mind that these approaches are most germane to our
model since it is recognized that Afro-Americans do
not constitute a sovereign political entity, and that
there are limits to a theory of Black political
development if such development must assume (which is
the case in developing nations) that an independent
political system is an essential element for a
sovereign people engaged in nation-building.

This thesis warrants greater elaboration. The political culture and social system approaches are important aspects of political integration for a people even who are not politically independent as a nation-state since such processes may occur irrespective and independently of the sovereign nation in which it occurs. These approaches are instrumental as well to this end (political integration) in a national subpolity which we have termed the cultural nation. Contrary to these approaches to political development, we would argue that the legal, administrative and economic approaches, if applied to Blacks or for that matter other ethnic groups, would be dependent completely upon the economic and political system to which they are tied. For example, if one were to look at Afro-American political development from the legal perspective, such development would depend upon the larger American political system which Blacks constitute a part of and the willingness of state and federal legislatures to pass laws that advance equality and development for Afro-Americans.

On the other hand, limitations would still have to be put upon the approaches utilized here with regard to political integration. As we pointed out earlier, it would be <u>naive</u> to argue that such integration should be to form a separate state or entity. Furthermore, a statement would be too simplistic that proposed political integration will take place uniformally among Blacks on the national level, or wholly in a community in an ideal sense. The causal relationship between our authority types and the levels of political integration established, not to mention other internal (as opposed to external) factors, tends to bear this out since they appeal to different segments of the masses. It is not suggested here, nevertheless, that political integration among Afro-Americans would not be just for "integration's sake." Safa points out that separation (using it in the context of our model) and assimilation need not be antagonistic trends among a people, that there are steps through which a group must pass in order to achieve a place for themselves in a pluralistic society.[1] Similarly, Carmichael and Hamilton, in stating a fundamental premise of their concept of Black Power, argue:

> Before a group can enter the open
> society, it must first close ranks.

By this we mean that group solidarity
is necessary before a group can operate
effectively from a bargaining position
of strength in a pluralistic society.
Traditionally, each new ethnic group
in this society has formed the route
to social and political viability
through the organization of its own
institutions with which to represent
its needs within the larger society.[2]

In summary, we may state that political integration in this context of separation may lead to greater
pluralism within American society if it results in
economic and political consolidation of resources
among an ethnic or racial group, in this case Blacks.
Initially, the important question that was posed in
constructing the axioms, that is the "puzzle" to be
solved, was determining and investigating the critical
components and variables of a model of Afro-American
political integration, employing holistic concepts.
It was assumed, for the purposes of making deductions
related to this end, that ceteris paribus was an
important part of our calculus even though no paradigm
in the social sciences can really assume a closed
system or calculus that accounts for all variables
affecting a dependent variable.

The deductive arguments made suggest that there
are important barriers to a theory of unified and
ultimate political integration existing within the
cultural nation with the CP clause. This is not to
say that factors external to the model of political
integration other than the concept of political
capacity would not effect this end and it would be
naive to think so. Rather, it assumes that even if one
could perceive a Black sovereign nation, there would be
serious obstacles to political integration as the result
of competing authority types. This would be contrasted
with the concept of a nation-state which, by definition,
would have political leadership centralized in an
authority figure. In many nation-states, however, there
are still serious problems related to political integration. This problem was taken note of earlier. But
due to historical, socio-economic and political factors
Afro-Americans have not evolved in the same way that
other developing nations have in the past. However,
from an academic viewpoint, it is positively asserted

that this model constitutes an important break with the colonial model, which has come to be a dominant model associated with Black politics. This does not mean that we have attempted to provide the critical linkage between a colonial society and a developing nation which involves political and violent revolutionary upheaval. It does suggest, with certain stipulations, looking at Black politics in the context of a developing nation.

Let us turn briefly to the concept of model and its employment in the social sciences, in order that it may clarify our usage and the limitations of it in the calculus. Rudner suggests that the term model has many meanings which include: 1) the terms model and theory used as synonyms, 2) a model as any theoretical formulation other than a theory, and 3) a model as a reference to extralinguistic entities involved in math and logic.[3] Furthermore, a model can provide a "model for a theory", in which it consists of an alternative interpretation of the same calculus for which the theory itself is an interpretation. In other words, a situation in which two interpreted theories are isomorphic is one involving two different deductive systems that are both interpretations of the same underlying calculus. In this case, one of the isomorphic theories will be the model of, or furnish a model for the other. This will depend primarily not upon structural features but merely the subject matter one is interested in.[4] Brodbeck states what is termed a "model for a new area" as being one involving an area about which we know a good deal that is used to suggest laws for an area about which little is known, where the familiar area providing a form of the laws is the model for a new area.[5] This is contrary to Hempel's concept of overdetermination as opposed to explanatory incompleteness, in which the former means that if two or more alternative explanations with nonequivocal explanan-sets are available for the explanandum, then one has overdetermined what is to be explained, whereas with Brodbeck's concept one uses an explanatory model to seek further investigation in an unknown area.[6] Hempel's notion of overdetermination is closer to Rudner's "model for a theory" than to Brodbeck's "model for a new area", since one has the option of which explanan-set to choose for the model and which one the investigator wants to choose for the theory.

Although in our particular logical construct a causal model was employed, in the stricter definitional sense (as opposed to merely descriptive), a model can be a reference to any of the above. It was noted that in our model we were concerned primarily with internal consistency as opposed to predictive power as the overall objective, which a theory must be able to provide (no doubt, the model does have relevance to the real world). At the same time, Brodbeck's phrase model for a new area is perhaps most applicable in the definitional realm since we have taken laws and postulates from political development theory in comparative politics and applied it to the American political system, and especially since few scholars have explored the concept of a developing nation among an ethnic or racial minority within the United States with a rigorous theoretical construct. Here we may encounter some heuristic overtones since the model may provide fertile grounds for further investigation of Afro-American political integration and development.

For example, developing nation-states in the Third World as pointed out have been assumed to go through stages of political development which include those in Figure 6-1.

Traditional ⟶ Colonial ⟶ Nationalist ⟶
Revolutionary-Independence ⟶ Drive Toward Modernity

Fig. 6-1 A unilinear model of political development

What is suggested in this unilinear pattern of development is that in the Nationalist stage various ethnic groups may ban together in order to achieve the Revolutionary Independence stage, or moving from a multitude of cultural nations (different ethnic groups) to one independent, and hence sovereign nation-state. We would say that the cultural nation becomes sovereign through revolution, or symbolically CN = SN in the process.

Nevertheless, to propose our model as a heuristic one might assume the following form in Figure 6-2. It may be stated that Afro-Americans, like Africans, began in a traditional (Trad.) society or stage and like Africans, were subjected to a period of social, economic and political subordination similar to

Fig. 6-2 A heuristic model of political
          integration

the colonial period (Colon.) in Africa. However, one
may have to substitute some other stage than that of
classical colonialism to explain the experience of
Blacks in America. In short, perhaps a paradigm other
than the classical colonial framework may explain the
nationalist (Natlist.) stage and the stage of cultural
independence (Cul. Indep.). This would represent a
significant break with the above stages of political
development both in questioning the colonial model as
stagnant rather than dynamic. It would allow one to
present other explanatory models of political change
although one may have to place limits on Afro-American
political development in a sequence that involves a
violent revolution for independence and the drive
toward modernity in the context of other developing
nations. Not only have we questioned how realistic it
is to think in terms of this type of revolution in
America, but the idea of Afro-Americans attempting to
"modernize" separately in what is already a modern
nation-state, appears contradictory. Hence, we might
state that the real revolution that may take place is
the cultural one that began in the mid-sixties with
the renewed emphasis upon Black pride, culture and
identity. In this respect, we could not say that CN =
SN in our model is the equivalent of developing nations.
Rather, with Afro-Americans we would state that $CN \neq$
SN, but that $CN_{t_1} = CN_{t_2}$.

In plain language, this would mean that the
cultural nation (CN) as we have defined it does not
equal, or result in, the sovereign nation (SN). Rather,
the cultural nation (type 1), in one stage takes
another form in the second stage (or type 2), which
assumes a more fully integrated subpolity in our model.

On the other hand, one could also employ Rudner's
notion of a model for a theory, since one could
undoubtedly deduce other implications and interpretations of our calculus. Although it is doubtful that
Hempel's statement of overdetermination would not seem
as plausible because it is doubtful if one could deduce

an alternative unequivocal explanatory set of variables from our calculus that would explain the phenomena of political integration from the same perspective.

Nontheless, there are criticisms of models and model-building in the social sciences that warrant our attention since we have advocated one for Afro-American political integration. Golembiewski et. al., propose eight criticisms of model-building, six of which are germane to our discussion:

1) models often attempt to get the best of all possible worlds, yet typically end up more or less with the worst of them;

2) model-building in political science tells us what we do know based upon what we do not know- new names are given wholesale to existing insights;

3) models sometimes are formulated in ways that are self-fulfilling and thus defy testing;

4) basic propositions of models are often of unestablished validity, and indeed may be in heated dispute;

5) because of the scope of models the most careful analysis is likely to be shot through with a large number of implicit propositions dealing with reality or a desirable state of affairs;

6) and Rapport's statement that the typical model-building enterprise at best aids in recognizing and categorizing phenomena, which constitutes only one component of the scientific event.[7]

While we do not want to dwell on criticisms of model-building, a summary discussion of them provides another means to clarify and critically perceive our model in explanatory terms. Number one was spoken of in some detail in the discussion of holism vs. reductionism, and needs no further mention here. Number two, coining neologisms to describe old phenomena, undoubtedly is part of our problem in the model since terms such as intra-integration is merely another way of stating the problem of political integration within polities but has another manifestation in the context of a bi-racial society as we define the cultural and sovereign nations.

197

Criticisms three and five above, involving models of
self-fulfillment and a desirable state of affairs, at
best could only be launched as a secondary criticism
of our model because we stated initially that we were
investigating political integration in normative and
subjective terms. The fourth criticism, regarding
propositions that are in dispute, surely is manifested
in our model since the debate continues to rage as to
whether a pluralist, elitest, and/or colonial model
(among others) is most applicable to the American
political system in particular, not to mention our
propositions which are couched in developmental integrative terms. Of course, the justification here is
that axioms are empirical laws whose truth for the
moment are accepted in order to make further deductions
from them.

Finally, the sixth criticism of model-building above
of the total of eight discussed by Golembiewski, et.
al., may be true in general but is not important in our
model, since we did not attempt to just clarify and
categorize phenomena but more importantly to establish
a causal network, establish rules of interpretations,
provide a set of interrelated axioms, and make references based upon them in our calculus which represents
a "scientific" endeavor in itself, in line with the
school of logical positivism.

In the process of deducing the various relationships
between our concepts and variables, we stated that
political integration and social mobilization among
Afro-Americans is likely to be a more enduring (e)
phenomena when political capacity and political culture
are affecting them simultaneously, although it will
ultimately take different forms. We may make a further
deduction from these inferences by returning to our
probability statement which we initially posed as:

$$PI = P(PC + PC^1 + SM \times (PA)^t).$$

Now, as a result of the deductions made, we could
represent this probability statement more precisely
with endurance (e) as an addendum, in which it would
take the following form:

$$(PI)^e = P(PC + PC^1 + SM^e \times (PA)^{ten}).$$

We could now say that the probability of political

integration is likely to be more enduring (PI)e among Blacks when PC and PC¹ act simultaneously upon social mobilization (SM) which is also likely to be more enduring. Further, the political authority (PA) types (t) that emerge as a consequence are likely to endure (e) longest who have the greatest appeal when our causal covariants act concomitantly, which tend to be our nationalist (n) types (in which these three letters are represented by the "ten" in the above equation). Specifically, these authority types would constitute the Religious and Cultural Nationalist leaders for reasons that we have articulated upon already. The most important aspect of our revived probability statement, other than the additional letters e and n added to our variables, is that we no longer have to stipulate our covariants acting independently upon social mobilization as part of the probability statement. The reasoning is that their location in the political equation in the manner represented is valid as it stands, since PC + PC¹ denotes their common occurrence.

Since there are certain demands manifested in deduction and logic, our probability statement is of no particular value, unless, we can translate its mathematical potential into a logical deduction. Therefore, we may interpret this statement in a deductive syllogism in the following manner:

1) Afro-American political integration is likely to be more enduring when political culture and political capacity act simultaneously as covariants in effecting social mobilization and political authority.

2) Political culture and political capacity are acting simultaneously as covariants in effecting social mobilization and political authority.

3) Therefore, political integration among Afro-Americans is likely to be a more enduring phenomena.

Of course, this deductive syllogism is hypothetical in nature and may not be applicable today. It will be applicable, however, if the eighties turn out to be like the sixties. The current policies of the Reagan administration suggest that this may be a reality, however, with his oppressive social policies.

However, we also hypothesized that Afro-American political integration could become self-perpetuating in the absence of political capacity; and, for analytical and deductive purposes let us suggest this also in the form of a probability statement, in which a positive identity would now play the chief role:

$$PI = P(PC + SM \times (PA)^{tn}).$$

This statement would show a significant difference in the duration of political integration with just political culture as the independent variable effecting the causal model of political integration. Hence, the e (for endurance) could be excluded from the equation and the variables since the covariants are not acting together, but we would still expect the letter (n) to remain since it is the nationalist types that have the greatest appeal to political culture.

Political culture could still precipitate political integration on the basis of two causal extrapolations implicit in the foregoing discussion. First, we attempted to show a circular model of causality using political culture as the independent variable in which political integration would constantly be reinforced in the circular network of concepts. Secondly, our authority types in the above probability statement of political integration regarding endurance would still arise and have the greatest effect when political culture is the causal or independent variable. Again, in order to maintain consistency in the deductive process, let us pose this last probability statement in the form of syllogistic logic:

1) Political integration is likely to increase when political culture is the independent variable causing social mobilization and political authority.

2) Political culture is the independent variable causing social mobilization and political authority.

3) Therefore, political integration is likely to increase.

Ultimately, three of our four leadership types are likely to fade (at least from their present form) like

a piece of colored material washed with white clothes
and a bleaching solution if the American polity moves
toward racial integration on a larger and more complete
scale. The Justice Department under the Reagan administration, however, has advocated policies contrary to
facilitating racial integration. However, these
leadership types may still take on a modified form of
the Traditional-Brokerage and therefore not be as
distinct as they are now. For example, our Religious
Nationalists may still use some form of political
religion to lobby support on a particular legistative
bill important to the masses (in the eyes of the
leader), depending upon the character of the leader and
the perception of the masses. Black nationalism in
many of its present forms would lose its appeal by
making reference to Whites as the "Devil" or other
denunciations involving "demonology", since they
(Whites) would no longer be associated with acts of
oppression and violence toward the Black community, or
what we have termed a part of political capacity.

The model that we have attempted to develop from
our axioms in order to deduce certain theorems that
logically entail, has focused upon the national level
and the Black masses in general, rather than a particular community (although we often made reference to
the community level) or region of the United States.
As such, one has to speak in generalities rather than
specifics, and perhaps a passage from Almond and Verba
best summarizes this approach. They state:

> It is as if that system were a large
> map on the wall of a darkened room,
> and all we know of it is what is
> revealed by one thousand separate
> pinpoints of light. These points of
> light...illuminate the spots on the
> map that they touch. But they light
> up only a small part of the map and
> leave the areas between the dots
> completely dark. We want to say some-
> thing, not merely about the points
> that are illuminated, but about the
> entire map itself.[8]

The Eighties: Ominous Signs of Mobilization

An important aspect of political theory and social

science, whether it be empirical or normative, is to make recommendations for public policy and further epistemological inquiry. Let us therefore make a few comments and suggestions with this in mind.

One may infer here that if the political capacity for alienation in the American political system should diminish, it does not logically follow that the need for Afro-American political integration should also seize. The civil and political rights movement and cultural identity and awareness which Blacks obtained in the sixties may serve as a viable tool for clout in the political arena if the movement for ethnic and racial cohesiveness should continue. In this regard, the concept of Black nationalism can play a positive role in the long struggle of Afro-Americans to find their "place in the sun." The implication of political integration à la Black nationalism as Blacks wanting or achieving a separate nation-state may increase if America should continue to turn its back on full equality and Black progress. Of course, one could argue, however, that increased alienation and oppression of Blacks surely could break down loyal ties to America and increase the possibility of mobilization for such a cause, but it is proposed here that such mobilization would only be miniscule compared to those who would continue their loyalty to the American system as long as the fruits and lure of the "American Dream" are tantalizingly hanging from the trees and branches of theoretical equality.

The outlook, though, for fulfilling the American dream is bleak today. As noted above, the Reagan administration has turned its back on racial equality and Black progress. This is an ominous note for political stability in the American political system. Ronald Reagan continues to show a lack of sensitivity or empathy for the poor in general and the Black masses in the ghettoes in particular in a number of areas. Food stamps, health services and hot lunch programs for the poor are being drastically cut by Reagan. Federal funding for summer employment programs have been cut back. The Reagan administration has supported tax-exempt status for parochial colleges and universities which have racially discriminatory policies. Reagan is against busing to achieve school integration and has shown reservations with regard to extending the 1965 Voting Rights Act. Reagan plans to completely phase out the CETA (Comprehensive Employment and Training Act) program which is vital to Black youth in the inner city and proposes to cut-off many other forms of grants and aid to urban America, most of which benefits the Black underclass. The list of "cruel and unusual" policies targeted for the urban poor and Blacks by the Reagan administration is endless.

Congress, meanwhile, has considered a constitutional amendment to forbid busing of children for the purpose of racial integration. Furthermore, Congress is considering diluting the 1965 Voting Rights Act, undoubted the single most important civil rights act for Blacks in the twentieth century.

White America in general, as well as the Reagan administration, has turned its back on Black progress. The Ku Klux Klan, once thought to be a dying entity in the late sixties, is growing in membership and more visible in protest and politics than at any time since the 1950's. Many racial confrontations between the Klan and Afro-Americans have taken place in the past several years in Jackson, Birmingham, Greensboro and many northern cities. At least two Blacks were found lynched and hanging from trees in Alabama and Georgia over the past two years. Challenges to affirmative action and equal opportunity have been witnessed in the De Funis, Bakke and Weber cases. Blacks continue to be the "last-hired, first-fired" and as the recession of 1982 gets deeper, Blacks are hurt in disproportionate numbers with regard to employment opportunities.

On the other hand, protest and marches reminiscent of the civil rights movement of the sixties has began anew. The Reverend Ralph David Abernathy has led a march from Alabama to Washington in support of extending the 1965 Voting Rights Act. Various groups, including "Ground Zero", are marching to protest increased arms build-up and the increasing threat of nuclear war. Increased alienation and mobilization against oppressive policies of the Reagan administration, particularly by Blacks, can only increase the possibility of social mobilization. Social mobilization will provide the opportunity for the political authority types in our model to increase their influence and leadership potential. The end result may well be greater political integration among Blacks. The

oppressive policies of the Reagan administration and
the various branches of the federal government, along
with increasing indifference by White America concerning
Black progress, could surely make the eighties like
the sixties--or perhaps worse.

Notes

1. Helen Iclsen Safa, "The Case for Negro Separatism", Urban
   Affairs Quarterly, 4, (September, 1968), pp. 45-63.

2. Stokley Carmichael and Charles V. Hamilton, Black Power, (New
   York: Vintage Books, 1967), p. 44.

3. Richard S. Rudner, op. cit., p. 23.

4. Ibid., pp. 24-25.

5. May Brodbeck, "Models, Meanings and Theories", p. 84.

6. Carl G. Hempel, "Explanatory Incompleteness", p. 405.

7. Robert T. Golembiewski, William A. Welsh, and William T.
   Crotty, A Methodological Primer for Political Scientists,
   (Chicago: Rand McNally and Co., 1969).

8. Gabriel Almond and Sidney Verba, op. cit., p. 73.

*****

SELECTED BIBLIOGRAPHY

Ake, Claude, A Theory of Political Integration,, (Homewood: The Dorsey Press, 1970).

Almond, Gabriel and Sidney Verba, The Civic Culture: Political Attitudes and Democracy in Five Nations, (Princeton: Princeton University Press, 1963).

Almond, Gabriel and James Coleman, The Politics of the Developing Areas, (Princeton: Princeton University Press, 1963).

Apter, David, The Political Kingdom of Uganda, (Princeton: Princeton University Press, 1963).

Apter, David, (ed.), Ideology and Discontent, (New York: Free Press, 1964).

Apter, David, The Politics of Modernization, (Chicago: University of Chicago Press, 1965).

Apter, David, Some Conceptual Approaches to the Study of Modernization, (Englewood Cliffs: Prentice-Hall, Inc., 1968).

Ashby, W. Ross, "Analysis of the System to Be Modeled", in The Process of Model-Building in the Behavioral Sciences, ed. by Ralph Stodgill, (Columbus: Ohio State University Press, 1970).

Bachrach, Peter and Morton Baratz, "Decisions and Nondecisions: An Analytical Framework", American Political Science Review, 57, (September, 1963), pp. 632-42.

Bailey, Ron, "Economic Aspects of the Black Internal Colony", The Review of Black Political Economy, 3, (Summer, 1973), pp. 43-69.

Balandier, G., "The Colonial Situation: A Theoretical Approach (1951)", in Social Change: The Colonial Situation, ed. by Immanuel Wallerstein, (New York: John Wiley and Sons, Inc., 1966).

Banfield, Edward C., The Unheavanly City, (Boston and Toronto: Brown, Little and Co., 1966).

Banton, Michael, "1960: A Turning Point in the Study of Race Relations", Daedalus, 103, (Spring, 1974), pp. 31-43.

Baraka, Imamu Amiri, "Toward the Creation of Political Institutions for All African Peoples", Black World, 21, (October, 1972),

SELECTED BIBLIOGRAPHY

pp. 54-78.

Baron, Harold M., The Demand for Black Labor: Historical Notes on the Political Economy of Racism, (Cambridge: Radical America, 1971).

Barth, Ernest and Donald Noel, "Conceptual Framework for the Analysis of Race Relations: An Evaluation", Social Forces, 50, (March, 1972), pp. 333-48.

Bergmann, Gustav, "Purpose, Function and Scientific Explanation", in Readings in the Philosophy of the Social Sciences, ed. by May Brodbeck, (London: Collier-Macmillan Limited, 1968).

Buecher, John, Public Administration,(Belmont: Dickinson Publishing Co., 1968).

Binder, Leonard, James S. Coleman, Joseph LaPalombara, Lucian Pye, Sidney Verba, and Myron Weiner, (eds.), Crisis and Sequences of Political Development, (Princeton: Princeton University Press, 1971).

Black, Max, Talcott Parsons, and Robert Bales, (eds.), The Social Theories of Talcott Parsons, (Englewood Cliffs: Prentice-Hall, 1961.

Blalock, Herbert M., Jr., Theory Construction, (Englewood Cliffs: Prentice-Hall, 1969).

Blasingame, John, The Slave Community, (New York: Oxford University Press, 1972).

Blauner, Robert, "The Ghetto as Internal Colony", Social Problems, 16, (Spring, 1968), pp. 393-408.

Boggs, James, Racism and the Class Struggle,(New York: Monthly Review Press, 1970).

Brecht, Arnold, Political Theory, (Princeton: Princeton University Press, 1959).

Bretton, Henry, The Rise and Fall of Kwame Nkrumah, (New York: Praeger, 1961).

Brodbeck, May, "Explanation, Prediction and 'Imperfect' Knowledge", in Readings in the Philosophy of the Social Sciences, ed. by

206

SELECTED BIBLIOGRAPHY

May Brodbeck, (London: Collier-Macmillan Limited, 1968).

Brodbeck, May, "Introduction", to Readings in the Philosophy of the Social Sciences, ed. by May Brodbeck, (London: Collier Macmillan Limited, 1968).

Brodbeck, May, "Models, Meanings and Theories", in Readings in the Philosophy of the Social Sciences, ed. by May Brodbeck, (London: Collier Macmillan Limited, 1968).

Brown, Robert, Explanation in Social Science, (Chicago: Aldine Publishing Co., 1963).

Bryce-LaPorte, Roy Simon, "The Slave Plantation: Background to Present Conditions of Urban Blacks", in Race Relations, ed. by Edgar C. Epps, (Cambridge: Winthrop Publishing Co., 1973).

Bullough, Bonnie, "Alienation in the Ghetto", in Black Political Attitudes, ed. by C.S. Bullock and H.R. Rodgers, (Chicago: Markham Publishing Co., 1972).

Carmichael, Stokeley and Charles V. Hamilton, Black Power, (New York: Random House, 1967).

Clark, Kenneth, Dark Ghetto, (New York: Harper and Row, 1967).

Clayton, Edward T., The Negro Politician, (Chicago: Johnson Publishing Co., Inc., 1964).

Cleaver, Elridge, "The Crisis of the Black Bourgeoisie", The Black Scholar, 4, (January, 1973), pp. 2-11.

Cloward, Richard A. and Frances Fox Piven, "Welfare for Whom?", in Black Politics, ed. by Edward S. Greenberg, Neal Milner and David J. Olson, (New York: Holt, Rinehart and Winston, Inc., 1971).

Conner, Walker, "Nation-Building or Nation-Destroying?", World Politics, 1, (April, 1972), pp. 319-55.

Conot, Robert E., Rivers of Blood, Years of Darkness, (Toronto and New York: Bantam Books, 1967).

Cox, Oliver C., Caste, Class and Race, (New York: Doubleday, 1948).

SELECTED BIBLIOGRAPHY

Cross, William E., "The Negro-to-Black Conversion Experience", *Black World*, 20, (July, 1971), pp. 13-27.

Cruse, Harold, *The Crisis of the Negro Intellectual*, (New York: William Morrow and Co., 1967).

Cruse, Harold, *Rebellion or Revolution*, (New York: William Morrow and Co., 1968).

Cruse, Harold, "Black and White: Outlines for the Next Stage", *Black World*, 20, (January, 1971) pp. 19-41.

Curtin, Philip D., "The Black Experience of Colonialism and Imperialism", *Daedalus*, 103, (Spring, 1974), pp. 17-28.

Dahl, Robert, "Critique of the Ruling Elite Model", *American Political Science Review*, 52, (June, 1958), pp. 463-69.

Dahl, Robert, "The Concept of Power", in *Politics and Social Life*, ed. by R.A. Dentler, Nelson Polsby and Paul A. Smith, (Boston: Houghton Mifflin Co., 1963).

Dalby, David, "The African Elements in American English", in *Rappin' and Stylin' Out*, ed. by Thomas Kochman, (Chicago: University of Illinois Press, 1972).

Dallin, A. and G. Breslauer, *Political Terror in Communist Systems*, (Stanford: Stanford University Press, 1970).

David, Wilfred L., "Black America in Development Perspective, Part I", *The Review of Black Political Economy*, 3, (Fall, 1972), pp. 89-103.

Davies, James C., "The Family's Role in Political Socialization", *The Annals of the American Academy of Political and Social Science*, 361, (September, 1965), pp. 10-19.

Deutsch, Karl W., "Social Mobilization and Political Development", *American Political Science Review*, 55, (September, 1961), pp. 493-514.

Deutsch, Karl W., *Nationalism and It's Alternatives*, (New York: Knopf, Random House, 1969).

Diesing, Paul, *Patterns of Discovery in the Social Sciences*, (Chicago and New York: Aldine-Atherton, Inc., 1971).

SELECTED BIBLIOGRAPHY

Dollard, John, <u>Caste and Class in a Southern Town</u>, (Garden City: Doubleday, 1957).

Donavan, Hedley, "Real Black Power", <u>Time Magazine</u>, (November, 1967), pp. 22-24.

Drake, St. Clair and Horace Clayton, <u>Black Metropolis</u>, (New York, Harcourt, Brace and World, Inc., 1970).

DuBois, W.E.B., <u>The Philadelphia Negro</u>, (New York: B. Blom, 1967).

Dye, Thomas, <u>The Irony of Democracy</u>,(Belmont: Wadsworth Publishing Co., Inc., 1970).

Easton, David, "The New Revolution in Political Science", in <u>Approaches to the Study of Political Science</u>, ed. by Michael Haas and Henry Kariel, (Scranton: Chandler Publishing Co., 1970).

Easton, David, and Jack Dennis, <u>Children in the Political System</u>, (New York: McGraw-Hill, 1969).

Eckstein, Alexander, "Economic Development and Political Change in Communist Systems", <u>World Politics</u>, 22, (July, 1970), pp. 475-95.

Edelman, Murray, <u>The Symbolic Uses of Politics</u>, (Urbana and Chicago: University of Illinois Press, 1970).

Eisenstadt, S.N., "Modernization and Conditions of Sustained Growth", <u>World Politics</u>, 16, (July, 1964), pp. 576-95.

Eisenstadt, S.N., "Breakdowns of Modernization", <u>Economic Development and Cultural Change</u>, 12, (July, 1964), pp. 576-94.

Elkins, Stanley, <u>Slavery</u>, (Chicago: University of Chicago Press, 1968).

Ellison, Ralph, <u>Shadow and Act</u>, (New York: Random House, 1964).

Emerson, Rupert, <u>From Empire to Nation: The Rise to Self-Assertion of Asian and African Peoples</u>, (Cambridge: Harvard University Press, 1960).

Emerson, Rupert, "Parties and National Integration in Africa", in <u>Political Parties and Political Development</u>, ed. by

SELECTED BIBLIOGRAPHY

J. LaPalombara, (Princeton: Princeton University Press, 1963).

Emerson, Rupert, and Martin Kilson, "The American Dilemma in a
Changing World: The Rise of Africa and the Negro American",
in The Negro American, ed. by Talcott Parsons and Kenneth
Clark, (Boston: Beacon Press, 1970).

Engstrom, Richard L., "Race and Compliance: Differential Political
Socialization", in Black Political Attitudes, ed. by C.S.
Bullock and H.R. Rodgers, (Chicago: Markham Publishing Company,
1972).

Erickson, Eric C., "The Concept of Identity in Race Relations:
Notes and Queries", in The Negro American, ed. by Talcott
Parsons and Kenneth Clark, (Boston, Beacon Press, 1970).

Fainsod, Merle, "Bureaucracy and Modernization: The Russian and
Soviet Case", in Bureaucracy and Political Development, ed.
by Joseph LaPalombara, (Princeton: Princeton University Press,
1967).

Fanon, Franz, The Wretched of the Earth, (New York: Grove Press,
Inc., 1966).

Fanon, Franz, Black Skin, White Mask, (New York: Grove Press, Inc.,
1968).

Fatouros, A.A., "Satre on Colonialism", World Politics, 17, (June,
1965), pp.703-19.

Frazier, E. Franklin, The Negro Family in the United States,
(Chicago: University of Chicago Press, 1939).

Frazier, E. Franklin, The Negro in the United States, (New York:
The Macmillan Co., 1949).

Frazier, E. Franklin, "The MacIver Award Lecture", Social
Problems, 4, (April, 1957), pp. 291-301.

Frazier, E. Franklin, Black Bourgeoisie, (Glencoe: Free Press,
1957).

Friedman, Neal, "Africa and the Afro-American: The Changing
Negro Identity", Psychiatry, 33, (May, 1969), pp. 127-136.

Frohock, Fred, The Nature of Political Inquiry, (Homewood: The

SELECTED BIBLIOGRAPHY

Dorsey Press, 1967).

Fyfe, Christopher, "The Legacy of Colonialism—Old Colony, New State", Phylon, 25, (September, 1964), pp. 247-53.

Glazer, Nathan, "Blacks and Ethnic Groups: The Difference and the Political Difference it Makes", Social Problems, 18, (Spring, 1971), pp. 444-60.

Goffman, Erving, Stigma: Notes on the Management of Spoiled Identity, (Englewood Cliffs, Prentice-Hall, 1963).

Golembiewski, Robert T., William A. Welsh, and William T. Crotty, (eds.), A Methodological Primer for Political Scienctists, (Chicago: Rand McNally and Co., 1969).

Gosnell, Harold, Negro Politicians: The Rise of Negro Politics in Chicago, (Chicago: University of Chicago Press, 1967).

Gottfried, Alex, "Political Machines", International Encyclopedia of the Social Sciences, 12, (1968), pp. 248-52.

Goulet, Dennis A., "Development for What?", Comparative Political Studies, 1, (July, 1968), pp. 295-310.

Graham, George C., Methodological Foundations of Political Analysis, (Waltham: Ginn and Co., 1971).

Greenberg, Edward S., "Black Children and the Political System", Public Opinion Quarterly, 34, (Fall, 1970), pp. 333-45.

Greenberg, Edward S., "Models of the Political Process: Implications for the Black Community", in Black Politics, ed. by Edward S. Greenberg, Neal Milner, and David J. Olson, (New York: Holt, Rinehart and Winston, 1971).

Greenberg, Edward S., "Orientations of Black and White Children to Political Authority Figures", in Black Political Attitudes, ed. by C.S. Bullock and H.R. Rodgers, (Chicago: Markham Publishing Co, 1972).

Greer, Scott, The Logic of Social Inquiry, (Chicago: Aldine Publishing Co., 1969).

Grundy, Kenneth, "Nkrumah's Theory of Underdevelopment", World Politics, 15, (April, 1963), pp. 438-54.

SELECTED BIBLIOGRAPHY

Guttentag, Marcia, "Group Cohesiveness, Ethnic Organization and
    Poverty", Journal of Social Issues, 26, (Spring, 1970),
    pp. 105-33.

Haas, Michael, and Theodore L. Becker, "The Behavioral Revolution
    and After", in Approaches to the Study of Political Science,
    ed. by Michael Haas and Henry Kariel, (Scranton: Chandler Pub-
    lishing Co., 1970).

Hah, Chong-Do, and Jeanne Schneider, "A Critique of Current
    Studies of Political Development and Modernization", Social
    Research, 35, (Spring, 1968), pp. 131-58.

Halpern, Manfred, "The Revolution of Modernization", in Compara-
    tive Politics, ed. by C. Macridis and Bernard E. Brown, (Home-
    wood: The Dorsey Press, 1968).

Hamilton, Charles V., "Conflict, Race and System Transformation
    in the United States", in Readings on the American Political
    System, ed. by. L. Earl Shaw and John C. Pierce, (Lexington:
    D.C. Heath and Co., 1970).

Hare, Nathan, The Black Anglo-Saxons, (London: Collier-Macmillan
    Limited, 1965).

Hassein, Margary, "'This is the Way': Muhammed", Muhammed Speaks
    (September, 1974), p. 12.

Hayden, Tom, "Colonialism and Liberation as American Problems",
    in Politics and the Ghetto, ed. by Roland Warren, (New York:
    Atherton Press, 1969).

Hempel, Carl G., "The Logic of Functional Analysis", Symposium
    on Sociological Theory, ed. by Llewellyn Gross, (New York:
    Harper and Row, 1959)

Hempel, Carl G., "Explanatory Incompleteness", in Readings in the
    Philosophy of the Social Sciences, ed. by May Brodbeck, (Lon-
    don: Collier-Macmillan Limited, 1968).

Hess, R.D., and J.V. Torney, The Development of Political Attitudes
    in Children, (Chicago: Aldine Publishing Co., 1967).

Holden, Jr., Matthew, The Politics of the Black "Nation", (New
    York: Chandler Publishing Co., 1973).

SELECTED BIBLIOGRAPHY

Holloway, Harry, The Politics of the Southern Negro, (New York: Random House, 1969).

Holt, Robert T., and John E. Turner, "The Methodology of Comparative Research", in The Methodology of Comparative Research, ed. by Robert T. Holt and John E. Turner, (New York: The Free Press, 1970).

Horowitz, Irving Louis, "Party Charisma", Studies in Comparative International Development, 1, (March, 1965), pp. 83-96.

Huntington, Samuel P., "Political Development and Political Decay", World Politics, 17, (April, 1965), pp. 386-430.

Huntington, Samuel P., Political Order in Changing Societies, (New Haven: Yale University Press, 1968).

Huntington, Samuel P., "The Change to Change", Comparative Politics, 3, (April, 1971), pp. 283-322.

Hyman, Herbert, Political Socialization, (Glencoe: Free Press, 1959).

Ilchman, Warren F. and Ravindra C. Bhargava, "Balanced Thought and Economic Growth", Economic Development and Cultural Change, 14, (July, 1966), pp. 385-99.

James, C.L.R., "Kwame Nkrumah: Founder of African Liberation", Black World, 21, (July, 1972), pp. 12-30.

Jennings, M. and R. Niemi, "The Transmission of Political Values From Parent to Child", American Political Science Review, 62, (March, 1968), pp. 169-84.

Jones, Rhett, "Blacks in Colonial America", Black World, 21, (February, 1972), pp. 12-30.

Jordan, Winthrop, White Over Black, (Chapel Hill: University of North Carolina Press, 1968).

Kammerer, G.M. and J.M. DeGrove, "Urban Leadership During Change", Annals of the American Academy of Political and Social Science, 357, (May-June, 1964), pp. 95-106.

Kantrowitz, Nathan, "Segregation in New York, 1960", American Journal of Sociology, 74, (May, 1969), pp. 685-95.

SELECTED BIBLIOGRAPHY

Kaplan, Berton, "Notes on a NonWeberian Model of Bureaucracy", Administrative Science Quarterly, 13, (December, 1968), pp. 471-83.

Karenga, Maulana Ron, "Which Road: Nationalism, Pan-Africanism, Socialism", Black Scholar, 6, (October, 1974), pp. 21-30.

Kautsky, John H., Political Change in Underdeveloped Countries: Nationalism and Communism, (New York: John Wiley and Sons, Inc., 1962).

Kesselman, Mark, "The Literature of Political Development as Ideology: Order or Movement", World Politics, 25, (October, 1973) pp. 139-54.

Killens, John, The Black Man's Burden, (New York: Trident, 1965).

Kim, Joungwon Alexander, "The Politics of Predevelopment", Comparative Politics, 5, (January, 1973), pp. 224-35.

Kinloch, Graham C., The Dynamics of Race Relations, (New York: McGraw-Hill, 1974).

Knowles, L. and K. Prewitt, Institutional Racism in America, (Englewood Cliffs: Prentice-Hall, Inc., 1969).

Kornhauser, William, The Politics of Mass Society, (New York: Free Press: 1959).

Kuhn, Thomas, The Structure of Scientific Revolutions, (Chicago: University of Chicago Press, 1970).

Kuper, Leo, "On Theories of Race Relations", in Ethnicity and Nation-Building, ed. by W. Bell and W.E. Freeman, (Beverly Hills: Sage Publications, 1974).

Ladd, Everett C., Negro Political Leadership in the South, (Ithaca: Cornell University Press, 1966).

Lane, Robert and David O. Sears, Public Opinion, (Englewood Cliffs: Prentice-Hall, 1964).

Langston, Kenneth P. and David A. Karns, "The Relative Influence of the Family, Peer Group and School in the Development of Political Efficacy", Western Political Quarterly, 22, (December, 1969), pp. 813-22.

SELECTED BIBLIOGRAPHY

Lasswell, Harold and Abraham Kaplan, Power and Society, (New Haven: Yale University Press, 1950).

Lasswell, Harold, Politics: Who Gets What, When and How?, (Cleveland: Meridian Books, 1958).

Leggett, John C., Class, Race and Labor, (New York: Oxford University Press, 1968).

Lerner, Daniel, The Passing of Traditional Society, (Glencoe: Free Press, 1958).

Levin, Jack and Gerald Taube, "Bureaucracy and the Socially Handicapped: A Study of Lower-Status Tenants in Public Housing", Sociology and Social Research, 54, (January, 1970), pp. 209-19.

Levy, Marion, The Structure of Society, (Princeton: Princeton University Press, 1952).

Lincoln, C. Eric, "Color and Group Identity in the United States", Daedalus, 96, (Spring, 1967), pp. 527-40.

Lincoln, C.Eric., "Joe Jipson", The Autobiography of a Southern Town, (no further citation given).

Lipset, Seymour M., Political Man: The Social Basis of Politics, (Garden City: Doubleday, 1969).

Lowi, Theodore, "Machine Politics-Old and New", in Black Politics, ed. by Edward S. Greenberg, Neal Milner and David J. Olson, (New York: Holt, Rinehart and Winston, 1971).

Lyons, Schley R., "The Political Socialization of Ghetto Children: Efficacy and Cynicism", in Black Political Attitudes, ed. by C.S. Bullock and H.R. Rodgers, (Chicago: Markham Publishing Co., 1972.

Magdoff, Harry, "Problems of United States Capitalism", The Socialist Register, ed. by Ralph Miliband and John Saville, (New York: Monthly Review Press, 1965).

Mannoni, O., Prospero and Caliban: The Psychology of Colonization, (New York: Praeger, 1964).

March, James, "Model-Building", in The Process of Model-Building in the Behavioral Sciences, ed. by Ralph Stodgill, (Columbus:

SELECTED BIBLIOGRAPHY

Ohio State University Press, 1970).

Matthews, Donald and James Prothro, Negroes and the New Southern
    Politics, (New York: Harcourt, Brace and World, Inc., 1966).

Mazrui, Ali A., "From Social Darwinism to Current Theories of
    Modernization", World Politics, 26, (October, 1968), pp. 69-83.

McCarthy, John D. and William L. Yancey, "Uncle Tom and Mr.
    Charlie: Metaphysical Pathos in the Study of Racism and Person-
    al Disorganization", in Race Relations, ed. by Edgar C. Epps,
    (Cambridge: Winthrop Publishers, 1973).

Meehan, Eugene E., The Foundations of Political Analysis, (Home-
    wood: The Dorsey Press, 1971).

Memmi, Albert, The Colonizer and the Colonized, (Boston: Beacon
    Press, 1954)

Memmi, Albert, Dominated Man, (Boston: Beacon Press, 1971).

Metzer, Paul, "American Sociology and Black Assimilation: Conflict-
    ing Perspectives", American Journal of Sociology, 76, (January,
    1971), pp. 627-44.

Michels, Robert, Political Parties, (New York: Dover, 1959).

Milbrath, Lester, Political Participation, (Chicago: Rand McNally
    Co., 1965).

Moynihan, Daniel P. and Paul Barton, The Negro Family: The Case
    for National Action, (Washington, D.C: United States Department
    of Labor, 1965).

Mtume, James and Clyde Halisi, The Quotable Karenga, (Los Angeles:
    US Organization, 1967).

Muhammad Speaks, (January 21, 1972), p. 32.

Murapa, Rukudzo, "Nkrumah and Beyond: Osagyefo: Pan-Africanist
    Leader", Black World, 21, (July, 1972), pp. 12-20.

Murphy, Russell D., Political Entrepreneurs and Urban Poverty,
    (Lexington: Heath Lexington Books, 1971).

Myrdal, Gunnar, An American Dilemma, (New York: Harper and Row,

SELECTED BIBLIOGRAPHY

1969).

National Advisory Commission on Civil Disorders, Supplemental
   Studies for the National Advisory Commission on Civil Disorders, (Washington, D.C: Government Printing Office, 1969).

Nimmo, Dan, The Political Persuaders, (Englewood Cliffs: Prentice-
   Hall, 1970).

Nye, Joseph, "Corruption and Political Development", American
   Political Science Review, 61, (June, 1967), pp. 417-26.

Organski, A.F.K., The Stages of Political Development, (New York:
   Alfred A. Knopf, Inc., 1965).

Packenham, Robert A., "Approaches to the Study of Political Development", World Politics, 16, (October, 1964), pp. 108-20.

Packenham, Robert A., "Political Development Research", Approaches
   to the Study of Political Science, ed. by Michael Haas and
   Henry Kariel, (Scranton: Chandler Publishing Co., 1970).

Parsons, Talcott, "The Position of Sociological Theory", American
   Sociological Review, 13, (April, 1948), pp. 156-64.

Pease, John, William H. Form, and John H. Rytina, "Ideological
   Currents in American Stratification Literature", American
   Sociologist, 5, (May, 1970) pp. 127-34.

Pettigrew, Thomas, "Complexity and Change in American Racial
   Patterns: A Social Psychological View", in The Negro American,
   ed. by Talcott Parsons and Kenneth B. Clark, (Boston: Beacon
   Press, 1966).

Piven, Frances Fox and Richard A. Cloward, "Black Control of Cities", in Black Politics, ed. by Edward S. Greenberg, Neal
   Milner and David J. Olson, (New York: Holt, Rinehart and Winston, 1971).

Poussaint, Alvin F., and Linda McLean, "Black Roadblocks to Black
   Unity", Black World, 18, (November, 1968), pp. 11-18.

Pye, Lucian and Sidney Verba, Political Culture and Political
   Development, (Princeton: Princeton University Press, 1965).

Pye, Lucian, "The Theory of Political Development", in Contemporary

SELECTED BIBLIOGRAPHY

Political Analysis, ed. by James C. Charlesworth, (New York: Free Press, 1967).

Lucian Pye, *Aspects of Political Development*, (Boston: Brown, Little and Co., 1966).

Riggs, F.W., "Bureaucrats and Political Development: A Paradoxical View", in *Bureaucracy and Political Development*, ed. by Joseph LaPalombara, (Princeton: Princeton University Press, 1963).

Rodgers, H.R. and G. Taylor., "The Policeman as an Agent of Regime Legitimation", in *Black Political Attitudes*, ed. by C.S. Bullock and H.R. Rodgers, (Chicago: Markham Publishing Co., 1972).

Rossi, Peter H., "Community Decision-Making", *Administrative Science Quarterly*, 1, (March, 1957), pp. 415-43).

Rudner, Richard S., *Philosophy of Social Science*, (Englewood: Prentice-Hall, Inc., 1966).

Runciman, W.G., *Social Science and Political Theory*, (Cambridge: Cambridge University Press, 1963).

Russett, Bruce M., "International Behavior Research: Case Studies and Cumulation", in *Approaches to the Study of Political Science*, ed. by Michael Haas and Henry Kariel, (Scranton: Chandler Publishing Co., 1970).

Rustow, Dankwart A., and Robert E. Ward, *Political Modernization in Japan and Turkey*, (Princeton: Princeton University Press, 1961).

Ryan, William, *Blaming the Victim*, (New York: Pantheon Books, Random House, 1971).

Safa, Helen Icken, "The Case for Negro Separation", *Urban Affairs Quarterly*, 4, (September, 1968), pp. 45-63).

Salamon, Lester M., "Leadership and Modernization: The Emerging Black Political Elite in the American South", *Journal of Politics*, 35, (August, 1973), pp. 615-46.

Shils, Edward, *Working Papers in the Theory of Action*, (Glencoe: Free Press, 1953).

Shils, Edward, *Political Development in the New States*, (The Hague:

Mouton and Co., 1962).

Sibley, Mulford Q., "The Limitations of Behavioralism", in Contemporary Political Analysis, ed. by James C. Charlesworth, (New York: The Free Press, 1967).

Singer, L., "Ethnogenesis and the Negro American Today", Social Problems, 29, (Winter, 1962), pp. 419-32.

Sjoberg, Gideon and Richard A. Farris, "Bureaucracy and the Lower Class", Sociology and Social Research, 50, (April, 1966), pp. 325-37.

Stampp, Kenneth, The Peculiar Institution, (New York: Alfred A. Knopf, 1956).

Staples, Robert, "Race and Ideology", Journal of Black Studies, 3, (March, 1973), pp. 395-420.

Stuckey, Sterling, The Ideological Origins of Black Nationalism, (Boston: Beacon Press, 1972).

Tabb, William K., The Political Economy of the Black Ghetto, (New York, W.W. Norton, 1970).

Tabb, William K., "Race Relations Models and Social Change", Social Problems, 18, (Spring, 1971), pp. 431-43.

Thompson, Daniel C., The Negro Leadership Class, (Englewood Cliffs: Prentice-Hall, 1963).

Toscano, James V., "Models in the Study of Political Integration", in The Integration of Political Communities, ed. by Philip E. Jacobs and James V. Toscano, (Philadelphia and New York: J.B. Lippincott, 1964).

Truman, David, The Governmental Process: Politcal Interest and Public Opinion, (New York: Alfred A. Knopf, 1951).

Tryman, Mfanya D., "Black Mayoralty Campaigns: Running the 'Race'", Phylon, 35, (December, 1974), pp. 346-58.

Unity and Struggle, "Fascist Police Repression: So. Bend, Ind.", (September, 1974), p. 8.

Valentine, Charles, Culture and Poverty: Critique and Counter-Proposals, (Chicago: University of Chicago Press, 1969).

SELECTED BIBLIOGRAPHY

Vorys, Karl Von, "Use and Misuse of Development Theory", in Contemporary Political Analysis, ed. by James C. Charlesworth, (New York: Free Press, 1967).

Walton, Hanes, Black Politics, (Philadelphia and New York: J.B. Lippincott, Co., 1972).

Warner, W. Lloyd, "American Caste and Class", American Journal of Sociology, 32, (September, 1936), pp. 234-37.

Weber, Max, The Protestant Ethic and the Spirit of Capitalism, New York: Scribner, 1948).

Weber, Max, The Theory of Social and Economic Organization, (New York: The Free Press, 1957).

Weed, Perry L., The White Ethnic Movement and Ethnic Politics, (New York: Praeger, 1973).

Weiner, Myron, "Political Integration and Political Development", Annals of the American Academy of Political and Social Science, 358, (March, 1965), pp 52-64.

Weisbord, R., "Africa, Africans and the Afro-Americans: Images and Identities in Transition", Race, 16, (January, 1969), pp. 305-19.

Whitaker, Jr., C.S. "A Dysrhythmic Process of Political Change", World Politics, 19, (January, 1967), pp. 190-217.

Wilhelm, Sidney, Who Needs the Negro?, (Cambridge: Schenkman Publishing Co., 1970).

Williams, Eric, Capitalism and Slavery, (Chapel Hill: University of North Carolina Press, 1944).

Willner, Ann Ruth, "The Underdeveloped Study of Political Development", World Politics, 16, (April, 1964), pp. 468-82.

Wilson, James Q., Negro Politics: The Search for Leadership, Glencoe: Free Press, 1960).

Winegarden, C.R., "Industrialization in the Black Economy: Industry Selection", Review of Black Political Economy, 1, (Autumn, 1970).

Yette, Samuel, The Choice: The Issue of Black Survival in America, (New York: G.P. Putnams and Sons, 1971).

ABOUT THE AUTHOR

Mfanya Donald Tryman was born January 26, 1948 in Montclair, New Jersey. He attended undergraduate school at California State Polytechnic University and graduate school at Florida State University. Dr. Tryman has taught at several colleges and universities, including Texas Southern University, Houston Community College, North Harris County College, the University of Houston, and Jackson State University

Professor Tryman holds a B.S. in Political Science, a M.A. in Government, an M.S. in Public Administration, and the Ph.D. in Government. He is the recipient of numerous community and professional awards and honors and is very active in community affairs. Professor Tryman has been a consultant and has engaged in research for government at the local and national level and has published over a dozen articles, primarily in the area of Black politics.

*****